Essays on Hegel's
Philosophy of Subjective Spirit

Essays on Hegel's
Philosophy of Subjective Spirit

Edited by

David S. Stern

Published by State University of New York Press, Albany

© 2013 State University of New York

All rights reserved

Printed in the United States of America

No part of this book may be used or reproduced in any manner whatsoever without written permission. No part of this book may be stored in a retrieval system or transmitted in any form or by any means including electronic, electrostatic, magnetic tape, mechanical, photocopying, recording, or otherwise without the prior permission in writing of the publisher.

For information, contact State University of New York Press, Albany, NY
www.sunypress.edu

Production by Ryan Morris
Marketing by Anne M. Valentine

Library of Congress Cataloging-in-Publication Data

Essays on Hegel's philosophy of subjective spirit / edited by David S. Stern.
    p. cm.
  Includes bibliographical references and index.
  ISBN 978-1-4384-4445-1 (hc : alk. paper)—978-1-4384-4444-4 (pb : alk. paper)
  1. Hegel, Georg Wilhelm Friedrich, 1770–1831. 2. Spirit—History—19th century.
3. Subjectivity—History—19th century. I. Stern, David S., 1956

B2949.S75E87 2012
193—dc23   2011052054

10 9 8 7 6 5 4 3 2 1

Contents

References and Abbreviations   vii

Editor's Introduction   ix
   David S. Stern

Anthropology, *Geist*, and the Soul-Body Relation:
The Systematic Beginning of Hegel's *Philosophy of Spirit*   1
   Angelica Nuzzo

Hegel's Naturalism or Soul and Body in the *Encyclopedia*   19
   Italo Testa

How the Dreaming Soul Became the Feeling Soul, between the
1827 and 1830 Editions of Hegel's *Philosophy of Subjective Spirit*:
Empirical Psychology and the Late Enlightenment   37
   Jeffrey Reid

The Dark Side of Subjective Spirit: Hegel on Mesmerism,
Madness, and Ganglia   55
   Glenn Alexander Magee

Hegel on the Emotions: Coordinating Form and Content   71
   Jason J. Howard

Awakening to Madness and Habituation to Death in
Hegel's "Anthropology"   87
   Nicholas Mowad

Awakening from Madness: The Relationship between
Spirit and Nature in Light of Hegel's Account of Madness   107
    Mario Wenning

Between Nature and Spirit: Hegel's Account of Habit   121
    Simon Lumsden

The "Struggle for Recognition" and the Thematization
of Intersubjectivity   139
    Marina F. Bykova

Freedom as Correlation: Recognition and Self-Actualization
in Hegel's *Philosophy of Spirit*   155
    Robert R. Williams

Hegel's Linguistic Thought in the *Philosophy of Subjective Spirit*:
Between Kant and the "Metacritics"   181
    Jere O'Neill Surber

The Psychology of Will and the Deduction of Right:
Rethinking Hegel's Theory of Practical Intelligence   201
    Richard Dien Winfield

The Relation of Mind to Nature: Two Paradigms   223
    Philip T. Grier

Contributors   247

Index   251

References and Abbreviations

Through this volume references to Hegel's works use the following abbreviations:

Enz. (1817)   G. W. F. Hegel, *Enzyklopädie der philosophischen Wissenschaften im Grundrisse* (1817), with collaboration of Hans-Christian Lucas and Udo Rameil, ed. Wolfgang Bonsiepen und Klaus Grotsch, *Gesammelte Werke*, vol. 13 (Hamburg: Felix Meiner, 2000).

Enz. (1827)   G. W. F. Hegel, *Enzyklopädie der philosophischen Wissenschaften im Grundisse* (1827), ed. W. Bonsiepen and H.-C. Lucas, *Gesammelte Werke*, vol. 19 (Hamburg: Felix Meiner, 1989).

Enz. (1830)   G. W. F. Hegel, *Enzyklopädie der philosophischen Wissenschaften im Grundisse* (1830), with collaboration of Udo Rameil, ed. Wolfgang Bonsiepen and Hans-Christian Lucas, *Gesammelte Werke* vol. 20 (Hamburg: Felix Meiner, 1992).

Enz III   G. W. F. Hegel, *Enzyklopädie der philosophischen Wissenschaften III*, in *Werke in zwanzing Bänden*, vol. 10, ed. Eva Moldenhauer and Karl Markus Michel (Frankfurt am Main: Suhrkamp Verlag 1986).

VPG   (1827–28) G. W. F. Hegel, *Vorlesungen über die Philosophie des Geistes.Berlin 1827/1828*, transcribed by Johann Eduard Erdmann and Ferdinand Walter. Ed. Franz Hespe and Burkhard Tuschling, *Vorlesungen. Ausgewählte Nachschriften und Manuskripte*, vol. 13 (Hamburg: Meiner Verlag, 1994).

LPS	(1827–28) G. W. F. Hegel, *Lectures on the Philosophy of Spirit 1827–28*, trans. and intro. Robert R. Williams (New York: Oxford University Press, 2007).
PSS	G. W. F. Hegel, *Hegel's Philosophy of Subjective Spirit*. 3 vols. Ed. and trans. M. J. Petry. (Boston: D. Reidel, 1978).
PM	G. W. F. Hegel, *Hegel's Philosophy of Mind*, trans. W. Wallace and A. V. Miller (New York: Oxford University Press, 1971).
PN	G. W. F. Hegel, *Hegel's Philosophy of Nature*, trans. A. V. Miller (Oxford: Clarendon, 1970).
Z	Refers to the *Zusätze* or additions based on lecture notes inserted as clarificatory material by Hegel's posthumous editors. The particular source in which the Zusatz appear will be indicated by the footnote itself.

Editor's Introduction

The present volume of essays is the first English-language collection devoted to Hegel's *Philosophy of Subjective Spirit*. The *Philosophy of Subjective Spirit* is the first section of the third part of Hegel's *Encyclopedia of the Philosophical Sciences*. First published in 1817, Hegel published two additional editions of the *Encyclopedia* in his lifetime, one in 1827 and the third in 1830, just a year before his untimely death. That he saw fit to devote his efforts to revising, expanding, and republishing the *Encyclopedia* provides a clear indication of the importance Hegel attached to the *Encyclopedia*, something not lost on Hegel scholars. But this recognition notwithstanding, the *Philosophy of Subjective Spirit* has remained until very recently what one scholar has justifiably called a "less-well-known, less well-understood area in Hegel's thought."[1] For a variety of reasons, including the editorial work associated with the publication of the new edition of Hegel's *Gesammelte* Werke, recent textual discoveries, and the saliency of issues in the philosophy of mind in contemporary philosophy generally, we have recently witnessed renewed interest in the *Philosophy of Subjective Spirit*. The essays in the present volume, all prepared for publication here, contribute to a growing body of new scholarship on the *Philosophy of Subjective Spirit* and Hegel's thought on some issues of central concern in contemporary philosophy of mind.

Prior to the 1970s there were virtually no studies of the *Philosophy of Subjective Spirit* in English. In 1975, John Findlay brought out a new edition of the 19th-century translation of the *Philosophy of Subjective Spirit* into English,[2] followed some three years later by the three-volume edition of the *Philosophy of Subjective Spirit* by Michael Petry.[3] Both of these included for the first time English translations of the *Zusätze* or supplementary material that Hegel's 19th century editor, Ludwig Boumann, compiled from notes, lecture transcripts, and other sources. Drawing on this new editorial and translation work, Willem deVries published an important study, *Hegel's Theory of Mental Activity*, in 1987, and Daniel Bertold-Bond authored *Hegel's Theory of Madness* in 1995.[4]

It is generally agreed that these supplementary materials enhance the intelligibility of the materials published by Hegel in the *Encyclopedia*, which was intended by him to serve as an outline for his lecture courses, and these English-language scholarly works may have been stimulated by the translation of the materials in English. Nonetheless, the editorial methods Boumann used in compiling the materials have confounded scholars. In creating the *Zusätze* he combined varying sources from different hands that were drawn from different years, based on as many as five different lecture courses offered by Hegel between 1816 and 1830 and that in some cases were based on the first edition of the *Encyclopedia* but were published together as Additions to the text of the third edition.

Many of the materials available to Boumann have, alas, been lost or destroyed. Though Hegel lectured on the philosophy of spirit five times between 1820 and 1830, we have available five transcripts based on three of the lecture courses. Three of the transcripts—by Hotho from 1822 and Griesheim and Kehler from 1825—have been known to scholars for quite some time and were reissued and translated into English by M. J. Petry in his invaluable three-volume edition noted just above. More recently, they have been definitively edited and published as a volume in Hegel's *Gesammelete Werke*.[5] None, however, presents a transcript of a complete lecture course. In 1994 two transcripts lost during World War II were rediscovered in Polish libraries. The publication of these transcripts by Franz Hespe and Burhard Tuschling constituted a major addition to the resources for understanding Hegel's *Philosophy of Subjective Spirit*, constituting the first publication of a complete transcript of one of Hegel's lecture courses from 1827 through 1828.[6] That transcript has now been translated into English by Robert Williams, who has also provided a very useful introduction.[7]

The editorial and philological stage has thus been set for a fresh philosophical encounter in English with Hegel's *Philosophy of Subjective Spirit*. The present volume of new essays, by scholars from the United States, Canada, Australia, Macau, and Italy constitutes a significant contribution to that encounter. As these essays reveal, there are far more than philological and historical reasons why such a new encounter is warranted. The *Philosophy of Subjective Spirit* is a rich work in which Hegel deals with a wide range of topics that have been central to the philosophy of mind, philosophical psychology, and philosophy of action, including discussions of feeling, consciousness, mind and body, emotions, memory, habit, free will, and rationality, among many others. But a reader new to this work may also be surprised to find that Hegel deals with a variety of other phenomena that one might not expect, including the paranormal, madness, dreams, and ganglia, to mention only a few. Moreover, Hegel does so by considering both historical and contemporaneous philosophical works on the one hand and contemporary science on the other. And finally, it should be noted that the *Philosophy of Subjective Spirit* contains detailed treatments of some of the most important Hegelian concepts such as the master/slave dialectic, recognition, and the relation between causality and freedom so central to Hegel's social and political philosophy. These treatments do not merely recapitulate what is available in the better known texts such as the *Phenomenology of Spirit* or the *Philosophy of Right*, but instead offer new approaches that sometimes differ markedly from the more familiar texts.

Given the extraordinary array of topics in the *Philosophy of Subjective Spirit*, the contributors included in this volume do not aim to provide a comprehensive study of all the important topics Hegel treats. Rather, they present concentrated analyses of some of the major topics Hegel considers in *Philosophy of Subjective Spirit* and associated lecture courses. In doing so, they take a range of approaches to Hegel; the most important are historical approaches that situate Hegel's thought and articulate its distinctive perspective within the history of philosophy, on the one hand, and essays that deal with contemporary topics and thinkers on the philosophy of mind, language, and action, on the other hand. The distinction is, however, an imperfect one, as several of the essays combine both approaches to advance our understanding of Hegel's sometimes strange and fascinating texts on subjective spirit. This fact is one that accounts for the appearance of repetition in the ground the essays cover. When this occurs, as for example in the essays by Williams and Bykova on recognition, or the essays that concern madness by Magee, Mowad, and Wenning, the authors write in differing and complementary ways that advance our understanding of Hegel's philosophy, its historical distinctiveness, and its contributions to contemporary philosophical debates.

Notes

1. LPS, 1.
2. PM.
3. PSS.
4. Willem deVries, *Hegel's Theory of Mental Activity* (Ithaca, NY: Cornell University Press, 1987); Daniel Berthold-bond, *Hegel's Theory of Madness* (Albany: State University of New York Press, 1995).

5. G. W. F. Hegel, *Gesammelte Werke*. Vol. 25, 1. *Vorlesungen über die Philosophie des Subjektiven Geistes*, ed Christoph J. Bauer (Hamburg: Felix Meiner Verlag, 2008). This volume contains the full texts of the 1822 transcript by Hotho and the 1825 transcript by Griesheim, with variants from the transcripts by Kehler and Pinder for the lecture course from 1825 noted.
6. VPG.
7. LPS, 1–56.

Anthropology, *Geist*, and the Soul-Body Relation

The Systematic Beginning of Hegel's Philosophy of Spirit

ANGELICA NUZZO

Introduced and defined as the "truth" of nature and thereby set unquestionably much "higher" than nature,[1] Hegel's concept of *Geist* does not cease to be determined throughout its development in relation to nature. While nature is indeed "sublated" in and by *Geist*, it is never entirely left behind in the articulation of spirit's reality. Freedom is spirit's most proper character, the guiding thread of its development; yet spirit's liberation *from* nature is more precisely its liberation *within* (and *with*) nature.[2] This predicament of Hegel's *Geist*—its necessary and ongoing entanglement with nature—is surprising and even irritating only for those interpreters who hold on to a (extrinsic) teleological reading of the progression of Hegel's system, cherish a forward-looking notion of *Aufhebung*, and ultimately read the *Philosophy of Spirit* as a renewal of older metaphysics in spite of Kant. On the contrary, a closer look at (and appreciation of) how constitutive the relation to nature is for Hegel's concept of *Geist* may help us gain an insight into the much more complex character of the dialectic-speculative development of spirit from its subjective to its objective sphere. In addition, it may allow us to revisit the question of Hegel's debt to the philosophical tradition in this part of his system, addressing it from a broader angle than the perspective of the Aristotle-Kant alternative.[3] In this essay, I discuss spirit's relation to

1

nature, taking as paradigmatic case in point the "Anthropology," the first division of the *Philosophy of Subjective Spirit*. More specifically, I examine the question of the relationship between "soul" and "body" that Hegel raises at the outset of the "Anthropology." My claim is that such relation remains the underlying basis of Hegel's entire philosophy of spirit. This constellation is crucial on several counts. First, in the *beginning* of the philosophy of spirit at stake is Hegel's presentation of the general notion of *Geist*, the concept that lays the foundation of the philosophy of spirit as such. Second, Hegel's indication of such beginning as "anthropology" is neither a self-evident nor an uncontroversial choice—both in terms of content (topic of the "Anthropology" is the *animal* soul or spirit, and not distinctively the human soul or spirit) and in relation to the philosophical tradition (the most recent referent being Kant's 1798 *Anthropology* with which Hegel's own "Anthropology" has very little in common).[4] Third, it is on this set of issues that the newly translated Erdmann *Nachschrift* of Hegel's 1827–28 lectures on the "philosophy of spirit" sheds a particularly interesting light.[5] The fact that J. E. Erdmann is the author of the 1837 *Abhandlung über Leib und Seele*, which develops a Hegelian theory of the soul/body relation as prolegomena to a general theory of spirit, gives us reason to think that in 1827–28 he may have been a particularly sensitive and attentive hearer of Hegel's lectures precisely on this topic.[6] In fact, by examining the text of Erdmann's introduction to the *Philosophy of Spirit* along with the first paragraphs of the "Anthropology," and by comparing it with the corresponding sections of the introduction to the philosophy of spirit and "Anthropology" of the 1827–21830 *Encyclopedia*, we shall see in what sense the relation *Seele/Leib* that opens the "Anthropology" specifies the more general relation between spirit and nature offering the genetic definition of *Geist* and establishing the point of departure of spirit's development. Such development offers Hegel's final transformation of Kant's critique of metaphysics, in particular of rational psychology, and specifies the perspective from which speculative philosophy takes up the central concepts of Aristotle's and Plato's metaphysics and psychology. Finally, the interpretation that I offer herein recommends itself also in relation to the current discussion on this part of Hegel's system. For brevity, I shall mention only Robert R. Williams' and Michael Wolff's positions.

In his introduction to the English translation of Erdmann's *Nachschrift*, taking stock of the status of the literature on Hegel's *Philosophy of Subjective Spirit*, Williams rightly stresses how this is by and large the least studied part of his thought. On his account, the fundamental significance of the *Philosophy of Subjective Spirit* lies in its constructing the systematic connection to objective spirit—to the concepts of right and intersubjectivity in particular.[7] Central to this task is the move from the *Phenomenology* to the *Psychology*. Ultimately, the *Phenomenology* (and its concept of recognition) is seen as orienting the overall movement of subjective spirit. However, from Williams' emphasis it follows that the discussion of the inner articulation of this division, projected onto the crucial issues of objective spirit, underplays both the anthropology and the relationship between subjective spirit and nature with which this part of the system begins. On this view, subjective spirit is ultimately relevant because of where it leads, not because of whence it arises. In my analysis, I propose the opposite, yet complementary, perspective. I argue that the anthropology is crucial for the entire *Philosophy of Subjective Spirit* because it provides its determinate entry point or a beginning that remains the permanent basis of spirit's development—from its subjective forms to its objective and absolute manifestations. More generally, I argue for the importance of dialectic's determination of spirit's structures *a parte ante*—and not only, teleologically, *a parte post*.

The second important reference in the literature with regard to my topic is Michael Wolff's extensive commentary to § 389 of the 1830 *Encyclopedia*.[8] My aim here is to revisit and rectify his interpretation of Hegel's position concerning the soul/body problem in light of the Erdmann *Nachschrift*. I shall make two points. First, I contend that Erdmann's text confirms the centrality of the anthropology for the entire philosophy of spirit and shows that Hegel still defines the anthropology in terms of spirit's relation to corporeality in 1827/28—while Wolff claims that this is no longer the case after 1817.[9] Second, I argue that unlike Kant (in the Paralogisms of the first *Critique*),[10] Hegel does not simply "dissolve" the traditional soul/body problem declaring it systematically irrelevant. Rather, he fundamentally reformulates it in new dialectic-speculative terms. This explains the reemergence or rather persistence of the problem in later Hegelianism.[11]

I proceed in two steps. First, I examine Erdmann's introduction to the *Philosophy of Spirit* with regard to the "beginning" of the sphere of subjective spirit comparing it with the 1827 and 1830 *Encyclopedia*. Second, I show how the "Anthropology" specifies the general relation between spirit and nature into the relation of the "soul" to "corporeality," thereby lending to the discipline of anthropology a new meaning.

The Introduction to the *Philosophy of Subjective Spirit*: Beginning with the "Anthropology"

The peculiar significance that Hegel attributes to the introductory sections of his works is generally discussed in the literature exclusively with regard to the logic, and in particular with regard to the relation between the 1807 *Phenomenology* and the logic as first part and foundation of the system of philosophy. However, the three editions of the *Encyclopedia* testify to Hegel's ongoing concern with the "introduction" to all three systematic spheres—the logic as much as the philosophy of nature and the philosophy of spirit. A comparison of the three versions of the *Philosophy of Spirit* of the *Encyclopedia* as well as a closer look at the Erdmann *Nachschrift* allows me to conclude that there is a specific problem of introduction to the philosophy of spirit connected to the larger issue of the introduction to the logic. Significantly, Hegel settles this problem in a somehow definitive way in 1827.[12] The 1817 *Encyclopedia* opens all three disciplines with a "*Vorbegriff*"—a "preconcept" or prefatory concept to the logic, philosophy of nature, and spirit, whose task is to present object, method, and aims of the respective discipline. The two successive editions (1827, 1830) instead reserve the *Vorbegriff* to the logic alone. In the spheres of nature and spirit Hegel replaces the "Preconcept" with an "Introduction,"[13] which in turn contains the general "*concept*" of the object proper to the incipient discipline. Such concept is genetically "deduced" from the preceding systematic sphere.[14] Thus, while the logic (or better *das Logische*) allows for a "preconcept," nature and spirit have a specific "concept." I have addressed the problems raised by the *Vorbegriff* to the logic elsewhere; here I want to briefly discuss the tasks, respectively, of the "introduction" to and the "concept" of the philosophy of spirit.

The introduction has a twofold function: it leads to the "philosophy of spirit" in general, that is, to the determination of the entire sphere of *Geist*; but it also specifies its starting point, which, in this case, is the beginning of the *Philosophy of Subjective Spirit* with the anthropology (and with spirit's anthropological determination as "soul"). This double function of the introduction is reflected in the somehow surprising opening of the Erdmann *Nachschrift*, which conflates the two functions: "Our object is the philosophy of spirit or anthropology and psychology".[15]—*pars pro toto*: the beginning and the end of the *Philosophy of Subjective Spirit* stand here for the philosophy of spirit in its entirety. In the encyclopedic "Concept of Spirit,"[16] Hegel turns to the systematic connection in which the corresponding concept has been obtained as the immanent result of the preceding development. Herein, the crucial relation between nature and spirit is brought to the fore as constitutive of spirit's general concept. The concept of spirit is, at this point, provided by its genetic definition or by its topological placement within the system: "For us—explains Hegel—*Geist* has nature as its presupposition; its truth and hence its absolute *primum* is spirit."[17] The relation to nature, however, defines also, at the same time, the starting point of subjective spirit in the anthropology, namely, spirit as "soul." In the beginning of the anthropology the proposition "*Geist* has become the truth of nature" leads to the first, anthropological determination of the soul: "The soul [. . .] is the universal immateriality of nature."[18]

The "Concept of Spirit" is the systematic place where the transition between nature and spirit (considered from the side of spirit) properly occurs, thereby providing the necessary conditions for the determinate beginning of the new sphere, namely, *subjective* spirit. From this the somehow ambiguous validity of these sections in the 1827/1830 *Encyclopedia* follows: the "Concept of Spirit" marks both the space of transition between the two successive spheres of nature and spirit (accordingly, it belongs to the introduction) and an immanent position within the development of speculative science (hence it is not introductory but already belongs to the philosophy of spirit). We can see how this ambiguity plays itself out in Erdmann's text. While in the published compendium the soul/body relation is a specific anthropological problem that does not directly belong to the general concept of spirit, which is defined only by its relation to nature, the introduction to Erdmann's *Nachschrift* draws the anthropological characterization of spirit to the center. Significantly—and coherently with the idea of the introductory concept of spirit—Erdmann's text develops the general concept of spirit and its anthropological specification within the larger framework of spirit's relation to nature. In this text, the anthropology proper begins only *after* the problem of the soul's immateriality—that is, the first appearance of the soul/body problem—has been raised as specification of the more general issue of spirit's arising from nature as its truth.[19] This shift, whereby what the *Encyclopedia* places in the anthropology proper, Erdmann places in the introduction, testifies of the greater significance that Erdmann's text (hence arguably Hegel's 1827/28 oral exposition of the *Encyclopedia*) recognizes to the soul/body problem: it is not just the topic of the anthropology, but, as part of the general "concept of spirit," it is the necessary condition that allows the anthropology itself to begin. In Erdmann's text, the introduction to the entire philosophy of spirit is bent toward the anthropology. Thus, one can conclude that in the Erdmann *Nachschrift* Hegel uses the anthropological presentation of *Geist* to frame the general problem of spirit as such—*pars pro toto* as we have seen. The "Anthropology" (and the soul/body problem with which this discipline begins) is not simply the first sphere of a philosophy of subjective spirit but serves Hegel to channel in, by way of introduction, the broader problem of spirit's relation to nature.

The centrality that spirit's relation to nature displays in the 1827/28 *Nachschrift* is significantly confirmed and specified by the definition that the anthropology receives at the outset of that text: "Anthropology as such considers spirit in its natural life, when spirit is still immersed in nature, and appears as spirit *in conflict with and in relation to corporeality* (*in Konflikt und Beziehung auf das Leibliche*)."[20] Hegel has indicated in the anthropology the first part of the "science of spirit" since the 1808 *Philosophische Enzyklopädie für die Oberklasse*. In this text, the anthropology is defined by the problem of spirit's relation to the body. This discipline, Hegel contends, thematizes spirit "in its natural existence and in its immediate connection with the organic body."[21] While Udo Rameil has shown that the conception outlined by this passage goes back, more likely, to later courses in Nürnberg (1815), Michael Wolff underlines that since 1817 Hegel abandons the definition of the anthropology in terms of the soul/body relation—this being yet another sign of the irrelevance of the problem for his view of spirit.[22] My conclusion, instead, is that Erdmann's *Nachschrift* confirms a different scenario: in 1827/28 Hegel still defines the anthropology in terms of the soul/body relation—a sign, I maintain, of the ongoing importance of the problem for Hegel's philosophy of spirit.

The Standpoint of the *Philosophy of Spirit*: Anthropology, Empirical Psychology, Pneumatology

The Erdmann *Nachschrift*, we have seen, defines the sphere of spirit by way of its "subjective" beginning and end—the anthropology and psychology—and indicates in spirit's relation to corporeality the achieved result of the transition from nature. We should now turn to a closer examination of the latter point. Let us look again at the beginning of Erdmann's text: "Anthropology as such considers spirit in its natural life, when spirit is *still* immersed in nature, and appears as spirit *in conflict with and in relation to corporeality*. Psychology has for its object spirit as it relates to and develops out of itself. The phenomenology of spirit, spirit as consciousness, stands between anthropology and psychology."[23] Although "spirit *has become* (*geworden*) the truth of nature,"[24] and is indeed declared "higher"[25] than nature, spirit as soul is *still* immersed in nature (*noch* in die Natur versenkt)."[26] Nature has not been left behind (or below, as it were). Spirit is still immersed in nature and truly "sunken" into it; it may be axiologically higher than nature, but existentially (and systematically) spirit is still in nature. Nature, however, has been transformed by that transition into the form of spirit's natural life and immediate existence. In its beginning, spirit *is* nature—it is indeed the "truth" of nature; this holds true, however, insofar as natural life or corporeality is, conversely, spirit's own initial and immediate truth. This is precisely the meaning of spirit's anthropological embodiment. The soul is necessarily embodied because spirit is (or has become) the truth of nature and is thereby "still immersed" in nature—just as the soul is immanent in the living body. Hence the anthropology's chief concern is to address the relationship of spirit to *Leiblichkeit*, a relation that Hegel further qualifies as being that of a "conflict." Psychology, on the contrary, develops spirit's relation to itself. Comparing the initial definitions of anthropology and psychology, one can already conclude that in the soul's relation to corporeality spirit is not yet spirit, is not yet in relation to itself, hence is not free. Although the body is the soul's body, *Leiblichkeit* is still spirit's natural "other." And yet corporeality is that which immediately constitutes spirit as *subjective*, finite spirit. To this extent corporeality is spirit's initial truth. Consciousness, the topic of phenomenology, is the result of the anthropological development of embodied spirit: consciousness will bring spirit to its body (or will bring corporeality to spirit), setting the conditions for the free self-relation developed by the psychology. Correspondingly, one can anticipate that in the psychological articulation of spirit's free development "out of itself" corporeality is neither excluded nor abandoned. In the psychology spirit's body has become itself spirit—has been spiritualized or rather "idealized" as Hegel indicates the specific perspective gained by the speculative standpoint.

Thus, anthropology and psychology—the former defined by spirit's conflict with corporeality, the latter by spirit's relation to itself—differ with regard to the position that spirit assumes toward its own body. While the soul is immersed in it and hence unfree and does not recognize corporeality as its own, the conscious spirit is free in its own body and capable of developing "out of itself" through it. The distinctive character of spirit's subjectivity and hence finitude is given by its intermediary position, by its standing "between two worlds"—as Hegel maintains in a seemingly Kantian fashion. Finite spirit stands between nature or its corporeality and the infinite and is characterized by a double movement: by a projection toward the external world (*Ent-äusserung*) and by a concentration within its own depths (*Er-innerung*).[27] In both respects the relation to corporeality remains the basis of spirit's development.

Given that *Geist*, in its first genetic determination, is the result and truth of nature and is defined by the relation to corporeality, how shall a philosophy of spirit address its topic? What shall the method and the perspective of a philosophy of spirit be? It is at this point, still in the introductory steps of the philosophy of spirit, that Hegel confronts the ancient and modern tradition in order to outline the specifically speculative standpoint assumed by his philosophy. It is here that the introduction to the *Philosophy of Spirit* of the 1827/1830 *Encyclopedia* properly starts.[28]

Taking up the "absolute command" of the Delphic oracle,[29] Hegel makes it clear that knowledge of spirit is both "knowledge of man (*Menschenerkenntnis*)" and "self-knowledge (*Selbsterkenntnis*)."[30] This already points to the disciplines in which the tradition has developed such knowledge, namely, anthropology and psychology. Unlike the text of the *Encyclopedia*, the Erdmann *Nachschrift*, coherently with the point made above, develops the reference to traditional "anthropological" knowledge in much more detail. Moreover, the comparison of the two texts shows that in the 1827/28 lecture course Hegel defines his speculative philosophy of spirit on the basis of a more *inclusive* and somehow less critical confrontation with traditional and contemporary disciplines.

The question of what constitutes spirit is the question of "what the determination of man (*Bestimmung des Menschen*) is."[31] Echoing the contemporary Fichtean and Kantian terminology, Hegel frames the issue of human determination or vocation in terms of the human being's use of her freedom: to ask what the determination of man is, is to ask "what man should make of himself."[32] However, while Kant in his pragmatic anthropology contrasted man's self-made condition to what nature makes of man,[33] Hegel sees the two sides as complementing and integrating each other. Even more significantly, what belongs to the anthropology is, for Hegel, precisely what spirit is in its natural, still unfree, and still only animal determination. It is necessary to start from nature's determination in order to advance to human self-determination. It is this transition that occupies Hegel's anthropology. To act freely and to determine itself according to freedom, the human being must know the "nature of spirit,"[34] which is first and foremost its natural condition or the condition of spirit sunken in its natural corporeality. Thus, Hegel's anthropology is the necessary condition to "self-knowledge" and to "knowledge of man" *precisely because* it does not deal specifically with the human being but with a merely "animal soul."[35] After all, as Hegel makes clear in the *Philosophy of Right*, of "*Mensch*" in the proper sense one can speak only at the level of objective spirit, for only within social structures and institutions does the human being satisfy its natural needs differently than do mere animals. At the level of the "System of Needs," Hegel explains emphatically: "It is here and also properly only here that for the first time" one can speak of *Mensch*.[36] Yet one should not forget that the "social anthropology" developed at the level of "ethical life" presupposes and is grounded in the "animal" anthropology of subjective spirit.

In Erdmann's text, Hegel criticizes three perspectives that the philosophical inquiry into spirit's nature has assumed in the tradition: first, the approach of "pragmatic history," second, that of empirical psychology, and last, that of rational psychology. Only empirical psychology and rational psychology are discussed in the *Encyclopedia* text.[37] Pragmatic history has indeed the merit of recognizing the historicity of spirit—and correspondingly the fact that the "science of spirit" is itself a historical product.[38] However, with its psychologizing tendency focused on abstract individuality, it misses, on Hegel's view, the *universal* dimension of spirit. Empirical and rational psychology integrate each other. Although the former has the merit of valuing the *concrete* character of spirit, its illusory pursuit of an allegedly 'pure' experience devoid of thinking, of categories, and indeed of "metaphysics" is responsible for the utter contingency of its manifold observations, which in turn makes it unable to grasp spirit's underlying *necessity* and *systematic unity*. In the perspective of empirical psychology, spirit is seen as a collection of many faculties and activities set randomly next to each other "as things in space."[39] Significantly, however, Hegel rejects the idea that the speculative standpoint is opposed to or in contradiction with empirical research. The task is rather to bring the speculative concept to bear on the results of empirical investigation.

Rational psychology is the part of metaphysics that deals with the "soul" and its attributes as well as with its relationship to the body (*Gemeinschaft, commercium*). In the Paralogisms of the first *Critique*, Kant provided the most sweeping critique of the discipline, arguing that the problem of rational psychology is based on a category mistake committed by reason. Of the "I" taken as pure unity of apperception, the determinations of simplicity, immateriality, substantiality, and so on cannot be predicated (for, transcendentally, the unity of apperception is rather the condition of all predication). Knowledge of the empirical I (or of the self "in life"),[40] on the other hand, is indeed possible. Yet, what we know of ourselves as empirical, natural phenomena is not that we are disembodied, simple, immaterial souls; it is only our embodied condition—our being in time, space, and appearances in nature.[41] Knowledge of the living self is knowledge of the embodied self, not knowledge of a disembodied "soul."[42]

In the "*Vorbegriff*" to the 1827/30 *Encyclopedia*, Hegel discusses the problem of pneumatology in the "First Position of Thinking toward Objectivity." Rational psychology is concerned with the "metaphysical nature of the soul." It deals, explains Hegel, with "*Geist* as a thing (*Ding*)."[43] The soul of Hegel's anthropology is not the soul-thing of rational psychology. The latter is spirit reduced to *res* or *ens*, that is, to a metaphysical substance to which attributes are supposed to inhere. As thing, however, the soul is not activity, is not even the possibility of activity (and hence of subjectivity). And it is precisely the latter point that interests Hegel and grounds the appeal of Aristotle's position: the "soul" of Hegel's anthropology is rather "like Aristotle's passive *nous*"[44] the possibility of all activity; it is the inner purpose of the organic body.

Hegel discusses rational psychology again in the "Second Position of Thinking toward Objectivity," in addressing Kant's philosophy. Hegel praises as "a great success of the Kantian critique that philosophizing on *Geist* has been liberated from the Seelen*dinge*, from the categories, and hence from the questions regarding the soul's simplicity or composition, materiality, etc."[45] Hegel's philosophy of spirit in general and the anthropology in particular start precisely from the results of Kant's critique. On Hegel's view, Kant has correctly seen that the mistake of pneumatology consists in replacing the empirical determination of the self (which makes sense only in reference to our empirical, phenomenal self) with thought determinations whose validity is abstracted from the reference to our embodied condition and claimed "absolute." What results are the metaphysical propositions that define the soul as a "thing": "a. The soul is *substance*, b. is *simple* substance, c. is *numerically identical* with regard to its existence in time, d. is placed in relations to space."[46]

Since Hegel praises Kant's critique of the metaphysical propositions of rational psychology for liberating the philosophy of spirit from the wrong approach to *Geist* as thing, it may be surprising that at the beginning of the "Anthropology" he takes up what seem to be the traditional metaphysical problems of the soul discarded so forcefully by Kant.[47] In fact, Hegel's anthropology entails a further, crucial correction of Kant's own position. While Hegel agrees with Kant that "self-knowledge" and indeed "knowledge of man" can be only knowledge of the embodied self—that spirit can know itself, develop freely, and be active only as embodied and because it is embodied, he does not follow Kant in dismissing the problem of the soul/body relation *tout court* (and with it the problem of the soul's attributes). Against Kant, Hegel advocates the "true standpoint" that corrects a "thought"—namely, the idea of the "soul"—which does not contain truth, instead of rejecting it as a mere empty thought.[48] To the truth of a concept belongs, for Hegel, its correspondence to a "real (*wirklich*)" object. The notion of "soul" should not be discarded as mere illusion but speculatively corrected, that is, related to the right actual object. Hence the task of Hegel's anthropology as part of a *Realphilosophie* (philosophy of real objects or reality): to show that as spirit can know itself and act freely only in the body, the soul is real only in relation to (and indeed "in conflict with" as Erdmann's text suggests) corporeality. Since the soul is spirit's immediate and natural relation to corporeality, *to be spirit is to be soul in a body*; this is the central thesis of Hegel's anthropology. It is this claim that in its progressive transformation remains the foundation of Hegel's entire philosophy of spirit. The concept of soul does not make sense if taken as designating a metaphysical, allegedly disembodied *ens* or *res*; it is instead a valid concept of a speculative philosophy of spirit designating the first, still natural, and only immediate embodiment of spirit. The soul is form of the body; it is the body's inner purpose and principle of life.

Nature and Spirit—Body and Soul

In addressing the consideration of spirit proper to pneumatology, the Erdmann *Nachschrift* draws the soul/body problem to the center. Claiming that the soul is immaterial and simple (hence lacking all relation to otherness), rational psychology makes its communion and interaction with the body (which is instead material and manifold, hence the soul's true other) into an unsolvable "contradiction." Once again, however, the chief error of rational psychology is to take the soul as a thing, a fixed, mere "*Seiendes*,"[49] of which immateriality, simplicity, and so on are then predicated. On the contrary, argues Hegel, the soul is something rich, active, and dynamic, and this is precisely what *Geist* designates. Hegel's correction of the mistaken perspective of metaphysics does not seem to rely here so heavily on Kant's critique but consists in complementing empirical and rational psychology—a move that brings Hegel back to Aristotle. "The concept of the soul includes both the simplicity of rational psychology, and the multiplicity, the rich content of empirical psychology. [Only] the two taken together amount to a full consideration."[50] However, it is still unclear at this point whether Hegel's replacement of the thing-like conception of the soul with the dynamic idea of the soul as *Geist* is meant to render the traditional issue of the soul's attributes and relation to the body inconsistent and hence to discard it, or rather to lend it a new meaning.

On the basis of an inclusive and comprehensive consideration of traditional psychology—empirical *cum* rational—Hegel's answer to the question What is spirit? consists in going back to the transition from nature, and to the initial determination of spirit and its freedom. The "essence of spirit is freedom";[51] but "freedom is the concept itself that has come to existence"[52] through its development in nature. The reality of freedom in spirit or its spiritual reality is measured, in the first place, by its contrast to nature, that is, by spirit's entanglement with corporeality. The fundamental claim from which Hegel's philosophy of spirit develops is obtained from the transition nature/spirit. Such relation is now the speculative "successor" of the soul/body relation of metaphysics. Spirit's presence within nature (initially, its being immersed in it) or the soul's immanence in corporeality (as its immanent purpose) is the point of departure of freedom's realization. By turning the connection between nature and spirit into the basis on which the anthropology institutes the soul/body relation, Hegel fundamentally transforms (indeed *aufhebt*) the alternative between "idealism" and "materialism," setting his own philosophy of spirit on a thoroughly different terrain.

"The determination of freedom is also what we call *ideality*: a difference is posited but its independence is at the same time *aufgehoben*."[53] Accordingly, the speculative standpoint is defined by a different consideration of nature and spirit than the one proper to traditional metaphysics and Kantian philosophy. In both these latter, nature and spirit (or, in metaphysics, body and soul) are set one next to the other or one over and above the other (as mere "things"). This placing—this *"nebeneinander,"* as it were—is the true root of all ontological dualisms, which Hegel rejects along with all monisms that simply erase difference. Since Hegel is well aware that it is not enough to claim that spirit is "higher" than nature,[54] when the speculative standpoint pronounces spirit higher, it truly commits itself, at the same time, to the crucial additional claim that spirit is "the ideality and the truth of nature." And *this* (rather than its alleged higher standing) is one with spirit's freedom.[55]

Within this conceptual framework Hegel examines the positions, respectively, of materialism and idealism. It is relevant to remark the different place that this discussion occupies respectively in the text of the 1827/30 *Encyclopedia* and in the Erdmann *Nachschrift*. In the compendium the discussion is concentrated in § 389 (remark and addition), at the beginning of the anthropology. The task is to define the "soul" in its relation to the body as chief concept of the "Anthropology."[56] In the 1827/28 course instead, the discussion of idealism and materialism takes place in the general introduction, whose function is to justify Hegel's idea of *Geist* as the result of the transition from nature. This comparison confirms that for Hegel the soul/body relation specifies the nature/spirit succession from the perspective of a speculative philosophy of spirit.

In the speculative framework, nature is nothing else but the activity "to idealize itself," "to be that from which spirit eternally issues (*der Hervorgang des Geistes*)."[57] Considered in the "metaphysical abstract sense" nature and the body are "matter."[58] Matter and spirit are clearly different. Hence metaphysics concludes to an ontological "dualism" that is squarely in contradiction with the unity of spirit. The attempt to solve the contradiction, Hegel argues, can go in two alternative directions, namely, "materialism" (or "naturalism") and "idealism, spiritualism."[59] Hegel's point is that neither position recognizes the significance of dialectic-speculative "ideality." For they both take one of the terms of the problem—either matter or spirit—as the only truth or the only true and independent existence, which, precisely in its being the only truth, in principle excludes and denies the other. Significantly, however, between the two standpoints Hegel values materialism over the more naïve position of spiritualism. "Materialism is much preferable to this spiritualistic idealism, since its view is that matter is independent and spirit dependent. The second standpoint has instead much against itself, because one needs only to touch matter in order to experience resistance, and it is folly to deny the reality of matter."[60] Because of this preference, Michael Wolff has rightly designated Hegel's own position as "Hylemorphismus" (rather than "idealism").[61] Hegel's philosophy of spirit denies neither the reality of corporeality and matter nor the fundamental dependence of mental and spiritual phenomena on bodily and material occurrences and conditions. In fact, such dependence is clearly affirmed in the "Anthropology." But how does Hegel correct the dead end of both materialism and idealism?

Hegel replaces those fixed alternatives with the claim that the speculative "science" of spirit traces the path of spirit's liberation from nature, and on this basis, he outlines three different relations of spirit to nature.[62] The division of the philosophy of spirit into "Anthropology," "Phenomenology," and "Psychology" follows accordingly. Hegel maintains that the "concept is the soul of nature"[63] whereby he means that although nature has no truth in itself, it does nonetheless have in itself the force that leads beyond the contradiction of the natural. Eventually nature "makes itself true,"[64] that is, makes the transition to spirit. The highest point of nature—namely, the notions of organism, life, and feeling—is the starting point of spirit. The living being in general already displays the dialectical unity and difference of body and soul: the soul penetrates the body in all its parts as the "one" form or *telos*.[65] The soul however, is nothing without the body. This relation describes Hegel's properly "speculative" standpoint against materialism and idealism. Against the claim that either matter alone or spirit alone is independent and true, Hegel maintains that matter has indeed its own truth and that such truth is its "ideality," namely, spirit.[66] Conversely, the ideality that spirit itself is because it arises from nature and takes place within nature is also the new meaning of the soul's "immateriality." On Hegel's view, the soul's immateriality simply designates its being the successor or truth of nature, that is, spirit's immanence within nature: "The soul is the universal immateriality of nature."[67] This is the starting point of the "Anthropology." But it is also the permanent basis of the entire philosophy of spirit. Even in its highest and most developed forms Hegelian *Geist* remains fundamentally connected to the body and to corporeality.[68]

By reframing the problem of rational psychology in terms of the speculative-dialectic relation of "ideality" connecting nature and spirit, Hegel lends a new meaning to the metaphysical propositions criticized by Kant. "The soul is not only for itself immaterial but it is the universal immateriality of nature."[69] The soul is not "simple"—a simple "thing"—as pneumatology claimed; it is "nature's simple ideal life." The soul is not *a* substance; it is "*the* substance" of nature—in the Aristotelian sense, the soul is the *eidos* of corporeality. The soul is not "numerically identical"; in its immanence within corporeality it is "identical ideality."

To sum up: The comparative study of the text of the *Encyclopedia* and of the Erdmann *Nachschrift* has allowed me to shed new light on two crucial issues regarding the beginning of Hegel's philosophy of spirit. First, I have shown the systematic importance of the "Anthropology" in presenting the result of the transition from nature to spirit as the beginning of the new systematic sphere. Erdmann's text places in the introduction to the *Philosophy of Spirit* what the compendium places in the first sections of the "Anthropology," thereby recognizing in it a more generalized validity. The anthropological consideration of spirit as "soul," that is, spirit in relation to corporeality, lays the foundation of Hegel's *entire* philosophy of spirit. Second, I have shown how Hegel transforms within his speculative consideration of spirit the traditional, early modern soul/body problem. My aim was to show in what sense Hegel's anthropology replaces traditional empirical and rational psychology as well as Kant's critique thereof. My claim is that the articulation of the soul/body relation should be read within the framework provided by the systematic transition between nature and spirit.

Notes

1. Enz. (1830), §§ 251; 388; VPG, 24–25.
2. See VPG, 19: "Freiheit vom und im Natürlichen."

3. For this debate as well as for the previous mention of some interpretations of Hegel's spirit/nature relation, see the discussion of the literature in Williams' introduction to his translation of the Erdmann *Nachschrift*.

4. See M. Wolff, *Das Körper-Seele-Problem, Kommentar zu Hegel, Enzyklopädie (1830)*, § 389, Frankfurt a.M., Klostermann, 1992, 29, who underlines, rather, Hegel's closeness to the idea of an "anthropology of inner sense" mentioned by Kant in § 89 of the third *Critique*. In addition, the soul/body relation is traditionally dealt with by empirical or rational psychology and not by the anthropology—this despite Hegel's claim that the topic of the first part of the *Philosophy of Subjective Spirit* is the object of what is "generally called anthropology." Enz. (1817), § 307.

5. LPS.

6. J. E., Erdmann, *Abhandlung über Leib und Seele. Eine Vorschule zu Hegel's Philosophie des Geistes* (1837), Leiden, Adriani,1902.

7. Williams, introduction, 22–27, 48–52.

8. Wolff, *Das Körper-Seele-Problem*.

9. Wolff, *Das Körper-Seele-Problem*, 32.

10. For a broad discussion of this connection see my *Ideal Embodiment: Kant's Theory of Sensibility* (Bloomington, Indiana Unviersity Press, 2008), chs. 1–3 in particular.

11. Wolff, *Das Körper-Seele-Problem*, 103–05.

12. I cannot address this issue in the present connection. It is however the topic of my forthcoming essay "Das Problem eines Vorbegriffs zu Hegel's Logik," ed. A. Denker, A. Sell (Freiburg: Alber, 2009).

13. Enz. (1827) (1830), §§ 245–46 (§ 245, Betrachtungsweisen der Natur") for the introduction to nature; Enz. (1827), (1830) §§ 377–80 for the introduction to spirit.

14. Enz. (1827), (1830) §§ 247–251, Begriff der Natur; Enz. (1827), (1830), §§ 381–84, Begriff des Geistes.

15. VPG, 3 (tr. 57).

16. Enz. (1830), §§ 381–84.

17. Enz. (1830), § 381.

18. Respectively, Enz. (1830), §§ 388, 389.

19. In other words, the text of Erdmann develops what corresponds to Enz. (1830), §§ 388–89 (the first sections of the "Anthropology") in the introduction (26–27).

20. VPG, 3 (tr. 5); my emphasis.

21. G. W. F. Hegel, *Werke in zwanzig Bände*, ed. E. Moldenhauer, H. M. Michel, Frankfurt a.M., Surhkamp, 1986, Henceforth, vol. 4, 42, § 129.

22. See U. Rameil, "Der systematische Aufbau der Geisteslehre in Hegels Nürnberger Propädeutik," in *Hegel Studien* 20 (1985): 173–98; Wolff, *Das Körper-Seele-Problem*, 32.

23. VPG, 3 (tr. 5); my emphasis.

24. Enz. (1830), § 388.

25. VPG, 4.

26. VPG, 3 (tr. 5); my emphasis.

27. VPG, 5. For a discussion of this issue, see my "Thinking and Recollecting: Logic and Psychology in Hegel," in *Mémoire et souvenir. Six etudes sur Platon, Aristote, Hegel et Husserl*, ed. A. Brancacci, G. Gigliotti, Napoli, Bibliopolis, 2006, 89–120.

28. See Enz. (1830), §§ 377–78.
29. Enz. (1830), § 377.
30. Enz. (1830), §§ 377; VPG, 7.
31. VPG, 6.
32. VPG, 6.
33. I. Kant, *Kants gesammelte Schriften*, ed. Preußische Akademie der Wissenschaften, Berlin, 1910ff., vol. 7, 119.
34. VPG, 6, 7.
35. The absence of the human in Hegel's anthropology has been remarked and criticized since Feuerbach and Marx. See Wolff, *Das Körper-Seele-Problem*, 29–30.
36. See *Grundlinien der Philosophie des Rechts*, § 190 Remark.
37. See Enz. (1830), § 378.
38. VPG, 5–6. Interestingly, this text suggests that "before" spirit comes not only nature but also a stage of history in which lack of freedom dominates so that spirit (and *Geisteswissenschaft*) is not properly there yet.
39. See VPG, 9: Hegel's claim is that "Empirie" is "gar nicht ohne Metaphysik"; that is, experience makes no sense without thinking.
40. See I. Kant, *Kritik der reinen Vernunft*, B 415.
41. See Hegel's rendering of Kant's position in Enz. (1830), § 47.
42. See the extensive discussion of Kant's position in my *Ideal Embodiment*, ch. 3.
43. Enz. (1830), § 34.
44. Enz. (1830), § 389; VPG, 27.
45. Enz. (1830), § 47 Remark.
46. Enz. (1830), § 47.
47. Enz. (1830), § 389. See for this, Michael Wolff's extensive commentary.
48. Enz. (1830), § 47 Remark. In this claim is my correction of Wolff's position (but see already Wolff, *Das Körper-Seele-Problem*, 152).
49. VPG, 11 (tr. 65).
50. VPG, 11 (tr. 65).
51. VPG, 12–13.
52. VPG, 15 (tr. 50).
53. VPG, 15 (tr. 51: translation slightly modified); my emphasis; see also Erdmann, 23: "Die Freiheit—Idealität alles andern [. . .]."
54. VPG, 15 (tr. 51) spirit should not be taken "bloß als das Höhere."
55. VPG, 15 (tr. 51).
56. This text is the object of Wolff's extensive commentary.
57. VPG, 16 (tr. 68; translation modified).
58. VPG, 16 (tr. 68).

59. VPG, 16–17.
60. VPG, 17 (tr. 69; translation modified); also 19 (tr. 70): "spiritualism has the disadvantage."
61. Wolff, *Das Körper-Seele-Problem*, cit., 14.
62. VPG, 19 (tr. 71).
63. VPG, 22.
64. VPG, 23–24.
65. VPG, 24–25.
66. VPG, 27: his claim is that "die Wahrheit des Materiellen ihre Idealität ist."
67. VPG, 26; Enz. (1830), § 389; see Wolff's extensive commentary on this claim.
68. For this suggestion, see Wolff, *Das Körper-Seele-Problem*, 119; see also Williams' introduction, 15–16, for the possibility of a "regress" from higher forms of spirit to the lower, anthropological ones.
69. Enz. (1830), § 389; see Wolff, *Das Körper-Seele-Problem*, 114–115, for a discussion of the two English translations of the first part of the proposition: Michael John Petry: "Not only is the soul for itself immaterial, but . . . ," which sees Hegel repeating the claim of pneumatology; J. N. Findlay and A. V. Miller: "The soul is no separate immaterial entity, . . . ," which instead sees rightly Hegel's fundamental correction of traditional metaphysics. For the reading of Enz. (1830), § 389, in relation to Enz. (1830), § 47 proposed below, see Wolff, *Das Körper-Seele-Problem*, 124.

Bibliography

Hegel, G. W. F. *Lectures on the Philosophy of Spirit 1827–8*, translated with Introduction by Robert B. Williams, Oxford, Oxford University Press, 2007.
Erdmann, J. E. *Abhandlung über Leib und Seele. Eine Vorschule zu Hegel's Philosophie des Geistes*, (1837)< Leiden, Adriani, 1902.
Nuzzo, A. *Ideal Embodiment. Kant's Theory of Sensibility*, Bloomington, Indiana Unviersity Press, 2008.
———. "Thinking and Recollecting: Logic and Psychology in Hegel." In *Mémoire et souvenir. Six etudes sur Platon, Aristote, Hegel et Husserl*, ed. A. Brancacci, G. Gigliotti, Napoli, Bibliopolis, 2006, 89–120.
———. *Logica e sistema*, Sull'idea hegeliana di filosofia, Genova, Pantograf, 1992.
Rameil, U. "Der systematische Aufbau der Geisteslehre in Hegels Nürnberger Propädeutik." In *Hegel Studien*, 20, 1985, 173–198.
Wolff, M., Das Körper-Seele-Problem, Kommentar zu Hegel, Enzyklopädie (1830), § 389, Frankfurt a.M., Klostermann, 1992.

Hegel's Naturalism or Soul and Body in the *Encyclopedia*

Italo Testa

A Glocal Question

The relation between soul and body, understood as a problem that demands a response through a constructive philosophical theory—capable of accounting for the possibility of the relation itself—never received full and systematic treatment in Hegel's work. Even though he did dedicate a great deal of space in his writings to the notions of *Seele, Geist, Leib, Körper,* and *Leiblichkeit* in the Jena writings on the philosophy of Nature and of Spirit, in the *Phenomenology*, and also in the various editions of the *Encyclopedia,* apart from occasional references in the *Lessons on the History of Philosophy* in just one passage of the *Encyclopaedia*—precisely in the *Anmerkung* to § 389—does Hegel come to grips with the problem—first posed, in his view, by modern philosophy—that calls into question the relation (*Verhältnis*) between soul (*Seele*) and body (*Körper*). For Hegel this question involves, fundamentally, the question of whether the soul is immaterial and the question of the *"community of soul and body (Gemeinschaft der Seele und des Körpers)."*[1] Hegel's response to these issues found, moreover, no particular echo in the Hegelian school—with the exception of Johann Eduard Erdmann[2]—or in the successive critical literature. Only recently has interest been taken in the importance of Hegel's position in relation to contemporary philosophy of mind and to its Aristotelian roots,[3] leading, with Michael Wolff, to the first modern monograph on the theme—in the form of a commentary on § 389 of the *Encyclopedia*.[4]

The minimal attention paid to Hegel's solution means neither that it was definitively comprehended by its interpreters nor that, within or outside Hegelian studies, prejudices reflecting a fundamental misunderstanding of the essential features of Hegel's thought did not take hold. In some respects, as we shall show, an adequate comprehension of the solution of this *local* problem in the economy of the system is destined to shed light on the *global* meaning of Hegel's philosophy, particularly with regard to what is called Hegel's idealism; that is why the problem of the relation between soul and body has a *glocal* meaning.

Redescription and Epistemological Strategy

The marginal position that the modern soul-body question holds in the Hegelian texts is, moreover, neither fortuitous nor attributable to an oversight, but is due to the fact that it is not of systematic interest.[5] This is because, for Hegel, it poses a false problem, the correct attitude to which does not consist in responding affirmatively or negatively to the dilemmas it implies (is the soul immaterial or material? is community of soul and body possible or impossible?) but rather in showing that the problem is only apparent and that not seeking a constructive response to it is, therefore, legitimate. Hegel's therapeutic-constructive attitude[6] leads to a solution strategy that demands, first, a redescription of the problem, and then its transcription in the more general question of the relation between *Geist* (mind, spirit) and *Natur*. The primary reason for this lies within the systematic division of Hegel's philosophy, which in the *Encyclopedia* is divided into three parts: "Logic," "Nature," and "Spirit." There is, however, also a substantial reason for such transcription: only if we topologically locate the soul-body problem at the systematic point that regards the transition from *Nature* to *Spirit* can we grasp the epistemological and ontological misunderstandings that create the appearance of an unsolvable problem. For Hegel, questions of *epistemology*, as theory of knowledge, can find adequate treatment only within the framework of a philosophy of subjective Spirit—which constitutes the first section of the *Philosophy of Spirit*. Here "Spirit as *cognitive*" (Geist als *Erkennend*)[7] is thematized from the standpoint of the cognitive powers and dispositions available to a finite, natural individual capable of self-reference, which is to say, a living individual that is first of all a natural organism. Reconstruction of the genealogy of our cognitive powers develops through "Anthropology," "Phenomenology," and "Psychology"—the sections into which *Subjective Spirit* is divided: in the same way, Hegel reconstructs the formal architecture of the different levels of Spirit, each one of which is deposited by the previous development but at the same time manifests an organizational logic that cannot be reduced to that of the level from which it genetically derives. It is thus in the context of the *Philosophy of Subjective Spirit* that Hegel makes his epistemological position explicit: "Spirit, *for us*, has *Nature* as its *presupposition* (Der Geist hat *für uns die Natur* zu seiner Voraussetzung)."[8] From the standpoint of the cognitive subject—the finite individual, endowed with cognitive powers—nature is given as presupposed. This position can be characterized as a form of *epistemological realism*:[9] it describes the phenomenological perspective of the cognitive subject, confronted with a reality that manifests itself to his eyes as independent and objectively accessible.

Against Ontological Dualism

Note that Hegel's *antidualistic ontological perspective* does not call epistemological realism into question, nor does his logical conception of objective thought. For Hegel reality is not the product of subjective categories at the disposal of individuals; however, we may interpret his conception that reality is fundamentally comprehensible—both as Nature and as Spirit—solely as a manifestation of the structure of the Idea. The fact, brought to light by the *Philosophy of Spirit*, that for Hegel theoretical and practical self-consciousness, the family, right (*Rechts*), and civil society are all social phenomena co-constituted by the recognitive interactions of individuals—are, in some respects, ontologically subjective—in no way diminishes their epistemological objectivity. At the same time it is clear that Hegel, as we see in his celebrated criticism of Kant's thing in itself—and even more paradigmatically in his criticism of Schulze's modern skepticism—was always averse to *metaphysical realism*: the fundamental objective of such aversion was not of itself the realism of knowledge—which, on the contrary, Hegel wishes to preserve—but, rather, its combination with a dualistic conception at the ontological level. This takes us directly back to the soul-body question itself, which, in fact, as Hegel tells us in the "Anthropology" section, is the poisoned fruit of the evil tree of ontological dualism. Hegel is particularly clear on the subject. The question of the immateriality of the soul and of its community with the body grows urgent only "if both are taken as *absolutely independent* of one another" (wenn beide als *absolut Selbständige* gegeneinander vorausgesetzt werden):[10] if, that is, Spirit is taken as "a *thing*" (ein *Ding*) and matter as "something *true*" (ein *Wahres*) that is opposed to it. Hegel states his opposition to this ontological dualism that pits spirit against matter, soul against body, as two realities existing independently of one another, as follows:

> here this *simplicity* of the soul is, primarily, to be determined as feeling, in which corporeity (*Leiblichkeit*) is contained. This determination must be upheld against the view that this corporeity, for consciousness and for the intellect, is a materiality whose parts are outside one another and outside the soul.[11]

The ontological objectivity Hegel opposes is clearly that of metaphysical realism and does not concern the conception of objective thought. In particular, Hegel is combating here the dualism of substances implied by the soul-body problem: the idea, already sharply attacked by Kant with his critique of paralogisms,[12] of the soul's being a thing, an *ens* having determinate properties (substantiality, simplicity, numerical identity, immateriality), with another type of being—material, corporeal substance—pitted against it. Once the soul, and Spirit in general (of which soul, in the Hegelian systematic topology, is a determination, a moment) is posited as a thing separate from the body, it becomes necessary to ask whether soul has material or immaterial nature and to ask how the community (*Gemeinschaft*) between soul and body is to be conceived. In fact, once the ontological dualism is posited, one ends up by conceiving the relation between soul and body as a form of causal interaction between two heterogeneous substances. In light of this approach, the community between soul and body becomes a paradoxical fact for modern philosophical theories, which attempt (Descartes, Spinoza, Leibniz) to account for it conceptually by introducing a *tertium*—God—as that which mediates and makes intelligible their otherwise impossible interaction, ending up, however, by declaring such communion to be an incomprehensible mystery:

> a cognate question is that of the *community (Gemeinschaft) of soul and body*. This community was assumed as a *fact (Faktum)*, and the only problem was how to *conceptually comprehend* it. The usual answer, perhaps, was to call it an *incomprehensible* mystery (ein *unbegreifliches* Geheimnis).[13]

Hegel's strategy does not consist in giving a solution to the two questions but rather in maintaining that we have the right not to answer them, since we do not necessarily have to accept the categorial framework implied by the interrogation. Hence it is necessary to redescribe the situation on the basis of the genetic and topological relation between Nature and Spirit: for Hegel, it is precisely at this level that the structure of the ontological dualism that generates the apparent problem can be identified and criticized. Note, also, that Hegel's solution to the question of the relation between Nature and Spirit is thematized in terms that render it independent of the ways in which the general theory of the Idea comes to be interpreted: whether it be interpreted as a theory that liquidates ontology through a dialectic dissolution of its reified categories or as a new type of second-degree constructive ontology. In fact, even if we leave this question of interpretation in abeyance, it remains true that for Hegel soul and body are not things of a different kind but refer to the same object, namely, the living individual. They are to be conceived, then, as different categories under which we find the same object: the fact that we have descriptions that are not located at the same level does not mean that we are confronted with two types of beings. Michael Wolff defined this position as a *theory of identity* between soul and body, in a nonreductionist sense of the term.[14] For Wolff, then, Hegel adopts neither a reductionist form of mentalist ontological monism (the only type of entity admissible, to which all others—including the material—are reduced, is the mental entity) nor a reductionist form of materialist ontological monism (the only type of reality admissible is material reality under a certain description of it: for example, the physicalist description).

Hegel's Naturalism

In our opinion, Wolff's reading is unsatisfactory insofar as it fails to illuminate the background that renders this conception of soul-body identity thinkable. In fact, the local problem of the soul-body relation can be grasped only against the global background of the relation between Nature and Spirit. In this perspective one must combat any conception that sees Spirit in its various degrees—Subjective, Objective, Absolute—as a type of being other than the natural, which subsists prior to and independently of the natural or which is added to it from outside. By contrast, Spirit for Hegel is "return out of Nature" (Zurückkommen aus der Natur), which is to say, Nature that returns to itself and awakens from its sleep.[15] Spirit, accordingly, far from constituting another type of thing, is for Hegel nothing other than a determinate constellation of relations of Nature itself as the one single reality. This thesis could be called *Hegel's naturalism*: the idea that there is one single reality—living reality—and different levels of description of it. For that matter, in the *Phenomenology of Spirit*, especially in the chapter "Observing Reason," Hegel had already maintained that every dualism between reason and nature, and in particular between reason and corporeal nature, must be combated. Hence his criticism of those philosophical theories that wish to obtain the independence of reason while prescinding from its fundamental dependence on embodiment:[16] on the contrary, the dialectic of dependence and independence, which Hegel begins to construct in the "Self-consciousness" section of the *Phenomenology*, requires that the autonomy of reason be obtained only on the basis of the recognition of its spheres of dependence. If, then, we concentrate on the conception of the genetic and topological relation between Nature and Spirit that emerges at the level of the System, we can affirm that here Hegel posits the need for a broad conception of Nature. On one hand, spiritual activities must be conceived in such a way that they do not prove to be something other than and independent of human natural being. On the other hand, there is need for a conception of Nature that is not restricted, a conception that accounts for the fact that the space of Reason does not necessarily have to be conceived on the basis of a sort of dualism between itself and the space of nature.[17] But this requires a broad conception of Nature, thought as something not reducible to the level of physicalist description to which modern materialist metaphysics wishes to reduce every legitimate description of reality.[18]

In this light we can see why for Hegel the question concerning the materiality or immateriality of the soul is badly put: any answer ends up by assuming ontological dualism, just as this assumption is inevitable for every reductionist conception that intends to reduce the mental to the material or the material to the mental. The question, rather, in conformity to the Hegelian strategy of redescription, has to be transcribed at the metalevel of the relation between Nature and Spirit. In this perspective we can grasp the meaning of Hegel's statement that

> the soul is not for itself immaterial, but is the universal immateriality of Nature, its simple ideal life (Die Seele ist nicht für sich immateriell, sondern die allgemeine Immaterialität der Natur, deren einfaches ideelles Leben).[19]

However, beneath the false problem concerning the soul's immateriality lies the more fundamental theme of the immateriality of Nature. But here Hegel by no means intends to affirm that natural beings are not made of matter, neither does he intend to deny that the activities of the soul and of Spirit in general are constituted by material conditions, emerge from such conditions, and always remain connected with them. The question, rather, is whether or not—to conceive Nature in its organization adequately, and thus also Spirit as Nature that returns to itself—every form of description, and every categorial apparatus, has to be reduced to the one we utilize to describe the material properties of bodies—a *first-natural naturalism*, for example under a physicalist description. Hegel's answer is, in that case, "no," since his analysis is, at bottom, dictated by the need to arrive at a broader concept of Nature, capable of embracing the totality of living realities—a broad or liberal naturalism capable of embracing the various levels of organization of living beings, including those phenomena of their social organization that we can also consider as spiritual second nature.

The Soul as Form of the Body

In this context we can now grasp the meaning of Hegel's affirmations in § 389 that the soul is "the *substance*" (die *Substanz*) of the body; later, however, we will also have to account for the affirmation that the soul is the substance of Spirit.[20] But to do so we must first determine the specific meaning of the notions of "Seele" and "Geist" more precisely than we have up to now. The doctrine of the soul is, in fact, part of the treatment of *Subjective Spirit* and, specifically, of its first part, "Anthropology," which examines immediate subjective Spirit: a type of self-relation that Hegel calls "*soul or natural spirit*" (*Seele* oder *Naturgeist*).[21] The different images Hegel uses to speak of the soul—natural Spirit, the sleep of Spirit, Spirit immersed in Nature—fundamentally express the idea that we are dealing here with a "*natural determinateness*" (*Naturbestimmtheit*).[22] The "Anthropology," as a doctrine of the soul, is thus concerned with the natural form of self-relation: the singularity of a natural individual that immediately refers to itself. Second, we note that the doctrine of soul, although defined here as "natural spirit," is not yet a fully integral part of the doctrine of Spirit: referring to this level of development, Hegel writes that "it is not yet Spirit, but *soul*."[23] Hence the "Anthropology" has to do with a genealogy of Spirit based on its natural conditions. Furthermore, it is important to recall that the soul considered here, following the Aristotelian approach of the *De Anima*—for Hegel the most important treatise of all time on this topic[24]—is understood as a being in the domain of *physis*, and thus as one of those beings that, having the principle of its movement in itself, is included in the manifestative horizon of nature. Clearly, Hegel's doctrine of soul has nothing to do with a religious doctrine or with any sort of "spiritualist" conception. It must also be kept in mind that the Hegelian doctrine is tripartite—*natural soul, feeling soul, actual soul*—and that fundamentally, while systematically located in the "Anthropology," the first two forms taken into consideration are not specifically human—again, a reference to Aristotle—but are proper more in general to living and animal nature, with only the third form constituting a clear transition toward intrinsically human powers. From this standpoint the doctrine of soul takes, fundamentally, a *naturalistic approach*: not only is the soul not understood as a type of entity other than the living and embodied natural individual, but even the different organizational forms of soul correspond to different organizational levels—and thus to different concepts—of nature (first nature as regards the first two forms, second nature for the third).

In this framework the soul is conceived as the substance of animal corporeity. In this first sense, however, soul is not a certain type of substance along with others—a relapse into ontological dualism—but rather "the *Substance*" (Die *Substanz*):[25] the sole substance of life. It is therefore substance as form of the body, which is to say as substantial form:[26] organizational form of the living body. We find this sense of the substantiality of soul in the passages where Hegel maintains that "in the corporeal, then, the soul is a simple *omnipresent* unity" (Sie ist darum in dem Leiblichem einfache *allgegenwärtige* Einheit).[27] "The soul is the ideal, subjective substantiality of corporeity."[28]

If the soul is to be understood as the simple unity of the body—its internal finality—then the question whether it is material or immaterial loses all meaning: the soul, here, is not a thing separate from the body—neither separate nor separable, contrary to certain interpretations of Aristotle—but rather its intrinsic organizational structure. Hence, maintaining that the soul is life, body, does not mean that it is reducible to material components or to states of excitation of the body itself: it is, rather, the substantial form of the body itself, the organizational structure that endures in its dynamism beyond any replacement of the individual's matter. In this respect the soul is the true "immateriality of nature." This, however, does not keep it from having the body's states of excitation as its material condition, but only means that its form is not reducible to them. As form of the body, the soul cannot, then, be understood as "a thing," a certain type of entity distinct from a corporeal being, but rather as an "*activity*" (Tätigkeit) of the body itself. In the "Anthropology" the activities of the soul analyzed by Hegel are, principally, "sensibility" (Empfindung)—in reference to the natural animal; "feeling" (Gefühl) and "self-feeling" (Selbstgefühl)—in reference to the "feeling soul" (fühlende Seele); and "habit" (Gewohnheit)—which regards the transition from the feeling soul to the actual soul. These activities are considered proper to the animal organism; moreover, as regards the natural and feeling soul, they are not seen as intentional activities, having propositional structure and contents. They are, nevertheless, activities that manifest a form of prereflexive self-reference, giving rise to a certain self-relation of the living being: in the feeling soul—which, we recall, is not specifically human—this prereflexive self-reference can be described as a form of the living being's self-feeling.

Habit and the Genealogy of Spirit

In general "Anthropology," along with "Phenomenology" and "Psychology," the other sections into which the *Philosophy of Subjective Spirit* is divided, respond to a naturalistic epistemological strategy, aimed at refuting the premises that generate the dualistic opposition between knowledge as the exercise of capacities proper to our natural being and knowledge as the exercise of rational activities. Hegel's effort is to redescribe our cognitive powers as manifestations of activities of the body: indeed, the specific aim of the "Anthropology" itself, as doctrine of the soul, is to delineate the genesis of these cognitive powers—and of the higher ones in particular, the spiritual powers, involving thought, judgment, linguistic normativity—on the basis of the sentient inferior powers. The program of the genealogical reconstruction of Spirit is expressed by Hegel with a strong Aristotelian echo: "Everything is in sensation (Empfindung); if you will, everything that emerges in spiritual consciousness and in reason has its source (Quelle) and origin (Ursprung) in sensation."[29]

To be sure, this affirmation is offset by a critique of sensualism or sensationism understood as a reductionist theory that admits just one level of description to which all the other levels are referred. But, then again, Hegel does accept at least these theses of sensualism: a) Spirit has its origin in sentient nature; b) even at its higher levels of development Spirit continues to have sentient nature as its condition, and therefore does not exist independently of it. Both theses are closely connected with the theory of "habit" (Gewohnheit) that Hegel introduces first in his treatment of the feeling soul—at a level, then, that is not yet specifically human—but that in other respects will then concern the full extent of the theory of Spirit.[30] In fact, for Hegel, habit is "the most essential thing for the *existence* of all spirituality in the individual subject, enabling the subject to be a *concrete immediacy*."[31] Even more significantly, Hegel adds that "the form of habit embraces all the kinds and all the grades of the activity of Spirit."[32]

Thus all spiritual activities in the proper sense of the word, endowed with intentional structure and propositional content—that is, our higher faculties, and particularly those proper to humans, having the structure of consciousness and of self-consciousness—not only presuppose the corporeal constitution of certain abilities (the habits produced through repetition and practice as corporeal mechanisms of self-feeling) but are always accompanied by these abilities at every level. Even the reflexive activities of Spirit, propositionally structured, accompanied by self-consciousness and expressible linguistically, must become habitual if they are to be exercised; that is, they must be embodied, to assume natural immediacy, and thus be exercised nonreflexively.

Second-natural Naturalism

Habit is thus described in § 409 as a mode of natural existence.[33] It is natural because proper to the first-natural beings studied by the "Anthropology." Furthermore, it is natural since it possesses nonreflexive immediacy, the spontaneity of the natural soul. Then again, the naturality of habit is the product of an activity through which the corporeal dispositions are modified and shaped, through repetition and practice, until they form abilities not already given of themselves. In this respect for Hegel habit is a "second nature" (zweite Natur)[34]; that is, a natural immediacy posited and produced through the mediation of other activities.[35] If he had not introduced a notion of "second nature" connected with the development of corporeal habits, Hegel could have accounted neither for the genesis nor, even, for the form of all the spiritual activities—from the upright posture to the self-conscious thought of self that modern philosophy has posited as proper to human being. Habit, as such, is not definable independently of corporeity—which, however, does not imply an objectified conception of the body, but rather an experience of a body proper (as *Leib*, then, rather than as *Körper*), subjectified: a body that, as ability shaped through practice, becomes an *expressive sign*. This is of particular interest for the question of the relation between soul and body. For Hegel the question of the community between soul and body is badly put insofar as the very idea of community, taken as a fact to be explained theoretically, assumes that soul and body be two separate entities whose relation must be thought in terms of a causal interaction—like the type of reciprocal action and reaction that can take place between two distinct physical bodies. The relation between soul and body is, by contrast, an expressive relation.[36] Furthermore, since the relation regards not two distinct entities but rather different descriptions of the same living individual, it can, rather, be considered as an expressive self-relation: especially since every expressive relation has a structurally self-referential form. This is the meaning of Hegel's idea that corporeity ought to be understood as "*Sign*" (*Zeichen*), "expression" (Ausdruck) and "artwork" (Kunstwerk) of the soul.[37] It is precisely this idea that signals the transition from the "*feeling soul*" (*die fühlende Seele*) to the third form of soul, namely, "*the actual soul*" (*die wirkliche Seele*), which prepares the transition to the structure of "consciousness"—which will be taken up in the next section, the "Phenomenology"—and thus to the distinction between the "I," the body proper, and the external world. It is precisely at this crucial point that Hegel writes:

> Thinking, too, however free and active in its own pure element it becomes, no less requires habit and familiarity (this impromptuity or form of immediacy), by which it is the property of my single self where I can freely and in all directions range. It is through this habit that I come to realize my *existence* as a thinking being. Even here, in this spontaneity of self-centered thought, there is corporeity (hence, want of habit and too-long-continued thinking cause headache); habit diminishes this feeling, by making the natural function an immediacy of the soul.[38]

Thus Hegel, in the clearest way possible, affirms the idea that all spiritual activities, while having a specific form of their own, remain linked to corporeity as their natural condition and as that which constantly accompanies their exercise. The *cogito* itself implies the body and the formation of corporeal habits: even the *cogito*, then, is a form of second nature. At this point we can clarify the meaning, left in abeyance earlier, of Hegel's affirmation that the soul is the "substance" of Spirit:

> Soul is the *substance* or fundamental basis of every particularization and individualization of Spirit, so that *Spirit*, in the soul, has all the material (Stoff) of its determination, and the soul remains the identical and pervading ideality of such determination.[39]

Here the notion of substance is used in a sense different from the passages in which Hegel speaks of soul as the substance of body. While in this second case it signifies "substantial form," in the first case, according to Michael Wolff's interpretation, Hegel utilizes the sense of substance as substrate.[40] Here, substance clearly indicates the *Grundlage,* the material basis to which the higher forms of spiritual determinations relate as to the substantial form with respect to matter. The idea that the natural soul is the substance of Spirit is thus essentially in agreement with what we said regarding the natural genealogy of spiritual activities:[41] the fact that Spirit cannot be conceived independently of "embodiment" (Verleiblichung) regards its genesis, its contents and, even, the very form of the activity in which these contents present themselves.

Embodiment and Philosophy of Mind

Now that we have shed some light on the nature of the relation between soul and body we may wonder what Hegel's position is on the problem of "mind"—which, as we shall see, does not coincide with "soul"—and of its relationship with body. *Geist* is the German term still utilized to translate the English word "mind": in fact "Philosophy of Mind" (in English), in the sense it is used today, is still rendered in German as "Philosophie des Geistes." Wallace and Miller, in their translation from the German, gave Hegel's "Philosophie des Geistes" the English title "Hegel's Philosophy of Mind." Nevertheless, the Hegelian notion of "Geist" is broader than the common notion of mind—not because it speaks of something entirely different, but rather because it implies a conception that is broader than the mental. This, first of all, is because the Hegelian analysis of Spirit includes the soul, which, properly speaking, is not yet fully Spirit, and which is understood as natural, sentient, and feeling activity, which is not intrinsically intentional. The doctrine of soul thus regards the cognitive activities of animal individuals and that type of proto-intentionality—*Selbstgefühl*—ascribable to such activities from outside but that cannot be self-ascribed. We are thus in the presence of what today might be called a natural theory of mind. Then, we must note that the further levels of subjective Spirit, involving the structures of the consciousness of objects and of self-consciousness, regard, rather, propositionally structured individual intentional mind. Nevertheless, in Hegel the domain of the mental extends also to the spheres of *objective Spirit* and of *absolute Spirit*. In the first case we have already to do with relations and activities that, while essentially involving individuals, and not being able to prescind from them, are nonetheless not methodologically and ontologically reducible to individuals. The holistic properties of individuals, and the social institutions themselves—family, law, civil society, State—thus express a form of spiritual activity that cannot be described as the mere aggregate of individual intentional activities. This poses the problem of the existence of a form of mental activity and of common, shared, and collective intentionality, whose properties cannot be explained solely on the basis of the properties of individual minds. If the Hegelian philosophy of Spirit reflects such an approach—some form of methodological and ontological holism—then we cannot claim to have dealt with the mind-body question adequately if we have concentrated exclusively on subjective Spirit. But this also presents us with a question of social ontology: what type of existence should we grant to this type of shared or collective spiritual activities? Are we perhaps confronted with a new type of incorporeal entities, distinct from such other entities as embodied individuals? And if this were the case, would we not end up by relapsing into some form of ontological dualism? Hegel had been aware of the problem ever since the *Phenomenology of Spirit*. In the sections "Reason" and then "Spirit" he did his best to avoid all dualism not only between reason and nature but also among reason, social reality, and nature. But, then, the problem of *Verleiblichung* is posed anew at this level as well, and an adequate response will have to be one that does not lead to a dualistic approach. Social space, then, in its historical development, has to be conceived as space that is adequate to express Reason, understood as a form of manifestation of spiritual activities. But, then again, social reality must not be understood as a type of entity other than natural reality—on pain of relapsing into some form of dualism—but rather as a determinate configuration of the expressive relations of living individuals as parts of a people. If habit is the universal form of Spirit, then also these spiritual expressive relations will have, in their turn, to be embodied. But, then again, the type of expressive embodiment required here differs from the one dealt within the analysis of subjective Spirit, since now we find ourselves not in the presence of physico-organic bodies but rather of social and institutional bodies regarding which it is problematic whether they can in some sense be considered as natural and living bodies.

Hegel's Social Naturalism

But at this point has not the very possibility of characterizing Hegel's position as a form of naturalism faded, even if expressed in terms of a second-natural naturalism? The situation is more complex than may appear at first blush. In the first instance we must recall that the Aristotelian thesis that sees man as a naturally social animal is implicit in Hegel's philosophy. Sociality itself, as an expressive configuration of Spirit, has a natural genesis for Hegel, insofar as it emerges from the natural determinations of living being; moreover, the social structures of Spirit themselves have the natural soul as their substance. In the second place, the thesis of natural sociality is, in the strong sense, grounded by Hegel also through the theory of the recognitive constitution of theoretical and practical self-consciousness that had already been formulated in the Jena writings and was taken up again in the major works. Nevertheless, if self-consciousness constitutes itself as such in recognitive interaction and thus has an intersubjective and social genesis and structure, then the spiritual activity that manifests itself in it will necessarily have to be embodied not only in the individual physical body but also in the social body of the forms of shared ethical life and of institutions. This means, moreover, that it is possible to ascribe some form of naturality also to the social body of immediate and institutionalized ethical life. In fact, for Hegel, institutions—as he argues in §§ 4 and 151 of the *Elements of the Philosophy of Right*—can be understood as a form of social second nature, and in this respect can be analyzed also in terms of habit. The social body and its institutions in one respect manifest a form of activity and of organization that is not reducible to the activity of individuals and that therefore presents a self-moving character. Furthermore, as Hegel argues in § 146 of the "Elements," the social body and its institutions present themselves to the individual as having a form of natural immediacy also insofar as they manifest an objectivity and a blind necessity—as far as the ends of individual intentional agents are concerned—analogous to that presented by the first-natural domain of physical nature. Appearing to the individual as an extraneous mechanism, the institutionalized social body manifests anew the structure of habit—defined as a mechanism of self-feeling. As connected to habits sedimented in social practices, the naturality of the social body is not in its turn independent of corporeity. Even though we may seem to be dealing with a nonmaterial body, this does not preclude the sense of living naturality, given the thesis of the universal immateriality of nature. Neither can it be taken for granted that the social body must be understood as something that prescinds from the corporeity of living organisms: the soul nevertheless remains the substance of Spirit, and Spirit, in its social articulation, is embodied exactly in the habits through which individual living bodies are socialized through education. Thus the hypothesis remains open that the second-natural social body is not to be understood as some other type of entity than living beings: it is, rather, an expressive configuration constituted through recognitive interactions and embodied in the habits of living individuals.

It is difficult, then, to characterize the philosophy of Hegel as a form of idealism. By no means does it express the conviction that everything there is can in the final analysis be reduced to ideal or mental entities. Hegel's opposition to reductionist materialism does not give rise to some type of spiritualism or reductionist mentalism: this outcome would be nothing other than the reversal of the previous position and would end up by suffering from the same basic dualism. The opposition to ontological dualism gives rise, rather, as De Vries and Wolff rightly maintained, to a philosophy that is hylomorphic.[42] It is unquestionable that Hegel pits himself against naturalistic approaches of a physicalist, reductionist, or eliminativist type. Nevertheless, in our opinion, Hegel's hylomorphism cannot be adequately conceived if one posits a dualism between organic natural reality and social reality: the form most adequate to characterize Hegel's comprehensive position is perhaps that of *social naturalism*, on the basis of which the institutions of social life are extensions and objectifications of human nature and of individual mind. This, at bottom, is the combined meaning of the Hegelian theses that soul is the substance of Spirit and habit is its universal form.

Notes

1. See Enz. (1827) § 389 Anm. I have modified the translation in PM throughout."

2. See J. E. Erdmann, *Abhandlung über Leib und Seele. Eine Vorschule zu Hegel's Philosophie des Geistes* (1837), new edition ed. G. J. P. Bolland (Leiden, 1902).

3. See C. Elder, *Appropriating Hegel* (Aberdeen: Aberdeen University Press, 1980); W. A. De Vries, *Hegel's Theory of Mental Activity* (Ithaca: Cornell University Press, 1988).

4. See M. Wolff, *Das Körper-Seele-Problem. Kommentar zu Hegel, Enzyklopädie* (1830), § 389 (Frankfurt am Main: Vittorio Klostermann, 1992).

5. See Wolff, *Das Körper-Seele-Problem*, 11–15.

6. On the different meanings of philosophical therapy, see M. Quante, "Spekulative Philosophie als Therapie," in *Hegels Erbe*, ed. Ch. Halbig, M. Quante and L. Siep (Frankfurt am Main: Suhrkamp, 2004), 329–33.

7. See Enz. (1827), § 387.

8. See Enz. (1827), § 381.

9. On Hegel's epistemological realism, from a perspective that combines pragmatism and moderate ontological holism, see K. R. Westphal, *Hegel's Epistemological Realism* (Dordrecht: Kluwer, 1989), 140–48; K. R. Westphal, "Force, Understanding and Ontology," *The Bulletin of the Hegel Society of Great Britain*, 57/58 (2008), 1–29. For a different, more traditional perspective—oriented

toward ontological monism—on Hegel's epistemological realism, see Ch. Halbig, *Objektives Denken. Erkenntnistheorie und Philosophy of Mind in Hegels System* (Stuttgart-Bad Cannstatt: frommann-holzboog, 2002); Ch. Halbig, "Das >Erkennen als solches<. Überlegungen zur Grundstruktur von Hegels Epistemologie, in *Hegels Erbe*, 138–63. W. Jaeschke maintains, moreover, that this epistemological realism necessarily presupposes a form of (nondualistic) ontological realism compatible with identity philosophy; see W. Jaeschke, "Zum Begriff des Idealismus," in *Hegels Erbe*, 180–82.

10. See Enz. (1827), § 389 Anm.
11. See Enz. (1827), § 403 Anm.
12. See Enz. (1827), § 321.
13. See Enz. (1827), § 389 Anm.
14. See Wolff, *Das Körper-Seele-Problem*, 100.
15. See Enz. (1827), § 381.
16. On the theme of embodiment see J. Russon, *The Self and Its Body in Hegel's Phenomenology of Spirit* (Toronto/Buffalo/London: University of Toronto Press, 1994), 14.
17. For a critique of this dualism see J. McDowell, *Mind and World* (Cambridge, Mass.: Harvard University Press, 1994; second edition 1996).
18. On the question of "broad or liberal naturalism," see *Naturalism in Question*, ed. M. De Caro and D. McArthur (Cambridge, Mass.: Harvard University Press, 2004).
19. See Enz. (1827), §389. In the *Anmerkung* to the same section Hegel then writes that "the question of the immateriality of the soul has no interest, except where, on the one hand, matter is regarded as something *true*, and, on the other, spirit conceived as a *thing*." Enz. (1827), § 389 Anm.
20. See Enz. (1827), § 389.
21. See Enz. (1827), § 387.
22. See Enz. (1827), § 390.
23. See Enz. (1827), § 388.
24. See Enz. (1827), § 378.
25. See Enz. (1827), § 389.
26. See Wolff, *Das Körper-Seele-Problem*, 140.
27. See Enz. (1827), § 403 Anm.
28. See Enz. (1827), § 409.
29. See Enz. (1827), § 400 Anm.
30. On the importance, and on the ambivalence, of the theme of habit also in the other sections of "Subjective Spirit" see B. Merker, "Jenseits des Hirns. Zur Aktualität von Hegels Philosophie des subjektiven Geistes," in *Subjektivität und Anerkennung. Festschrift für Ludwig Siep*, ed. B. Merker, G. Mohr and M. Quante (Paderborn: Mentis, 2003), 157–84. On the relation between habit and language see Thomas A. Lewis, "Speaking of Habits: The Role of Language in Moving from Habit to Freedom," *The Owl of Minerva* 39, nos. 1–2 (2007): 25–53. A. Ferrarin, in his remarkable essay on *Hegel and Aristotle* (Cambridge: Cambridge University

Press, 2001), reads the Hegelian theory of habit within an interpretation that postulates a clear-cut discontinuity between nature and spirit: the process through which spirit returns to itself from the exteriority of nature is, for him, nothing other than a movement of idealization in which nature must be negated and die if it is to be able to give life to spirit (Ferrarin, *Hegel and Aristotle*, 237–38). In this light Ferrarin sees the formation of habits as a unilateral process of rupture with the corporeity in which nature ceases to be an external given and becomes an ideal possession of spirit (Ferrarin, *Hegel and Aristotle*, 278ff.). It must, however, be noted that the process of idealization in Hegel is always accompanied—as, indeed, the theory of habit attests—by a complementary movement of embodiment: in this respect, habit is not just the activity that "produces spontaneity in receptivity" (Ferrarin, *Hegel and Aristotle*, 280), but is also the moment in which spontaneous activities are embodied in second-nature receptivity. The dualistic (and idealistic) readings of the relation between nature and spirit in Hegel spring, in my opinion, precisely from the tendency to neglect this second aspect and to accentuate unilaterally—in the idealist-subjective sense—the moment of idealization.

31. See Enz. (1827), § 410 Anm.
32. See Enz. (1827), § 410 Anm.
33. See Enz. (1827), § 409.
34. On second nature in Hegel and in contemporary philosophy, see I. Testa, "Selbstbewusstsein und zweite Natur," in *Hegels Phaenomenologie des Geistes*, ed. K. Vieweg and W. Welsch (Frankfurt: Suhrkamp, 2008), 286–307; I. Testa, "Criticism from within Nature. The Dialectic from First to Second Nature between McDowell and Adorno," *Philosophy and Social Criticism* 33, no. 3 (2007): 473–97.
35. See Enz. (1827), § 410 Anm.
36. On the critique of soul-body dualism in the *Phenomenology*, see P. Stekeler-Weithofer, *Philosophie des Selbstbewußtseins. Hegels System als Formanalyse von Wissen und Autonomie* (Frankfurt am Main: Suhrkamp), 2005, 412–19.
37. See Enz. (1827), § 411.
38. See Enz. (1827), § 410 Anm.
39. See Enz. (1827), § 389.
40. See Wolff, *Das Körper-Seele-Problem*, 126ff.
41. See Enz. (1827), § 392.
42. See De Vries, *Hegel's Theory of Mental Activity*, 45; Wolff, *Das Körper-Seele-Problem*, 14, 154.

How the Dreaming Soul Became the Feeling Soul, between the 1827 and 1830 Editions of Hegel's *Philosophy of Subjective Spirit*

Empirical Psychology and the Late Enlightenment

JEFFREY REID

Between the second, 1827, edition of his *Encyclopedia of Philosophical Sciences* and the ultimate 1830 edition, Hegel made a number of what might be considered minor changes, particularly in comparison with the extensive revisions undertaken between the first, 1817, edition and the second, "mature, if penultimate formulation," as Robert Williams writes.[1] One change that does occur between 1827 and 1830 takes place in the *Philosophy of Subjective Spirit*,[2] where Hegel changes the section heading at § 403 from "The Dreaming Soul" ("*Die traümende Seele*") to "The Feeling Soul" ("*Die fühlende Seele*"). This chapter explores the significance of this revision, which, although apparently minor, is hardly superficial. In fact, by calling attention to the original title, the change from "dreaming" to "feeling" invites us to investigate the origins of Hegel's thought on this crucial section, whose insights into the particularities of the human soul remain largely unchanged, in spite of the heading change. My first object of investigation will therefore be the sources of the dreaming soul.

Discovering these origins will then enable to me to propose an answer to why Hegel later changes "dreaming" to "feeling."

The section under discussion falls within Hegel's presentation of the soul (*Seele*), in the chapter entitled "Anthropology." The soul, in the 1830 edition, is presented in three main articulations: a) "The Natural Soul" (§§ 391–402); b) "The Feeling Soul" (§§ 403–10); c) "The Actual Soul" (§§ 411–12). Out of the actual soul arises rational consciousness, through a skeletal reenactment of Hegel's famous *Phenomenology of Mind*, perhaps a better translation than "Spirit" for *Geist*, in this subjective context (§§ 413–39). The outcome of the *Philosophy of Subjective Spirit*, in Psychology, is rational consciousness articulating itself in theoretical intelligence (*Verstand*) and practical will, both of which are shown to be ultimately grounded in freedom. The 1830 "Feeling Soul" section begins with a short introduction (§§ 403–04) before being divided into three subsections: (i) the "Feeling Soul" in its immediacy (§§ 405–06); (ii) "Self Feeling" (§§ 407–08); and "Habit" (§§ 409–10), which will not be discussed here.

Although the actual content of §§ 403 to 408 remains largely unaltered between the second and third editions, along with the change of heading from dreaming to feeling soul, Hegel does make several discrete additions or substitutions that serve to further accentuate the new emphasis on feeling. Notably, the term "feeling" (from *fühlen*) is substituted for the earlier "sentient" (from *empfinden*) in the main texts of §§ 403–406. In the same sense, the subheading for § 405 is changed from "The Passive Totality of the Individual" (1827) to "The Soul That Feels in Its Immediacy" (1830), and its Remark is lengthened to include new reflections on feeling.

To understand where the dreaming soul comes from, it is necessary to return to a far earlier Hegel text—his 1794 manuscript on psychology (MS)—to which Hoffmeister gave the appropriate title of "Materien [building blocks] zu einer Philosophie des subjektiven Geistes."[3] Although the possible relation between the early manuscript on psychology and the mature editions of the *Philosophy of Subjective Spirit* is noted by Petry, in his 1978 translation of the work,[4] substantial investigation into the MS as a source of Hegel's later work has remained neglected. Perhaps this is because of the nondiscursive, fragmentary nature of the untranslated manuscript, the fact it is largely written in point form, with many abbreviations. It is nonetheless remarkable that much of the content of the dreaming or feeling soul section of the mature *Philosophy of Subjective Spirit* appears to reprise the contents of a text penned by Hegel thirty-six years before subjective spirit's ultimate expression. What is even more remarkable is that the seminal text was actually composed by someone other than Hegel.

I will return to the crucial question of provenance later. For now, let us look briefly at the content of the 1794 MS and compare it with the later editions of the *Philosophy of Subjective Spirit*. Not only will this establish the early manuscript as a source, but it will also shed light on the origins of the dreaming soul and help us understand why it is replaced by feeling in the 1830 edition of the *Encyclopedia*.

Although the 1794 MS is pregnant with references to psychological theoreticians of the time,[5] the MS appears, above all, born under the sign of Kant's transcendental esthetic, through his interpreters Johannes Schultze and Karl Reinhold. The latter's contribution explains why the first part of the MS deals with the mind as productive of representations (*Vorstellungen*), either as representations of sentience (*Empfindungsvorstellungen*), derived from the five outer senses, or as representations from the inner life of the human organism. The latter enable us to feel inner changes, inner states, and include "representations from the soul, not worked on by consciousness." The "fundamental power of the soul" (*Seele*)[6] to generate unbidden, raw representations haunts the entire middle section of the MS, from about lines 150 to 540 in Hoffmeister's edition, whereupon the section on the understanding (*Verstand*) and its concepts puts an abrupt end to the soul's representations of Phantasie.[7] Indeed, the MS's central project concerns how to rationally explain the unconscious resurgence (*Wiedererweckung*) of forgotten, outer-produced representations and of unbidden inner representations. While the understanding will actively recall inner, conserved representations through remembrance (*Erinnerung*), this does not explain the resurgence of representations "ohne Erinnerung," as experienced, for example, by the sleepwalker or the cataleptic.[8]

The underlying goal of the central part of the 1794 MS, which includes the section that pertains directly to the question raised in this chapter, is consequently an attempt to impose reason on the unreasonable, to assign rational causes to the irrational manifestations of the soul. If we can establish what brings about spontaneous representations of the imagination or Phantasie, we may control them. The MS presents a number of possible laws and causes for the unbidden resurgence of representations.[9] The explanations include deformation of the brain, physical illness (hypochondria), fever, passion, light and darkness, weather and drunkenness. The general cause favored by the MS, however, is a weakening of conscious memory (*Gedächnis*), brought on by illness.[10] In sickness, weakened consciousness is "overpowered" by the soul and its "arbitrary" representations, now forming delusional trains of thought according to Phantasie's own "laws of association."[11]

Those familiar with the articulations of the *Philosophy of Subjective Spirit* will have already recognized common elements in the 1794 MS. The references to sleepwalking, to rational thought as remembrance (Erinnerung), are echoed in the content of the mature *Philosophy of Subjective Spirit*. The idea of the soul as an unstable store of preserved inner- and outer-generated images prefigures the "indeterminate pit" (*Schacht*) that forms the soul of each individual, in *Philosophy of Subjective Spirit* § 403, and that is the source of dreams, illusions, and madness. Above all, the conflictual nature of the relation between conscious mind and the "laws of Phantasie" (line 286 Hoffmeister),[12] where any weakening on the part of the former allows dominance by the latter, is clearly echoed in the 1830 edition of *Philosophy of Subjective Spirit*, § 405, where Hegel presents the pathological state of *Gemüt* as arising from an unnatural predominance of the soul over rational subjectivity.[13] As well, in the 1794 MS, the soul already displays a recalcitrant, stubborn nature, a tendency to fixate on ideas and resist change, only accepting "the new" through "unpleasant exercise [and] habit,"[14] an idea the *Philosophy of Subjective Spirit* introduces in § 409.[15] On a broader scale, one might also argue that the 1794 MS's stark juxtaposition between the dreamlike imaginings of the unconscious soul and the immediately subsequent section on conscious understanding is later developed into the dialectical transition between anthropology and psychology that Hegel presents in the *Philosophy of Subjective Spirit*'s "Phenomenology" section.

This is not the place to examine all the differences between the 1794 MS and the mature versions of the *Philosophy of Subjective Spirit* as a whole as, for example, the fact that the MS puts representation in the context of anthropology, rather than presenting it, along with intuition, as a function of conscious mind or that the MS goes on to evoke such apparently extraneous Kantian elements as reflective esthetic judgments and cosmology. Nor is there space to discuss further parallels in content, such as the MS's references to *Phantasie* as productive of literary discourse (*Dichtungskraft*) and the understanding's capacity to produce linguistic signs, discussions taken up in the *Philosophy of Subjective Spirit* § 458.[16] Now, I want to focus on the section within the MS that concerns me most, where Hegel most clearly finds the building blocks (*Materien*) for his later discussion of the dreaming soul, which will become the feeling soul, in 1830.

The section that I am particularly interested in, because it pertains directly to the Dreaming/Feeling Soul in the *Philosophy of Subjective Spirit*, runs from lines 363 to 538 in Hoffmeister's *Dokumente zu Hegels* Entwicklung[17] and immediately follows the lines that I have just been discussing, on the reasons and laws governing the spontaneous resurgence of the soul's representations. The section is entitled, "Use on Certain Conditions Where *Phantasie* Takes Part: Dreams, Somnambulism, Madness (*Verrückung*)[18] Premonitions, Visions." In fact, this MS text actually begins with a subsection entitled "Sleep," includes references to clairvoyance as well as to premonition, and ends with a final subtitled section on religious fervor (*Schwärmerei*) and enthrallment (*Enthusiasmus*). The content found in this well-defined section of the 1794 MS is all covered in the *Philosophy of Subjective Spirit*'s "Dreaming/feeling Soul" subchapter, in §§ 403 to 408, and particularly in §§ 405 and 406.[19] This correspondence is, of course, more obvious in the 1827 edition, where Hegel still refers to dreaming, which, as mentioned above, is an actual heading in the 1794 MS. Furthermore, at the end of § 390 of the 1827 edition, Hegel still refers to the following section (from §§ 391 to 402) as dealing with "the sleeping soul," a reference that is dropped in favor of "the natural soul," in the 1830 edition. In other words, the 1827 edition clearly displays the mature *Philosophy of Subjective Spirit*'s (*both* editions') debt to the 1794 MS, in which the sleeping soul is presented as a condition where *Phantasie* has free play, bringing forth both clear and obscure representations that are easily confused with those derived from the senses. The sleeping soul of the MS is one that hears and sees things that are not there. It dreams and walks in its sleep, which may be "magnetic";[20] it may become melancholy, mad, or deranged; have premonitions or visions; and may even fall into the worst excesses of religious fervor. Significantly, these *"Zustände"* (conditions) are pathological, not because sleeping and dreaming are, in themselves, symptomatic of illness but because they represent a state where conscious "power over the imagination" (*Macht über die Einbildungskraft*)[21] is lost. It is the pathological divagations of the dreaming soul that come to an abrupt halt, when it is snapped awake at the end of this passage, by the stark, unyielding title of the following MS section: *"Verstand."* Similarly, in *Philosophy of Subjective Spirit*'s §§ 403 to 408, the dreaming/feeling soul is one whose "determinations are *not* developed in conscious content arising from the understanding."[22] In fact, as Hegel puts it in the § 404 Remark, we are clearly dealing with a pathological "condition [*Zustand*] where the development of the soul, having already arrived at [. . .] consciousness and understanding may once again relapse."[23] The mature *Philosophy of Subjective Spirit*'s presentation of dreaming, somnambulism, folly, premonitions, visions, and religious fervor as pathological states appears to be derived from the "building blocks" of the 1794 MS. The 1827 edition's references to the sleeping and dreaming soul make this particularly evident. However, another, more peculiar shared reference establishes the MS's paternity, beyond any doubt.

In the 1794 MS, at the beginning of the section on sleep, there appears the single word, or rather name "Haller," followed by the words, "incapacity to move freely."[24] I suspected the text referred to the famous 18th-century physician Albrecht von Haller but could not grasp the reference nor see what it had to do with the topic treated: how our imagined representations may actually be clearer, more distinct than our empirical ones. In fact, the name Haller appears again in the 1827–28 lecture notes, recently translated by Robert Williams, however not in the principal Erdmann manuscript but in the Walter notes from the same lectures, which Williams helpfully adds in footnotes. The Walter notes add an even more enigmatic reference, writing, "Haller and the glass leg."[25] The lengthy Boumann *Zusatz* to *Philosophy of Subjective Spirit* § 408 also refers to "someone who imagined he had glass feet [being] cured by the staging of a pretended robbery."[26] Googling "Haller and glass feet or legs" will give you some very strange results, but it will not give you the solution to the enigma, which is found in Petry's edition of the *Philosophy of Subjective Spirit*, specifically in the lecture notes taken by Griesheim and Kehler, in the subjective spirit lectures of 1825.[27] Here, we discover that Dr. Haller in Göttingen (therefore indeed Albrecht von Haller) cured a patient who believed he was incapable of movement because he believed he had glass legs, by having some of Haller's students attack him and his patient while the two were riding in a carriage. Haller ran off; the patient did likewise and was thus cured. Incidentally, the fact that the Erdmann manuscript chooses not to include what may simply be taken as a colorful anecdote occults the fact that much of the content of the *Philosophy of Subjective Spirit* "Anthropology" *Zusätze* is inspired by writings in what was known at the time as empirical psychology. I will return to this later. For now, it is enough to have proven that Hegel used the 1794 manuscript on psychology more than thirty years after transcribing it, in his lectures accompanying the *Encyclopedia*, at least as late as 1827.

Besides clearly influencing Hegel in his determination of dreamlike states as pathological conditions, it is above all the general context of the MS that reveals an essential aspect of the mature *Philosophy of Subjective Spirit*, one that will explain the move from "dreaming" to "feeling" soul. This aspect is discovered in the fact that both the MS and the *Philoso-*

phy of Subjective Spirit consider the same mental pathologies as arising from a power struggle between rational understanding and the imagination, where the former loses its mastery and is overcome. The pertinence of this struggle, however, only becomes clear if we return to a question left in suspense above, that is, the question of provenance. Where does the 1794 MS come from, and what do its origins signify?

The editors of the critical *Gesammelte Werke*, having analyzed the MS's handwriting and the paper's watermark, conclude it was penned while Hegel was in Bern, probably in 1794.[28] However, Hoffmeister had already speculated that the actual content of the MS was derived from a course Hegel had taken while at Tübingen, from someone in the "Abel'schen Kreis."[29] Referring to the testimonial of Hegel's fellow student Betzendörfer, Hoffmeister supposes the source of the MS to have been the Tübingen professor J. F. Flatt, whose course in empirical psychology Hegel followed, in 1789/90.[30] The MS on psychology therefore seems to be the later transcription of course notes that Hegel took while attending Flatt's lectures four or five years earlier. This supposition seems confirmed by Dieter Henrich, who in 1964 discovered the course notes of Friedrich Klüpfel, another fellow Tübingen student of Hegel who also took Flatt's course in 1790.[31] The content of the Klüpfel course notes is virtually identical to most of the 1794 psychology MS, including that portion of the manuscript under discussion here that deals with the pathological imaginings of the sleeping and dreaming soul and that informs, I have shown, the mature *Philosophy of Subjective Spirit*. This means that much of the inspiration for *Philosophy of Subjective Spirit* §§ 403 to 408, on the dreaming/feeling soul, actually comes from J. F. Flatt.[32]

Such a conclusion may be unsettling and even distasteful to those who see Flatt as the "Scrooge of Tübingen," as Frederick Beiser calls him in his *Fate of Reason*.[33] Flatt is best known as the assistant of the dogmatic theology professor G. C. Storr, famous for his anachronistic and quixotic defense of orthodox religion and the literal truth (i.e., Revelation) of the Bible, the Trinity, and miracles, in the face of the Kantian critiques. Surely, both Flatt and Storr are included in the disparaging remarks Hegel and Schelling share in their correspondence of late 1794 and early 1795, on the poor state of theology at Tübingen. However, as Beiser himself points out, there are, in fact, two Flatts, the "reactionary" professor of theology, defender of supernaturalism[34] and the earlier version, a champion of Leibnizian/Wolffian late Enlightenment reason, against Kant's critique of metaphysical thought. In his famous polemical reviews of Kant's work (1788 and

1789),³⁵ Flatt is arguing for the objective reality of transcendent causation and the consequent possibility for a cosmological proof of the existence of God. In other words, Flatt defends the Enlightenment reason of Leibniz, Wolff, and Mendelssohn against the limitations imposed by Kant's first *Critique*. It is this J. F. Flatt who put together the lecture notes on empirical psychology. My contention is consequently that the *Philosophy of Subjective Spirit* section on the dreaming/feeling soul, which Hegel derives from Flatt's 1790 lectures, is thoroughly informed by Flatt's Enlightenment project, the defense of reason against its perceived opposite: the excessive claims of Phantasie, including somnambulism, premonitions, clairvoyance, and religious fervor (*Schwärmerei*, as a form of mental illness).

The *Philosophy of Subjective Spirit* sections on the dreaming/feeling soul are particularly clear expressions of this Enlightenment project championed by the early Flatt, because those sections correspond so well to the part of the 1794 MS under discussion, entitled "Use on certain conditions where Phantasie plays a part." What is being *used* here is empirical psychology, and the goal of this application is to show that these supposedly exalted, paranormal conditions may be explained scientifically and reasonably, as pathologies. This becomes evident when we understand where Flatt found the material for this discrete part of his lectures. Curiously, this is the one part of the MS where Hoffmeister, in his exhaustive analysis of its diverse references, renounces finding a source.

In fact, a clue to discovering Flatt's source for this section can be found, although somewhat circuitously, in a case of *Seelenkrankheit* (sickness of the soul) referred to in the addition to *Philosophy of Subjective Spirit* § 406.³⁶ In the *Zusatz*, Hegel mentions a case of a soldier who deserted his post and hurried to his mother in a town some distance away, because he had the clear premonition that she was "being tied up by robbers." Although this case attained some notoriety in late 18th Century Prussia, probably because the soldier was only lightly punished,³⁷ I found the original account in C. P. Moritz's *Magazin zur Erfahrungsseelenkunde*, a popular review published in Berlin between 1783 and 1793. While the *Magazin* may possibly claim the title of first journal of psychiatry, it is certainly the first journal of anthropology, as Hegel understands that science in the *Philosophy of Subjective Spirit*. An original Moritz footnote to this account (*Desertion aus einem unbekannten Bewegungsgrunde* [Desertion for an Unknown Motive]) is highly revealing of the *Magazin*'s overall mission and its impact on Hegel's *Philosophy of Subjective Spirit*, through Flatt's course material on the dreaming soul.³⁸ In his note, Moritz explains that such accounts of visions or clairvoyance are symptomatic of a "sick condition of the soul," where it is allowed to express its natural qualities too strongly. Although the *Magazin* regularly presents speculations on the nature of the soul and reflections on "speech from a psychological point of view," most of the volumes are dedicated to recounting testimonials of dreams, nightmares, somnambulism, and what we might call parapsychological or even paranormal experiences. Most significantly, the *Magazin* then brings these cases into the realm of scientific explanation, debunking them, one might say, by presenting them in terms of pathology, in order that we may reasonably know those aspects of the self that seem to lie beyond reason.[39] The often colorful, highly subjective anecdotes and accounts are the stuff of empirical psychology or empirical anthropology, in the sense of the journal's scientific concept of *Erfahrungsseelenkunde*. The picturesque examples that nourish a number of the *Philosophy of Subjective Spirit*'s *Zuzätze* are drawn from the *Magazin* and other similar sources. In spite of all the obvious qualities of Erdmann's 1827 lecture notes, his philosophical decision to concentrate exclusively on Hegel's conceptual discourse while leaving out the empirical psychology material is not without consequence. We thus tend to forget the intellectual impetus that motivates these sources: the late Enlightenment's struggle against supernatural religious fervor, enthrallment, and fanaticism, taken together under the term *Schärmerei*. In empirical psychology, in Flatt's lectures and the 1794 MS, as well as in the mature *Philosophy of Subjective Spirit*, this conflict is played out within the human psyche, in the constant power struggle between rational understanding and the dreaming soul, that defines sanity and madness.[40]

Flatt's 1789/90 lectures on empirical psychology were certainly inspired by the *Magazin*'s late Enlightenment mission of using "modern" anthropology to show that the excess of Phantasie and, particularly the manifestations of *Schwärmerei*, are pathological conditions of the soul. In this light, it should be no surprise that Moses Mendelssohn served as an early advisor to the review.[41] If indeed Hegel's 1794 MS is informed, through Flatt, by this aspect of the Enlightenment project, and if the MS informs the mature *Philosophy of Subjective Spirit*, then it may also be useful in explaining the move from the dreaming soul to the feeling soul, which takes place in the mature *Philosophy of Subjective Spirit* between the 1827 and 1830 editions. My hypothesis is that Hegel espouses the Enlightenment dimension of the section on the sleeping and dreaming soul in his struggle against the *Gefühlsreligion* of his Berlin rival, the theologian Schleiermacher, whose religion of feeling can now be seen as a type of

Schwärmerei, and thus as a pathological condition of the dreaming soul. Reference to Schleiermacher's religion of feeling in this section would explain the changing of the section's title to "The Feeling Soul" and the attendant alterations to the section's content.

Much has been written on the Hegel-Schleiermacher conflict at Berlin, but this is not the place to revisit it.[42] In order to support the likelihood of my idea that Hegel makes the change from "dreaming" to "feeling" as a result of this conflict, it is necessary to show three things: 1) that Hegel associates Schleiermacher with expressions of feeling, 2) that Schleiermacher's religion of feeling is referred to in the *Philosophy of Subjective Spirit* section on the feeling soul, and 3) that Hegel had a Schleiermacher-related reason to change the title of the section between 1827 and 1830.

1

Although Hegel refers to Schleiermacher, or to his writings, in his early essays, the *Difference Between the Systems of Fichte and Schelling* (1801) and *Faith and Knowing* (1802), and briefly in the *Philosophy of Right* (1820), his main and most polemical treatment of his Berlin colleague and rival is found in the preface Hegel wrote to H. F. W. Hinrichs' *Philosophy of Religion* (1822). Tracing the trajectory of these references, it may be argued that the evolution of Hegel's attitude toward Schleiermacher follows the latter's own progression from a religion of intuition, an expression he uses in the first edition of the *Speeches on Religion* (1799), to a religion of feeling, a term he introduces in later editions of the *Speeches* and develops fully in his *Dogmatics* (1821),[43] where the essence of religion is defined as the feeling of dependency toward God. In parallel, Hegel moves from a position of Schelling-influenced intellectual intuition, not entirely dissimilar to Schleiermacher's early idea of religion as an intuition of the universe, to a mature position where intuition tends to be assimilated into feeling, which is thought of as subjective, arbitrary, and naturally debased. The progression of Hegel's own thought in this area consequently allows him to caricature Schleiermacher's mature thought as revealing what it has been from its very origins in the *Speeches*, a religion of natural, subjective feeling. Thus, Hegel is able to famously write, in the preface to Hinrichs' *Religion*, "If, in man, religion is based entirely on feeling [. . .] the dog would then be the best Christian, for the dog [. . .] lives mainly within feeling," and further on, "[a] dog also has feelings of redemption when its hunger is satisfied by a bone."[44] The central argument of the preface consists in a genealogical demonstration that presents Schleiermacher's religion of feeling as symptomatic of a contemporary malaise, where modern cultures of empiricism and skepticism have fostered the belief that feeling is the only way to experience the truth.

2

How does religion, and more specifically, the religion of feeling, appear as a form of mental pathology, in the dreaming/feeling soul section of the *Philosophy of Subjective Spirit*? As mentioned above, the final part of the dreaming soul section of the 1794 MS deals with religious fervor and enthusiasm, a fact that is perfectly coherent with the pro-Enlightenment aspect of the MS's source. As the MS already puts it, the "religious pretension" of having access to "supernatural sources of knowledge" (übernaturalische Erkenntnisquellen) is, in fact, a form of "natural and transcendent ignorance." There is no mention of religious feeling in the MS because what will later be described as *Gefühl* and its pretension to immediate, absolute knowledge of the divine is, in 1794, still assigned to the delusional representations of Phantasie. Nonetheless, early religious fantasy shares with the later expression of *Gefühl* the character of naturalness, regarding both origin and pathological morbidity. Thus, in the MS, the cause of the *Schwärmerei* condition is either an "irritability of the organs" or an "over-stimulation of the imagination," and, in its worst excesses, morbid religious fanaticism actually leads to murder.[45] This natural aspect of *Schwärmerei* is clearly echoed in Hegel's preface to Hinrichs' *Religion*, where the practitioner of the religion of feeling (i.e., Schleiermacher) is repeatedly described as "the natural man" who claims to know God "without knowing anything at all."[46]

Feeling takes on increased importance between the 1827 and the 1830 editions of the *Philosophy of Subjective Spirit*, as reflected in the change of title at § 403. In the 1827 *Philosophy of Subjective Spirit*, Hegel does not make the distinction between sentience (*Empfindung*) and feeling (*Gefühl*). As we find articulated in the Erdmann lecture notes, "There is no great distinction to be made between sentience and feeling."[47] However, in § 402 of the 1830 edition, Hegel does come to make this distinction, which then allows him to introduce the new feeling-related section headings in that same edition—"The Feeling Soul" (§ 403), "The Feeling Soul in Its Immediacy" (§ 405, where he also substantially lengthens the Remark, on feeling)—and to replace the term "sentient" with "feeling" twice in § 407 (self-feeling). In a lengthy and instructive note, Williams provides a commentary on Hegel's later distinction between *Empfindung* and *Gefühl*.[48]

Williams remarks that Hegel regards *Gefühl* as more active than the other concept, allowing Williams to associate *Selbstgefühl* with the first inchoate articulations of self-consciousness or "self-awareness,"[49] thereby downplaying the essential natural, animal aspect of the concept. As we see in the preface to Hinrichs' *Religion*, however, feeling, like sentience, remains natural, although the former seems particularly given to inwardness. In the 1830 *Philosophy of Subjective Spirit*, this natural quality of interior feeling is assured by its intimate bond to *Leiblichkeit* (corporeity or "bodilyness").[50] For our purposes, it is perhaps enough to say that the dreams of the sentient soul take place in sleep while the feeling soul gives rise to waking dreams that are forms of folly. Although self-feeling may mark the first instance of self-distinguishing necessary for subsequent differentiation in consciousness, Hegel presents it as an immediate, "magical" division or judgment (*Urteilen*, as original dividing), which is inherently unstable in its lack of syllogistic mediation. This is why self-feeling is open to fixed conditions (*Zustände*) of derangement, alienation, and madness.[51]

References to religion in the 1827 Erdmann lecture notes on the dreaming soul section of the *Philosophy of Subjective Spirit* deal with *Schwärmerei* in the form of enthrallment and fanaticism. In these notes, Hegel refers to the surprising fact, gleaned from Pinel's Parisian experiences, that one-fifth to one-fourth of all those in mental asylums suffer from religious delusions.[52] These references in Erdmann's notes are found in the paragraphs immediately preceding the discussion of "Habit" (*Philosophy of Subjective Spirit* § 409) and thus correspond perfectly to the position of the subsection on *Schwärmerei* in the last part of the dreaming soul section of the 1794 MS. As well, Walter's notes from the 1827 lectures actually echo the MS's reference to religious fanaticism and murder.[53] However, it is important to see that by 1827, Hegel apparently considers the *Phantasievorstellungen* (delusional representations) of religious fanaticism as either marginal or largely a thing of the past. They are not mentioned in the body of the *Encyclopedia* text and are only alluded to briefly in the accompanying lectures. In this sense, Griesheim's notes (1825) refer to it being "no longer the case" that "a lot of people" suffer from mental derangement through "religious representations (*Vorstellungen*)." This does not mean, however, that religious delusion has disappeared. It has merely changed form. The pathologies of religious fervor, of *Schwärmerei*, originally discussed in the 1794 MS as conditions of the dreaming soul, are now present in the contemporary culture of feeling, whose perfect expression is found in Schleiermacher's *Gefühlsreligion*.[54] "Life in feeling," writes Hegel in § 406 of the 1830 edition, "as a form or state of the self-conscious, cultivated man, is a sickness where the individual relates immediately to his own concrete content." This is a form of folly or derangement because the "feeling individual" as "simple ideality" (§ 403), is, in fact, feeling his own particularity. He thinks he has an intuition of God when he is actually only feeling himself; he is thus symptomatic of "the perversion, the particular arrogance and absolute egoism that have surfaced in our time."[55]

Above all, Schleiermacher's religion of feeling is an affront to reason and science. It betrays "an animal ignorance" (*tierische Unwissenheit*), as Hegel writes in the preface to Hinrichs *Religion*.[56] The fact that precisely the same term (*Unwissenheit*) is found in the 1794 MS, with reference to *Schwärmerei*, at the end of the section on the dreaming soul[57] not only reveals the late Enlightenment source of Hegel's critique, it is also an indication that Schleiermacher's religion of feeling should be understood as a privileged manifestation of the mental pathology Hegel comes to call feeling.

3

Finally, what happened between 1827 and 1830 that would make Hegel want to change the heading of § 403 from "Dreaming Soul" to "Feeling Soul," and to clearly distinguish feeling from sentience, as a form of mental derangement? The answer, I believe, is found in Hegel's correspondence from the fall of 1829. Letters between Hegel and several of his collaborators on the *Journal of Scientific Criticism* reveal Hegel's preoccupation with recent critical attacks against the 1827 edition of his *Encyclopedia*. He clearly associates these attacks with Schleiermacher. "It seems the [anonymous] Letters Against the Encyclopedia are from Schleiermacher," he writes in a letter to Daub, on September 27, 1829. In his response on October 11, Daub writes that he also supposed the anonymous author to be Schleiermacher. A letter from Rust, on October 7, 1829, in which he excuses himself for not yet having delivered his critical review of several dogmatic works from the Schleiermacher camp, refers to fighting "with sharp weapons the pretensions and arrogance of the school of feeling," (*Gefühlsschule*) promising to "expose the pathetic activity of the Pietists and superficial theologians." Consequently, it is safe to say that Hegel revised the 1827 edition of the *Encyclopedia* at a time when he felt it was under attack by Schleiermacher and his *Gefühlsschule*. What better response than to let the object of the attack, the *Encyclopedia of Philosophical Sciences*, show his rival's position to be not only deeply unscientific but also symptomatic of a delusional feeling soul?[58] The formulation of such a response is perfectly consistent with the pro-Enlightenment flavor of the earlier articulations of the dreaming soul, which we discovered through the empirical psychology roots of the 1794 MS and reason's stand against religious enthrallment and fanaticism.

Notes

1. LPS, 6.

2. In this chapter, *Philosophy of Subjective Spirit* refers to the *Philosophy of Subjective Spirit* as presented in both 1827 and 1830 editions. When I need to distinguish between these editions, I shall do so explicitly.

3. An early edition of the 1794 MS can be found in Johannes Hoffmeister, *Dokumente zu Hegels Entwicklung* (Stuttgart-Bad Cannstart: Fromman-Holzboog, 1974 [1936]), 194–217. Cf. the later critical edition, which I will also refer to: G. W. F. Hegel, *Gesammelte Werke, Herausgegeben von der Rheinische-Westfälischen Akademie der Wissenschaften*, vol. 1, F. Nicolin, G. Schüler eds. (Hamburg: Felix Meiner, 1989) [= GW1], 165–92.

4. PSS, vol. 1, 1.

5. See Hoffmeister, 453.

6. GW1, 172, lines 6, 14. All translations are my own, unless otherwise noted.

7. GW1, 173, line 10.

8. GW1, 172, lines 17–18.

9. GW1, 175–177, line 19.

10. GW1, 175–177, lines 3–13.

11. GW1, 175–177, lines 3–13.

12. GW1, 177, line 8.

13. The remark to § 405 in the 1830 edition is substantially longer than in 1827, reflecting its new heading: "The Feeling Soul in Its Immediacy," which replaces "The Passive Totality of the Individual." This new heading and the added content on feeling is coherent with the section's change of title, which I am discussing, in § 403. The lengthened remark represents one of the more significant differences between the two editions and reflects the new emphasis on feeling as opposed to dreaming and thus falls under the subject of this chapter.

14. GW1, 173, line 9.

15. The section I am discussing from the 1827 and 1830 editions of the *Philosophy of Subjective Spirit* can be found in the 1817 edition, from §§ 320 to 326, where Hegel presents many of the same mental particularities (somnambulism, dreaming, clairvoyance, etc.) and habit, found in the last editions of the *Philosophy of Subjective Spirit* and that can be traced back to the MS. It is perhaps

worth mentioning that none of this material can be found in the 1822 fragment on anthropology (translated in Williams and in Petry), nor, as Petry points out, in any of the "spirit" material from the prephenomenological Jena period. I would simply add that, in the 1822 fragment, Hegel does refer to the "self-sentient soul" (*sich empfindende Seele*) in terms of a power struggle between the soul (which cannot control itself) and free, self-controlling consciousness. As I mentioned, this is the theme of both the central part of the MS and the later dreaming/feeling soul section of the *Philosophy of Subjective Spirit*. See PSS, vol. 1, 134–35.

16. Enz. (1817), § 380.

17. Hoffmeister, *Dokumente*, 205–10; GW1, 179–84.

18. GW1, 179. Cf. Hoffmeister, who reads the manuscript as *Verzückung* (rapture), which does not fit with the actual content of the section.

19. Enz. (1830), § 408 reflects, to a greater extent, later influences and readings, for example, in Z. Philippe Pinel's seemingly arbitrary theoretical nosography of mental illness (1798, 1803, 1807, etc.) is reorganized and "conceptualized" here by Hegel.

20. GW1, 181, line 15.

21. GW1, 181, line 3. In the mature *Philosophy of Subjective Spirit* magnetism is ambiguously presented as both an illness and a cure. Besides the dialectical truth of this fact (i.e., the addition of more negativity, i.e., of sickness, overcomes the sickness and effectuates the cure), the curative properties of magnetism are probably inspired by Hegel's reading of the works of the Marquis de Puységur, who is much more interested in this aspect than is his mentor, Antoine Mesmer. Puységur's Mémoires pour servir à l'histoire et à l'établissement du magnétisme animal was published in 1785.

22. Enz. (1830), § 404, at the beginning of the Remark; my emphasis.

23. This passage provides a seldom remarked key to Hegel's discussion of psychopathology. It is thought of in terms of a regression, and it is only as such, as pathology, that these "abstract configurations" of the soul become for us. In other words, Hegel is not saying that the development of human consciousness necessarily passes through madness and then is cured. He is saying that the unconscious level of the soul is always present and because of its power, represents a possible condition into which rational mind may relapse. As well, Hegel seems to be saying, in the same remark, that it is through observation of these relapses in other minds that science is able to study the unconscious soul. Hegel explicitly recognizes a fact now taken for granted in psychiatry: knowledge of the mind is developed through study of human psychopathologies. There has been much recent interest in Hegel's theory of madness. English language studies include: Daniel Berthold-Bond, *Hegel's Theory of Madness* (Albany: State University of New York Press, 1995); Kirk Pillow, "Habituating Madness and Phantasying Art in Hegel's Encyclopedia," *Owl of Minerva* 28, no. 2, 183–215; Jon Mills, *The Unconscious Abyss: Hegel's Anticipation of Psychoanalysis* (Albany: State University of New York Press, 2002).

24. GW1, 179, line 19.

25. LPS, 152, n. 269. Another reference is found in Walter's notes on p. 145 n. 236, referring to "feet of glass."

26. PPS, vol. 2, 383.

27. PPS, vol. 2, 385.

28. GW1, 483–87.

29. Hoffmeister, 453. On Tübingen professor J. F. Abel's interpretation of Kant's first Critique, see George di Giovanni, *Freedom and Religion in Kant and His Immediate Successors* (Cambridge: Cambridge University Press, 2005), 311–12.

30. The course was officially listed as either "empiricam psychologicam" or "Psych. empiricam" in the Tübingen course calendar. GW1, 484–85.

31. The fact that Rozenkranz makes no mention of having found a Hegel notebook from Flatt's course has led some to surmise that such a notebook did not exist and therefore that Hegel must have borrowed the notes from another fellow student, F. H. Mögling, who was also a house tutor in Bern around 1794. However, H. S. Harris's explanation for the fact Rozenkranz does not mention finding Hegel's course notes for Flatt's course is convincingly elegant: Hegel had simply thrown out his notes after having transcribed what he wanted from them, in 1794! H. S. Harris, *Hegel's Development*, vol. 1, 83–84. See also GW1, 484–85. The editors of the GW volume helpfully include the text from Klüpfel's notes in the *Anmerkungen* section.

32. Hoffmeister, in *Dokumente*, analyzes the multitudinous references in the 1794 MS and recognizes Flatt as synthesizing them into lecture notes.

33. Frederick C. Beiser, *The Fate of Reason* (Cambridge Mass.: Harvard University Press, 1987), 210.

34. "Reactionary" is from Beiser, 11. The supernaturalism of Storr/Flatt used Kant's first critique in a tendentious way: Because the noumenal realm is beyond empirical knowledge, its content must be known by Revelation.

35. In other words, while he was preparing his lectures on empirical psychology, he wrote his *Fragmentarische Beyträge zur Bestimmung und Deduktion des Begriffs und Grundsätze der Causalität* and the *Briefe über den moralischen Erkenntnissgrund der Religion*. See Beiser, 211–14.

36. PSS, vol. 2, 291.

37. PSS, vol. 2, 545.

38. All 13 volumes have been edited by Petra and Uwe Nettelbeck (Nördlingen: Franz Greno, 1986). For the case in question, see volume 2, 17–18. Petry presents a helpful list of contemporary German works on anthropology, PSS, vol. 1, lxiii–lxvi.

39. The full title of the *Magazin* is actually *Gnothi sauton* (in Greek letters = know yourself) *oder Magazin zur* . . .

40. Another sign of Hegel's interest in empirical psychology around the time he copied out his Flatt lecture notes to form the 1794 manuscript is his request, at the end of his Christmas Eve 1794 letter to Schelling that his friend have the "review of Mauchart's Repertorium" sent to him in Berne. Mauchart was a former teaching assistant at the Tübingen Stift. His *Allgemeines Repertorium für empirische Psychologie* (1792–) was a journal very similar in content and motivation to Moritz's *Magazin*. Perhaps Hegel's earliest sign of an interest in *Seelenkunde* is the excerpt

he copied from Campe's *"kleine Seelenlehre für Kinder"* in October 1786. See Hoffmeister, *Dokumente*, 101.

41. See the informative doctoral thesis on the *Magazin* by Kim Soo-Jung, "Vorhersehungsvermögen und Taubstummheit: Zwei Aspekte der Leib/Seele-Problematik" in Karl Philipp Moritz' "Magazin zur Erfahrungsseelenkunde" (Kiel: Christian-Albrechts-Universität, 2001). On Mendelssohn, see p. 15. Another late Enlightenment figure is pivotal in the understanding of mental illness as a struggle between reason and unreason: Kant's well-read "Von der Macht des Gemüts durch den blossen Vorsatz seiner krankhaften Gefühle Meister zu sein," published in periodicals in 1796 and again in his *Conflict of the Faculties*. This work and Kant's precritical (1770) essay "Versuch über die Krankeiten des Kopfes" are often neglected by philosophers writing on Hegel's theory of madness.

42. See, for example, Jeffrey Hoover, "The Origin of the Conflict between Hegel and Schleiermacher at Berlin," *The Owl of Minerva* 20, no. 1 (1988), 69–79 and Eric Von Der Luft, *Hegel, Hinrichs and Schleiermacher on Feeling and Religion* (Lewiston, N.Y.: Mellen Press, 1987). See also the chapter "Schleiermacher and Postmodernity" in my *Real Words: Language and System in Hegel* (Toronto: University of Toronto Press, 2007), 104–16.

43. *Der christliche Glaube nach den Grundsätzen der evangelischen Kirche im Zusammenhange dargestellt*. In anticipation of the publication, Hegel writes to Daub (May 9, 1821), "One can pay with markers for a long time, but sooner or later one must pull out one's purse. Will not more markers fall from that purse? We shall see!"

44. G. W. F. Hegel, *Werke in 20 Bänden* vol. 11, E. Moldenhauer and K. M. Michel eds. (Frankfurt am Main: Suhrkamp, 1970), 58.

45. GW1, 184, lines 10–15.

46. *Werke in 20 Bänden* vol. 11, 58, 61. As Von der Luft points out, the reference to natural man is from Luther's translation of the Bible, 1 Cor. 2:14.

47. LPS, 110.

48. LPS, 110 n. 94.

49. This is how Petry translates *Selbstgefühl*, thereby losing all its natural connotations.

50. Enz. (1830), § 404 Remark.

51. Here, as elsewhere, Hegel shows himself to be the great reconciler of two opposing contemporary scientific visions. The bond between the feeling soul and "bodilyness" allows Hegel to grasp mental illness as both physically derived (hypochondriac, for men, hysterical, for women, according to the scientific traditions of the day) and morally (psychically) caused, according to Pinel. The earlier German theoretician, G. E. Stahl, advocates a position similar to Hegel's: mental illness is the result of "an abnormal relationship between mind and body." Ilza Veith, *Hysteria, The History of a Disease* (Chicago: University of Chicago Press, 1965), 187.

52. LPS, 147. The reference Williams discovers is to Pinel, whose work was very influential (as was Puységur's) in the development of Hegel's mature *Philosophy of Subjective Spirit*.

53. LPS, 147 n. 250.

54. In *Faith and Knowing*, Hegel already describes Schleiermacher as a "exponential" expression (*Potenzirung*) of Jacobi. *Werke in 20 Bänden* vol. 2, 391.

55. Preface to Hinrichs' *Philosophy of Religion*. Hegel, *Werke in 20 Bänden* vol. 11, 60. To the extent Hegel associates Schleiermacher with the mental pathology of feeling, he is symptomatic of a generalized social condition.

56. *Werke in 20 Bänden* vol. 11, 65.

57. GW1, 184, line 15. Hoffmeister, *Dokumente*, line 537.

58. The 1829 *Jarbücher für wissenschaftliche Kritik* (no. 10) announces a review, by Hegel, of the "Letters against the *Encyclopedia of Philosophical Sciences*" but does not include it. In the same journal, Hegel does review favorably a book of aphorisms by K. F. Gösche and uses the occasion to reiterate many of the criticisms of contemporary theology (without mentioning Schleiermacher) that he makes in his preface to Hinrichs' *Religion*. *Werke in 20 Bänden* vol. 11, 353–389, 390 n.

The Dark Side of Subjective Spirit

Hegel on Mesmerism, Madness, and Ganglia

GLENN ALEXANDER MAGEE

Introduction

Hegel's treatment of animal magnetism constitutes one of the most extensive discussions of any topic in the *Philosophy of Subjective Spirit*. That Hegel took a strong interest in such an unusual subject is never denied by scholars—but seldom also do they consider what its true importance is for Hegel's philosophy. In this chapter I will present an overview of Hegel's treatment of animal magnetism and its place in the *Philosophy of Subjective Spirit*. Elsewhere I have dealt at greater length with the details of Hegel's discussion of animal magnetism.[1] In the present essay I will focus on why the topic was so important for him and what its place is in the Hegelian system. Specifically, I will argue that Hegel saw his ability to explain animal magnetism as a confirmation of the truth of speculative philosophy—and simultaneously a refutation of science done from the standpoint of the Understanding. I also believe that it is now possible to identify one of the major sources for Hegel's understanding of animal magnetism: the strange speculations of G. H. Schubert in his seminal 1814 work *Die Symbolik des Traumes*.

Hegel on Magic

The "Anthropology" section of the *Philosophy of Subjective Spirit* deals with "Nature-Spirit" (*Naturgeist*), that part of us that is deeper and prior to self-aware mind.[2] Hegel's technical term for this is "the soul" (*die Seele*), which he characterizes as the "sleep of Spirit"—Spirit in its most rudimentary, primal form.[3] Soul is further divided into "natural soul" (*natürliche Seele*) "feeling soul" (*fühlende Seele*), and "actual soul" (*wirkliche Seele*). The natural soul is all that which works within us below the level of consciousness. Feeling soul is a conglomeration of sensations and impressions: consciousness in its most primitive form, prior to the distinction of subjective from objective. The transition to actual soul involves the development of individual subjectivity out of this infantile confusion.

Hegel places his discussion of what we would call today "paranormal phenomena" under "feeling" because he claims that feeling can occur without the participation of the senses at all. This discussion, in fact, constitutes the bulk of the section "Feeling Soul." Hegel states that "feeling, or the subjective way of knowing, dispenses wholly, or at least in part, with the mediations and conditions indispensable to an objective knowledge and can, for example, perceive visible things without the aid of the eyes or without the mediation of light."[4] This is the reason why psychic phenomena such as clairvoyance or precognition (the ability to see the future) seem to involve the acquisition of knowledge without the mediation of the senses. Hegel also tells us that when the individual is at the level of feeling soul another subject may exercise control over it. Hegel calls this controlling, external entity the subject's *Genius*. In infancy the individual lives largely at the level of feeling soul, and another person, such as its mother or father, may act as its genius. Adults may, under certain circumstances, return to the level of feeling soul for a time. Under such conditions, another individual may act as their genius and control them. This idea is central to Hegel's theory of animal magnetism. He says, further, that all such relationships involve "a magic tie," and that they may display "magnetic phenomena."[5]

Hegel explains his use of the word "magic" in a *Zusatz*: "[T]his term connotes a relation of inner to outer or to something else generally, which dispenses with any mediation; a magical power is one whose action is not determined by the interconnection, the conditions and mediations of objective relations; but such a power which produces effects without any mediation is 'the feeling soul in its immediacy.'"[6] A magical relationship is, first of all, unmediated. Second, it annuls the distinctions of time and space. As Hegel makes clear later on, this means that magic is incomprehensible to the Understanding and can only be understood by speculative philosophy. Magic for Hegel includes paranormal phenomena, but it is not confined to these. For instance, Hegel describes the power of a stronger mind over a weaker, and even the power of the mind to spontaneously move the body as "magical."[7]

Hegel next distinguishes two different forms of the magical relationship, and it is here that we encounter Hegel's lengthy treatment of animal magnetism and paranormal phenomena. Hegel names the first of these magical relations "the formal subjectivity of life," which comprises the "life of the child in the womb." He offers some truly memorable illustrations of how the mother may influence the child *in utero*, most of which would today be classed under the rubric of the paranormal:

> This influence is revealed in those phenomena called birthmarks. Many of the phenomena classed under this head may well have a purely organic cause. But as regards many physiological phenomena there can be no doubt that these derive from the feeling of the mother and that, therefore, they have a psychic cause [*psychische Ursache*]. There are, for example, reports of children being born with an injured arm because the mother either had actually broken an arm or at least had knocked it so severely that she feared it was broken, or, again, because she had been frightened by the sight of someone else's broken arm. Similar examples are too familiar to require mention here.[8]

Hegel asserts that this magical relationship continues after the birth of the child. He alludes to cases where parents and children who had been separated at birth met again and "unconsciously felt a mutual attraction."[9]

In the second form of the magical relationship ("the real subjectivity of the feeling soul") the subject is now oriented outward toward the world, albeit in a still-unconscious fashion, whereas in the womb and also in dreams, by contrast, subjectivity is still implicit or withdrawn into itself. Hegel's principal illustration of this is animal magnetism.

Hegel on Animal Magnetism

Hegel writes in paragraph 406, "In this summary encyclopedic account it is impossible to supply a demonstration of what the paragraph states as the nature of the remarkable condition produced chiefly by animal magnetism [*tierische Magnetismus*] — to show, in other words, that it accords with experience."[10] Hegel goes on to address the problem of scientists and other learned men who doggedly refuse even to grant that the phenomena associated with animal magnetism exist. The reason for this, he argues, is that they are caught at the level of the Understanding; hence, animal magnetism is not intelligible to them: "The *a priori* conceptions of these inquirers are so rooted that no testimony can avail against them, and they have even denied what they have seen with their own eyes. In order to believe in this department even what one's own eyes have seen and still more to understand it, the first requisite is not to be in bondage to the hard and fast categories of the Understanding."[11] Hegel is well aware that he is challenging scientific orthodoxy.

The *Zusatz* that follows paragraph 406 goes on at great length and deals not just with animal magnetism, but also with a variety of paranormal phenomena, including clairvoyance, precognition, and metal and water dowsing. Hegel illustrates his discussion with a number of colorful examples, some unintentionally amusing. He recounts, for example, the tale of a French *savant* who could read when a book was pressed against his stomach. Surprisingly, this phenomenon is widely reported in older accounts of animal magnetism.[12] However, this particular gentleman was unique in that his stomach could also read a book from the next room. Hegel discusses the case of a girl who did not know her brother's whereabouts. In a vision, however, she saw accurately that he was sick and confined to a hospital in Spain. Hegel also discusses premonitions, remarking that "people have been awakened and impelled to leave a room or a house by a premonition that the ceiling or the house was about to collapse, which it subsequently did."[13] It is clear that he regards many such stories as credible.

The bulk of Hegel's discussion is devoted to animal magnetism, or mesmerism. Franz Anton Mesmer (1734–1815) was a Swabian physician practicing in Paris who discovered that passing magnets or magnetized objects over his patients not only sometimes improved their conditions, but also had the unintended consequence of putting them into a trance. Mesmer, believing that this might be the means to even greater therapeutic effects, created a new technology for inducing the trance state. One of his inventions, the *baquet*, is described by Hegel as consisting "of a vessel, with iron rods which are touched by the persons to be magnetized, and constitutes the intermediary between them and the magnetizer."[14] Mesmer later found that he could produce the same effects simply by passing his hands over his subjects. In an attempt to explain how these phenomena were possible, he posited the existence of an invisible fluid force which he called *magnétisme animal*.

A French commission led by Benjamin Franklin investigated mesmerism in 1784 and declared the phenomenon pseudoscience. However, numerous favorable studies of mesmerism later appeared in Germany—hence the widespread interest of German intellectuals in the topic. Both Schelling and Hegel had been interested in paranormal phenomena for many years. In an exuberant letter to Hegel dated January 11, 1807, Schelling discusses dowsing and suggests that Hegel perform certain experiments himself. Schelling says of these phenomena, "It is an actual magic incident to the human being, no animal is able to do it. Man actually breaks forth as a sun among other beings, all of which are his planets."[15] A little more than two months later, Schelling wrote to Hegel again, suggesting that Hegel consult an article by his brother Karl on animal magnetism. Karl Eberhard Schelling (1783–1854) was a physician who had studied with Hegel in Jena in 1801–02. In 1807 he published two articles on animal magnetism in the *Jahrbücher der Medicin als Wissenschaft*.

In 1810, Hegel discovered that another of his students from Jena, Peter Gabriel van Ghert, had become interested in animal magnetism. Hegel wrote the following to him:

> I was very interested to hear that you are occupying yourself with animal magnetism. To me this dark region of the organic conditions seems to merit great attention because, among other reasons, ordinary physiological opinions here vanish. It is precisely the simplicity of animal magnetism which I hold to be most noteworthy . . . . Its operation seems to consist in the sympathy into which one animal individuality is capable of entering with a second, insofar as the sympathy of the first with itself, its fluidity in itself, is interrupted and hindered. That [sympathetic] union [of two organisms] leads life back again into its pervasive universal stream. The general idea I have of the matter is that the magnetic state belongs to the simple universal life, a life which thus behaves and generally manifests itself as a simple soul, as the scent of life in general undifferentiated into particular systems, organs, and their specialized activities.[16]

The views expounded in Hegel's letter to van Ghert are, as we shall see, very similar to the theory of animal magnetism he set forth later.

Hegel asserts in the *Philosophy of Subjective Spirit* that in order to produce a mesmeric trance state the will of the magnetizer must be stronger than that of the subject. He states, "The main feature of this magical relationship is that a subject works upon an individual inferior to it in respect of freedom and independence of will . . . It is for this reason that strong men are especially adept at magnetizing female persons."[17] Here we see Hegel drawing on the aforementioned concept of "genius" in order to explain how animal magnetism works. (We shall see, however, that he offers other explanations which go much deeper than this.) At one point in the remarks, Hegel discusses the magnetizer's technique of passing his hands over the subject: "The hand is moved from the head toward the pit of the stomach and from there towards the extremities; care must be taken to avoid stroking backwards because this very easily gives rise to cramps . . . The magnetizer can tell whether he is still effective at a particular distance by feeling a certain warmth in his hand."[18] Hegel's remarks on animal magnetism are so detailed that one suspects he may have had firsthand experience of the phenomenon. Indeed there is a report, quoted in the volume *Hegel in Berichten seiner Zeitgenossen*, that while in Heidelberg Hegel attended mesmeric sittings with Franz Josef Schelver.[19]

Hegel is convinced not only of the reality of animal magnetism, but also of its value for medicine. He states that "in modern times men of unimpeachable integrity have performed so many cures by magnetic treatment that anyone forming an unbiased judgment can no longer doubt the curative power of animal magnetism."[20] Hegel does not, however, issue any calls for further scientific study of the phenomenon. Instead, he remarks that "this subject is now so thoroughly understood that essentially new phenomena are no longer to be expected."[21] What Hegel means by this, however, is that the phenomena associated with animal magnetism are well known; there are abundant testimonies as to its reality and its typical behavior. Nevertheless, exactly *how* it is possible remains a mystery. Hegel believes that he can solve this mystery, however, by situating animal magnetism within the context of his account of Subjective Spirit.

Hegel's Explanations of Animal Magnetism: The Hidden Influence of Schubert

Briefly, Hegel argues that in paranormal states the "feeling" part of the soul temporarily usurps the higher-level, "mental" functions.[22] In a sense, one identifies one's self—again, temporarily—with the most primordial part of the soul. In this identity with the feeling soul ordinary spatiotemporal distinctions are overcome, and along with them, the distinctness of individuals. As a result, Hegel theorizes, phenomena like clairvoyance and mind reading become real possibilities. He states that we can never understand animal magnetism "so long as we assume independent personalities, independent of one another and of the objective world which is their content—so long as we assume the absolute spatial and material externality of one part of being to another."[23]

However, Hegel makes it very clear that he regards psychic states as an aberration of Spirit, not as an elevation of it: "a degradation of Spirit below the level even of ordinary consciousness."[24] Hegel's discussion of insanity in the *Philosophy of Spirit* directly follows his discussion of the paranormal, and he offers a very similar theory to explain insanity. Daniel Berthold-Bond writes:

> Anticipating Freud, Hegel sees madness as a regressive turn backwards into archaic states of mind, a "reversion" or "sinking back" of the developed, rational consciousness into the more primitive world of instincts and drives, or what Hegel calls "the life of feeling" (*Gefühlsleben*) . . . The most general characteristic of madness is this motion of withdrawal into the soul, or the unconscious life of feeling, and the corresponding displacement of the usual relationship with reality.[25]

Hegel states emphatically that "the magnetic state is an *illness* (*Krankheit*)."[26]

However, in addition to these philosophical explanations of mesmerism and madness, in the *Zusätze* we also find Hegel offering bizarre physiological conjectures. Hegel states that "the function exercised by the brain in the waking state of the intellectual consciousness is taken over by the reproductive system during magnetic somnambulism."[27] He states further that in the magnetic trance state, "the soul's activity descends into the brain of the reproductive system, namely into the ganglia (*die Ganglien*), those heavily nodulated nerves in the abdomen."[28]

These physiological speculations seem so strange and incongruous, so out of character, that they make one wonder whether Hegel was drawing on some unacknowledged source here (for indeed he credits these ideas to no one). Turning to M. J. Petry's invaluable annotated edition of the *Philosophy of Subjective Spirit*, we find only the following: "This explanation of animal magnetism began to gain ground in Germany about 1814" (followed by citations of two authors, neither of whom Hegel cites in this context and one of whom he dismisses elsewhere as "superficial").[29]

However, almost certainly the reason this ganglionic theory of animal magnetism became popular around 1814 was the publication that same year of a work Petry seems unfamiliar with: *Die Symbolik des Traumes* (The Symbolism of the Dream) by Gotthilf Heinrich Schubert (1780–1860). We know that Hegel was acquainted with Schubert's other works, and he refers to him briefly in the *Philosophy of Nature*. Though largely forgotten today, Schubert caused a sensation among the *Naturphilosophen* of his time and was highly influential.[30]

As a teenager in Weimar, Schubert had been a pupil of Herder. In Leipzig he studied medicine and theology, then transferred to Jena in 1801 where he became an enthusiastic devotee of Schelling. Schubert practiced medicine for a time, but his heart was not in it. He wrote a novel, *Die Kirche und die Götter* (The Church and the Gods), and then in 1806 a speculative scientific treatise on the nature of life as such, *Ahndungen einer allgemeinen Geschichte des Lebens*. In 1807 Schubert decided to give up medicine and, at the urging of a friend, relocated to Dresden. There, he attracted the attention of Heinrich von Kleist, who was the organizer of a series of lectures on science and art. Kleist invited Schubert to give the 1807–1808 winter lecture series. Schubert, who was only 27 years old at the time, was asked specifically to lecture on animal magnetism, but instead he gave a series of 14 talks which aimed at offering a theory of nature as a whole. The lectures were entitled *Ansichten von der Nachtseite der Naturwissenschaft* (Perspectives on the Night Side—or Dark Side—of Natural Science) and were published under that name in 1808. Schubert dealt over the course of 14 evenings with the "dark side" of such subjects as botany, chemistry, geology, physics, zoology, and most significantly, anthropology. The lectures—only one of which actually dealt with animal magnetism— were well attended by Dresdenites of all sorts, including several members of the nobility.

Schubert, whose father was a Lutheran pastor, had originally wanted to study theology, and his theory of the natural sciences had a distinctly theological flavor. As Frederick Gregory points out, Schubert had been strongly influenced by Schelling—but unlike Schelling he was an old-fashioned theist who did not tend toward pantheism.[31] Very much like Schelling, however, Schubert lays out an account of a scale of nature, with humanity at the apex and lower life forms understood as approximations to the human. He writes that "the life of the entire animal kingdom appears to drive itself onward in a constant striving [*ein stetes Vorwärtsstreben*] toward the human and, just the same, to yearn for it."[32]

When Schubert comes to the topic of human nature and human history, he speculates that we began in a state of primal unity with nature—a unity that has since been broken. Schubert argues that the earliest humans possessed advanced knowledge in many areas. He infers this, in part, from the complexity of ancient languages and religions, as well as from ancient people's knowledge of astronomy. Schubert suggests that originally there was one advanced human society, which then broke up. This society was located, he speculates, near the North Pole, though at a time when the climate there was considerably warmer. Schubert refers to this early, prelapsarian period of unity with nature as the "nighttime" of the human race from which we have since emerged into the light—at the price of losing this original Eden, this unity with nature. Our emergence into the light took many centuries, however, and in the process the human race had to suffer much in the form of internecine conflicts and the degeneration and death of cultures. We were partially guided during this time by dim recollections of the lost, primordial nature wisdom. According to Schubert, however, Christianity has renewed the human race and bestowed on us a better, higher wisdom. He also asserts that our sciences, though they have made great advances in the modern period, are still largely in the service of merely practical ends and are in need of a doctrine that might confer unity upon them.

At the end of his lecture series, Schubert finally got around to the topic of animal magnetism—which played a crucial role in his overall argument. Quite simply, Schubert argues that in animal magnetism—specifically in the trance state of the subject—we see a glimpse of the primordial state of the human mind: not truly conscious, in the sense we understand, and in mysterious, psychic connection with all things. In short, animal magnetism for Schubert involves our consciousness sinking down into a primal state in which it transcends individual personality and the limitations of space and time. As Frederick Gregory notes, "As a result [of the trance state] the soul viewed a nexus of forces normally closed to it, one in which the present and future were linked. The external magnetic forces that attracted the body of the one magnetically treated usurped a portion of the soul, leaving the subject in a dream state."[33] Further, Schubert regards this state not as a "higher," more exalted form of consciousness but as, in effect, a sickness of the soul. In his account, Schubert reviewed numerous case studies of persons who had been magnetized, including some that seemed to suggest that the subjects had precognitive powers. The published version of these lectures was enthusiastically received by Schelling and by two other individuals who were important for Hegel: K. J. H. Windischmann and Franz von Baader. The lectures were also popular with the public and went through four editions.

Schubert returned to the topic of a primordial form of human consciousness in *Die Symbolik des Traumes*. There, he theorizes that the ganglionic system and the cerebral system play opposite roles in the consciousness of the human organism. The cerebral system is responsible for abstract reasoning and the grasp of the moral law. The ganglionic system, on the other hand, is *chthonic*: it ties us in a direct, nonrational fashion to nature itself. One is, in effect, Apollonian, the other Dionysian. Schubert conjectures further that the ganglionic system was much more developed prior to the Fall of Man, an event that resulted in the consciousness of the organism shifting to the upper, cerebral center. Nevertheless, the ganglionic system remains as a kind of vestigial "sixth sense organ," and under certain circumstances it allows us to transcend the limits of space and time through various forms of paranormal phenomena, and especially in the phenomenon of "magnetic clairvoyance." "But," Schubert writes, "these configurations are only a poor echo of the primal power" (*des anfänglichen Vermögens*).[34] Not surprisingly, however, given the position taken in his earlier work, Schubert's ultimate judgment of the ganglionic system and the phenomena it makes possible is highly negative. He regards the ganglionic consciousness as inferior to the cerebral and sees many perils awaiting those who would explore the powers of this mysterious organ.

As I have already noted, Schubert's theories were very influential on the romantic *Naturphilosophen* of his time, and they proved remarkably durable. In the second (1844) volume of *The World as Will and Representation*, for example, Schopenhauer refers to "the unconscious [of the individual], namely the vegetative life with its ganglionic system, into which brain consciousness disappears in sleep," and declares that amongst other things it makes mesmerism possible. Schubert's theories later became influential in theosophical circles, as reflected in James Morgan Pryse's 1910 work *Apocalypse Unsealed*, which attempts to link the *chakras* of Kundalini yoga to the ganglionic system (as well as to the seven seals of the Book of Revelation). This book, in turn, was one of the sources for D. H. Lawrence's odd 1921 work *Fantasia of the Unconscious*, in which his description of the function of the ganglionic system is remarkably similar to Schubert's.

To return to Hegel, though it seems likely that he is drawing on Schubert in his strange aside about the "ganglia," we must ask exactly what use he has made of Schubert's ideas. Needless to say, Hegel did not believe in the "Fall of Man" as a literal event. Nevertheless, he did believe—well before his encounter with Schubert—in a historical process by which, in effect, self-conscious Spirit had gained ascendancy over a naïve and unselfconscious "naturalness," which has it root in what Hegel calls "the soul." The soul, as we have seen, is the "sleep of Spirit," the raw material out of which true Spirit is formed. Hegel's usual approach to this is historical and phenomenological; yet in the *Philosophy of Subjective Spirit* he tries to complement this approach with physiological speculations. Rejecting Schubert's naïve biblical literalism, Hegel nonetheless seems to have seized on his treatment of the ganglionic system in order to identify the probable seat of the soul. Further, Hegel's evaluation of the soul and its ganglionic body is remarkably similar to Schubert's. Like Schubert, he is quite clear in his view that the ganglionic system and the consciousness it engenders are inferior to the higher levels of Spirit.

Hegel's treatment of the soul is entirely in keeping with his rejection of the tendency in his time to romanticize prerational forms of consciousness as a source of "higher wisdom." Nevertheless, given the attention Hegel devotes to paranormal phenomena and the structures of consciousness that make them possible, one must wonder if Hegel's judgment on the matter is entirely negative or whether he sees something important in these phenomena. In the next section I will address this issue.

Philosophy and the Paranormal

Hegel states, "The soul pervades everything, it does not exist merely in a particular individual; for as we have previously said, the soul must be grasped as the truth, as the ideality, of everything material, as the wholly universal being in which all differences are only ideal and which does not one-sidedly stand over against its other, but overarches it."[35] As I mentioned earlier, Hegel believes that spatio-temporal limitations are cancelled in paranormal states. He states that, "when the free, intellectual consciousness sinks to the form of the merely feeling soul, the subject is no longer tied to space . . . Secondly, the clairvoyant soul also rises above the condition of time no less than that of space."[36] Again, because we leave behind ordinary space-time distinctions in such unusual states, distinctions between individuals are left behind as well. Therefore, someone in a paranormal state is able to exercise an unmediated influence over (or gain unmediated knowledge of) persons and things.

Surprisingly, Hegel asserts that these considerations indicate a certain kinship between paranormal phenomena and philosophy. Hegel states this in his remarks on the "Introduction" to the *Philosophy of Spirit* itself: "in the visible liberation of Spirit in those magnetic phenomena from the limitations of space and time and from all finite associations, there is something akin to philosophy . . ."[37] This is surprising because Hegel has made it quite clear that he regards paranormal states as retrogressive, while philosophy is, of course, the highest level of Spirit. Nevertheless, the dialectical nature of Hegel's philosophy means that lower levels are sublated in the higher; they are not simply left behind, they are taken up and, in some fashion, preserved in higher forms. Philosophy, like the paranormal, effectively cancels time and space: the Logic "is the exposition of God as He is in his eternal essence before the creation of nature and a finite Spirit."[38] Hegelian philosophy transcends the Understanding, which not only absolutizes commonsense space-time distinctions, but also insists on rigid distinctions between individuals and ideas. Hegel nevertheless insists that the "absolute elevation" above the Understanding occurs only in "the conceptual recognition of the eternal" (*nur in dem begreifenden Erkennen des Ewigen*)—in other words, not in a primitive, preconceptual experience.[39]

However, there are other, more significant reasons why Hegel believes that paranormal phenomena are important for philosophy. Hegel explicitly states that the ability of his philosophy to explain the paranormal is an important proof of its explanatory power. Further, since Hegel believes that *only* speculative philosophy can explain the paranormal, this constitutes proof of the bankruptcy of science and philosophy done from the standpoint of the Understanding. Hegel makes this point up front, in the introduction to the *Philosophy of Spirit*: "In modern times especially the phenomena of animal magnetism have given . . . a lively and visible confirmation of the underlying unity of soul, and of the power of its ideality. Before these facts, the rigid distinctions of the Understanding are struck with confusion; and in order to dissolve the resultant contradictions a speculative approach is shown to be necessary."[40] In the *Zusatz* following this passage, Hegel remarks that "animal magnetism has played a part in ousting the untrue, finite interpretation of Spirit from the standpoint of the Understanding."[41]

In short, the existence of animal magnetism (and, by extension, the other paranormal phenomena Hegel deals with) simply cannot be explained by science and philosophy that is still caught at the level of the Understanding. In these phenomena the ability of Spirit to transcend space and time is "manifest in sensuous existence itself."[42] Hegel consequently regards his ability to explain these dark matters as yet another verification of the power of speculative philosophy.

Conclusion

Since Hegel became interested in the paranormal so early in his career, it is tempting to speculate about whether his interest might have played a role in the development of his philosophy. For example, could Hegel's knowledge of animal magnetism have played a significant role in convincing him of the inadequacy of the approach to science typical of the Understanding? Such conjectures are interesting but difficult to prove. It is quite clear, however, that Hegel's interest in peculiar matters such as animal magnetism—and in peculiar authors such as Schubert—is part of a larger pattern.

Scholars of the history of philosophy tend to want to understand canonical figures exclusively in relation to other canonical figures, and they resist especially the idea that a philosopher could have had an interest in the "irrational." Hegel is, of course, typically understood to have arrived at his philosophy through his encounter with Kant, Fichte, and Schelling. But the truth of the matter is far more complex. Hegel's intellectual development was not marked solely by the study of other philosophers, but also by forays into all sorts of subjects and authors, many surprisingly *outré*. Hegel's fascination with Jacob Boehme is probably the best-known case. We know, in addition, of his interest in other mystical and occult authors such as Meister Eckhart, Giordano Bruno, Paracelsus, and Franz von Baader. Hegel's writings display a fair knowledge of alchemy, and there is evidence that both he and Schelling were influenced by the Swabian school of "speculative pietism" (especially the Christian Kabbalist author F. C. Oetinger).[43]

Given these sorts of interests, Hegel's enthusiasm for animal magnetism seems unsurprising. Further, that he had such interests is entirely in keeping with the principles of his own philosophy. Hegel very clearly holds that truth is not just to be had in philosophy (or *Wissenschaft*) alone. There are other forms of Absolute Spirit—of humanity's attempt to achieve self-knowledge and knowledge of the whole (which, for Hegel, comes to the same thing). These other forms have the same content, though not the same form, as philosophy.[44] True to his word, Hegel sought truth in all forms, even in what had been scorned and derided by the "enlightened" thinkers of his day. Hegel's own love of wisdom evinces, in fact, far greater openness and intellectual curiosity than is often displayed by his modern interpreters.

Notes

I wish to thank Ardis Collins, Allegra de Laurentiis, Gregory R. Johnson, and Richard Winfield for their helpful comments and constructive criticism.

1. See Glenn Alexander Magee, *Hegel and the Hermetic Tradition* (Ithaca: Cornell University Press, 2001; revised paperback edition, 2008), 213–22; and Magee, "Hegel on the Paranormal: Altered States of Consciousness in the Philosophy of Subjective Spirit," *Aries: Journal for the Study of Western Esotericism* 8 (2008): 21–36.

2. Enz III, § 387; PM (reference is by page number). I have corrected Wallace and Miller's translation in many places. Among other things, they translate *Geist* as "mind" rather than "Spirit." They also do not translate *Verstand* in a consistent manner.

3. *Enzyklopädie*, § 389; PM, 29.
4. *Enzyklopädie*, § 406 Z; PM, 107.
5. *Enzyklopädie*, § 405; PM, 95.
6. *Enzyklopädie*, § 405 Z; PM, 97.
7. *Enzyklopädie*, § 405 Z; PM, 97.
8. *Enzyklopädie*, § 405 Z; PM, 99.
9. *Enzyklopädie*, § 405 Z; PM, 100.
10. *Enzyklopädie*, § 406; PM, 101.
11. *Enzyklopädie*, § 406; PM, 101.
12. I owe this observation to Adam Crabtree.
13. *Enzyklopädie*, § 406 Z; PM, 113.
14. *Enzyklopädie*, § 406 Z; PM, 116.
15. See Hegel, PSS, quoted in Petry's commentary, vol. 2, 517.
16. G. W. F. Hegel, *Briefe von und an Hegel*, ed. Johannes Hoffmeister (Hamburg: Felix Meiner Verlag 1952–81), letter 166; *Hegel: The Letters*, trans. Clark Butler and Christianne Seiler (Bloomington: Indiana University Press, 1984), 590.
17. *Enzyklopädie*, § 406 Z; PM, 117.
18. *Enzyklopädie*, § 406 Z; PM, 117.
19. *Hegel in Berichten seiner Zeitgenossen*, ed. Günther Nicolin (Hamburg: Felix Meiner Verlag: 1970), 157.
20. *Enzyklopädie*, § 406 Z; PM, 121.
21. *Enzyklopädie*, § 406 Z; PM, 117.
22. *Enzyklopädie*, § 406 Z; PM, 106.
23. *Enzyklopädie*, § 406; PM, 105.
24. *Enzyklopädie*, § 379 Z; PM, 7.
25. Daniel Berthold-Bond, *Hegel's Theory of Madness* (Albany: State University of New York Press, 1995), 26.
26. *Enzyklopädie*, § 406 Z; PM, 115.
27. *Enzyklopädie*, § 406 Z; PM, 118.
28. *Enzyklopädie*, § 406 Z; PM, 118.
29. PSS, vol. 2, 523.
30. My account of Schubert's ideas and their reception owes a great deal to an unpublished essay by Antoine Faivre, "'Magical eloquence,' or Narratives by Somnambules of Their Visions on the Highest Levels of the Beyond, as Commented on by Some Theosophically Oriented Naturphilosophen (A Contribution

to the Study of Animal Magnetism in German Romanticism)." It was Faivre who first brought Schubert to my attention.

31. Frederick Gregory, "Gotthilf Heinrich Schubert and the dark side of natural science," NTM Zeitschrift für Geschichte der Wissenschaften, Technik und Medizin 3, no. 1 (December 1995): 255–69; 258. There are few sources on Schubert in English, and this is one of the best available. I am greatly indebted to Professor Gregory's account of Schubert's thought, and to Professor Gregory himself for making a copy of the article available to me.

32. G. H. Schubert, Ansichten von der Nachtseite der Naturwissenschaft, 4th ed. (Dresden and Leipzig: Arnoldischen Buchhandlung, 1840), 156–57.

33. Gregory, 265.

34. Schubert, Die Symbolik des Traumes (Bamberg: C. F. Kunz, 1821; second, corrected edition), 229.

35. Enzyklopädie, § 406 Z; PM, 109.

36. Enzyklopädie, § 406 Z; PM, 111–12.

37. Enzyklopädie, § 379 Z, 16; PM, 7.

38. G. W. F. Hegel, The Science of Logic, trans. A. V. Miller (London: George Allen and Unwin, 1969), 50; Wissenschaft der Logik, 3 vols., ed. Hans-Jürgen Gawoll (Hamburg: Felix Meiner Verlag, 1986–1992), vol. 1, 33–34.

39. Enzyklopädie, § 406 Z; PM, 112.

40. Enzyklopädie, § 379; PM, 4–5.

41. '[Der] tierische Magnetismus dazu beigetragen, die unwahre, endliche, bloß verständige Auffassung des Geistes zu verdrängen' (Enzyklopädie, § 379 Z; PM, 6).

42. Enzyklopädie, § 379 Z; PM, 7.

43. I discuss all these matters in Hegel and the Hermetic Tradition. See also Magee, "Hegel's Philosophy of History and Kabbalist Eschatology" in Hegel and History, ed. Will Dudley (Albany: State University of New York Press, 2009).

44. It should be noted here that mysticism is clearly a form of Absolute Spirit, a subcategory (perhaps) of Religion. This fact has so far not been explored extensively by Hegelian philosophers. Hegel, of course, identified the speculative with "the mystical" in several places. See, for example, Enzyklopädie, § 82 Z.

Hegel on the Emotions

Coordinating Form and Content

JASON J. HOWARD

Emotion remains one of the most hotly contested issues not only in contemporary philosophy, but in psychology and the biological sciences as well.[1] Simply put: What is emotion? What function does it play? Are emotions only instincts and physiological processes, or do they have a distinct intentional content irreducible to bodily affections? That emotions help determine the quality of our lives is a point most would concede, yet there is much less consensus as to the "why" and "how" of this determination.[2]

Turning to Hegel for some elucidation here might seem a wise choice. Hegel certainly makes a strong case for the importance of feeling and passion against the moral asceticism of Kant. But how far can Hegel help us clarify the distinctions among emotions, or the difference between the affective and cognitive aspects of emotion? It is far from obvious that Hegel even has a developed theory of the emotions. Indeed, he rarely distinguishes between sensations (*Empfindung*) and feelings/emotions (*Gefühl*) in a systematic way, a point Robert Williams emphasizes in his recent translation of Hegel's *Lectures on the Philosophy of Spirit* from 1827 through 1828.[3] Despite such confusion in terminology, it is my contention that Hegel does have a theory of the emotions and that his theory is considerably innovative to the extent it anticipates many of the most pertinent distinctions in contemporary work on emotion. Yet it is a theory that also suffers one major drawback.

The best way to approach Hegel's take on the emotions is to query what "emotions" are supposed to accomplish. To ask that question is to ask what function emotions serve in developing subjective spirit in its genesis from natural soul to individual thinking consciousness. The simple answer is that emotions enable subjective spirit to know itself in a way that is concrete, individuated, and meaningful. To know how emotions accomplish this is to know Hegel's theory of emotions. If we focus on the various levels at which affective occurrences operate in Hegel's account of subjective spirit and pay special attention to the pivotal place of habit in the serialization of physiological processes, we can avoid some of the terminological confusions in Hegel's account. This approach will enable us 1) to better chart the genesis of emotions, distinguishing them from instinct, sensation, and irritability and 2) to say something definitive about emotions in particular and why Hegel thought them so important.

For expository convenience, I want to review some of the distinctive and innovative features of Hegel's approach to emotion before I turn to the details of his account. First, it is clear that Hegel does not see emotion as antirational, or destructive of rationality, but rather as helping in the determination of cognition, although emotion is not sufficient in itself for cognitive experience. Second, because emotion does not inherently destroy cognition, but at least partly constitutes it, emotion can be amended and corrected. Third, given the amendable character of emotions, and their indispensable role in motivating agents, emotions play a central role in a healthy moral life. Fourth, emotions themselves have no justificatory content. Emotions are neither true nor false, neither good nor bad; rather, an emotion is appropriate depending on its application and the extent to which it promotes the autonomy of subjective spirit.

Considering these features, how would we translate Hegel's position on emotion into contemporary terminology? Hegel provides an "evaluative" theory that explains how emotions underwrite cognition and motivate us and help us cultivate healthy and fulfilling human lives.

I now want to explore the conceptual architecture that underwrites Hegel's approach, highlighting some of its specific implications. I will also examine one of the most troublesome errors in Hegel's approach—the priority Hegel allots to physiology in distinguishing types of emotion. Evidence suggests that Hegel is wrong to insist that emotions always have some physiological determinant that helps to distinguish one emotion from another. Rather than being a minor setback in his theory of emotion, this mistake threatens to derail the coherency and plausibility of his position.

In the 1827–28 lectures on the *Philosophy of Spirit* Hegel clarifies the domain of feeling in the following way: "Feeling is the being for self of the individual soul, so that it is at the same time dissolved in its universality."[4] Feeling, he reclarifies, is "the most particularized uniqueness of the subject . . . so far as my determinateness is a being, this determinacy is feeling."[5] It is the brute immediacy of being embodied that designates the general sphere of sensation or feeling. This definition is not, however, what we ordinarily understand as emotion, but simply a general description of our natural status as corporeal. From Hegel's standpoint, the most distinctive feature of the human organism's sensorial capacity lies in its malleability and adaptability, that inherent to the immediacy of brute sensation is its capacity for idealization. Alfredo Ferrarin explains this point in the following way: "[T]he passivity inherent at first in sensation is progressively transformed into a possession for spirit that uses it in its psychic life. All connections, relations, and order among objects *we* thematize are those we set up, not those we have found."[6]

As Hegel clarifies in § 402 of the 1830 *Enzyklopädie*, although it is true that sensation (*Empfindung*) and feeling (*Fühlen/Gefühl*) are often used interchangeably, we still tacitly recognize an important difference between the two. For example, we say people have moral feelings, but not moral sensations, about themselves and toward their duties.[7] It is our bodies that register sensations, but it is our feelings or emotions that value what is sensed.

One of the basic distinctions within the field of sensation is between inner and outer sensations. As the natural soul or psyche develops, the distinction between inner and external sensations becomes more pronounced, which makes fuller reintegration of these sensations possible. Hegel contends that inner sensations are "affections originating in the mind," that leave their imprint at the physiological level.[8] According to Willem De Vries, Hegel's distinction between "inner" and "outer" sensation at the early stages of development is bound to be misleading if it is taken literally, since it implies a distinct sensorial agency that has yet to arrive. Rather, the distinction between inner and outer for Hegel rests in the etiology of the sensation. De Vries explains, "External sensations are those determined by causal processes originating in some physical object and affecting the sense organs."[9] The implication is that in Hegel's model inner sensations—which Hegel designates regularly with the term "feeling" (*Gefühl*)—develop as a nascent network of mental affections that are expressed physiologically. Hegel comments that the organization of inner feelings systematizes itself with the same specificity and necessity as do our five bodily senses.[10] Hegel even suggests that a new science of "psychical physiology" is needed to index all the emotive feelings and their corresponding physiological disturbances.[11] As we shall see later, the fact that Hegel saw such an indexing project as feasible raises questions about the plausibility of his account of emotion. Hegel claims that feelings develop in a necessary configuration, which is determined by the requirements of greater mental facility. This claim can help us grasp the place of emotion with more precision.

If we want to know precisely when inner feelings cease being registered as brunt physiological phenomena or "reflexes" and become endowed with a distinct meaning that makes them capable of eventually bearing explicit cognitive content, we need to consider Hegel's account of habit. For Hegel, emotive life begins with habit but certainly does not end there. Hegel says that with habit the self is no longer immersed in the vicissitudes of feelings, as is the case with the natural soul. Habit allows the self to distinguish itself from the pull of its own desires. As Hegel puts it, "the self is to be stamped upon, and made appear in, this life of feeling (*Gefühlsleben*), yet so as to distinguish itself from the particular details, and be a realized universality."[12] Since initially the self has no will to instantiate itself against the pull of feeling, or individuated "I," how can this "self" make its mark? Because habit designates only a formal capacity, there is no conscious attempt to integrate one's feelings with an external world. At this level, as Ferrarin clarifies, "corporeal and natural habits" persist "as products of the soul's inadvertent and pre-intentional activity," being the "immediate presupposition for consciousness."[13] The psyche does not "resist" the reality of its affective life but becomes indifferent, or desensitized, to its feeling-states of arousal.[14] It is the familiarization of the self-feeling soul with its own corporality, its integration of desires and appetites within an established routine of existence, that regulates the visceral pull of inner feelings, altering internal affections into more regular feeling states.

As Richard Dien Winfield makes clear, the psyche or feeling soul plays an indispensible role in the transition to consciousness; the psyche signals the instantiation of mental activity without being itself fully cognitive.[15] This process explains how consciousness can arise even if the self does not possess language. In this regard the transition of the self-feeling soul into habit is crucial because, as Winfield says, habit allows the psyche to "overcome its own passivity and modify the content of feeling and the way it feels."[16] Winfield implies that at this level the psyche registers feeling states, but no emotion per se, since there is no "qualitative discrimination" beyond the "neurophysiology of the animal organism."[17] I concur that there is yet to be established any sense of distinct reflexive emotions at this level (such as remorse, shame or pride), but I think Hegel's account is plastic enough that it will allow for some basic differentiation of feeling that qualifies as emotive at this stage and that, in fact, his account requires it.

First, Hegel is clear that habit is not determined naturally but something that the soul posits (*Setzen*). What is posited is a higher type of unity of self-possession that can "negate" the magnetic draw of feeling. That negation lets the soul attend to its own corporeity in a different manner. Hegel's definition reads as follows: "The soul's making itself an abstract universal being, and reducing the particulars of feelings (*Gefühle*) (and of consciousness) to a mere feature of its being is Habit."[18] The soul possesses its affectivity by acclimating itself with its own bio-rhythms. As Hegel emphasizes in the 1827–28 lectures on the *Philosophy of Subjective Spirit*, the liberation that habit provides consists "not in the particular satisfaction" of any one feeling, but in the "satisfaction of being self-related."[19] Thus, habit is the primitive experience of being at home with oneself in preserving the identity of the feeling self, yet habit is not without feeling, for it is the experience of self-satisfaction. The enjoyment the self registers when it transcends immediate corporeal urges is a basic blueprint for emotive experience. Hegel explains, "Habit is essentially a reproduction of enjoyment out of myself as this enjoyment is a feeling."[20]

Habit is more than just a repetition, a continual distancing from the natural immediacy of feeling. Habit is a repetition that establishes meaningful behavior. That is, habit signals the crystallization of internal physiological alterations into a basic emotional repertoire through integrating feelings within a central drive towards psychic development and normalization. It is only by being assigned to specific sensorial patterns that the physiological disturbances of hunger, sexual desire, fear, and the like can be resisted or idealized. Hegel makes it explicit that the acclimation of the soul with its corporeality is at the same time the "impressing and molding" (*Ein- und Durchbildung*) of corporeality "which enters into the modes of feeling" (*den Gefühlsbestimmungen*).[21] The soul can be indifferent to its bodily affectivity only because this is constantly in the process of serialization, an unconscious familiarity with patterns of sensorial stimuli whose specific episodic character can be negated only because it is localizable, and so reducible to a moment of the whole. Once they are distinguished from psychic self-concentration, feelings become aspects of one's identity rather than simply biological conditions. What alters is not the quality of the feeling, but its hold within the psychic order.

As Hegel emphasizes in the 1827–28 lectures and again in 1830, habit has an expansive influence. Through this expansive network of integration, feelings become "owned" by the soul. Hegel describes the process in the following way:

> [H]abit is indispensible for the *existence* of all intellectual life in the individual, enabling the subject to be a concrete immediacy, an "ideality" of soul—enabling the matter of consciousness, religious, moral, etc., to be his as *this* self, *this* soul, and no other, and be neither a mere latent possibility, nor a transient emotion or idea, nor an abstract inwardness, cut off from action and reality, but part and parcel of his being.[22]

I think this passage makes a strong case for habit as the starting point for the transformation from raw feeling states to basic emotions. In engendering the ownership of our interior life, habit allows feelings to become aspects of our identities, allows us to recognize discrete feeling states as our responses, a recognition that makes emotional life possible. Although it is true that habit creates neither the diversity nor the intensity of emotional life, we feel self-satisfaction through habit. Because this feeling is less fleeting and less distracting than other inner feelings, because it yields a distinctive physiological response, and because it arises as we subordinate sensation in general, this satisfaction serves as an implicit model for how emotions will inform our interior life.

Habit is nourished, in part, by the psyche's acclimation to its own body, changing the nature of corporeality from a brute given into the expression of subjective life. As recorded in the *Zusatz* to § 410 of the 1830 *Enzyklopädie*, we have "an ever-growing capacity" for "embodying" "inner intentions" (*innerlichen Bestimmungen*) in our bodily expressions, which reveals our mental and emotional states accordingly. Our corporeality is brought under a psychic "rule" (*Regel*) of self-organization. This rule is "transmitted" to the multiplicity of bodily activities. Thus, the experience of satisfaction that designates habit eventually becomes united with interest in general, creating an almost "mechanical" unity that perfects itself the less pronounced its expression.[23]

Up to this point in my account I have outlined the transition from blind feeling states to the rudimentary conditions for later emotions, but I have yet to tackle the role emotions play in an ordinary human life. I turn to that issue now. It is really only at the level of "practical feeling" (*Das praktische Gefühl*) that feelings become "emotive," only at this level that they operate in recognizable patterns that can be anticipated, amended, meaningfully shared, and consciously coordinated with the objective world. Prior to integrating with the will as the vehicle of self-determination, feelings were things we "underwent." They made up our disposition and personality, no doubt, but they could motivate us only situationally and unconsciously. As the feeling will transforms into the reflexive thinking will, emotion becomes part of a coordinated referential system that anchors us to the world of others. With every increase in the theoretical powers of the soul (intuition, representation, and thought) comes more precise indexing of emotional states.

Consequently, if we want to know what emotion is for Hegel, we should look to those affective experiences he designates under the general term "practical feeling" (*Das praktische Gefühl*). These affective experiences are closest in functional equivalence to what most theorists today would call emotions. In fact, the idea of practical feeling that emerges in the 1830 *Enzyklopädie* matches many influential contemporary accounts of emotion, such as that defended by Ronald de Sousa. De Sousa claims that "emotions are determinate patterns of salience among objects of attention, lines of inquiry, and inferential strategies."[24] Put otherwise, emotions organize experience by providing a range of intentional distinctions under specific affective sets that anchor motivation and behavior. And this anchoring is precisely what the rise of practical feeling accomplishes.

Agents recognize their emotions not just as chemical episodes they passively undergo but also as the experience of enjoyment (*Genuß*), for it is in terms of enjoyment that emotions most actively draw us out of ourselves.[25] If I follow Hegel correctly, the brute experience of enjoyment our emotions initially yield becomes indexed with increasing precision to an external reality beyond subjectivity. Hegel indicates that this indexing occurs in three phases, that of immediate practical feeling, impulses, and finally the pursuit of happiness. Practical feeling or the feeling will firmly establishes the relationship between the objective world and the inner world of emotion. We live our emotions as responses to a world of experience that we reference through feeling states. This coordination between the interiority of affective life and the externality of a world beyond is not the result of reflection per se; it is lived as the reality of subjective existence.

With practical feeling, then, we have the establishment of emotion as regulatory and motivational, yet agents still cannot mediate their emotions by consciously investing them in particular pursuits. Consequently, although their content is no longer "irrational" but determinate patterns of attention and interpretation that stem from personality traits and desires, the content remains "natural, contingent and subjective."[26] It is only with "impulse" (*Trieb*) that subjects recognize that the agreement between emotions and their objects is something that "ought" to be established by agents, rather than happening unconsciously.

Hegel's discussion of impulses in terms of the "practical ought" is the principle way he differentiates between types of emotions and their existential value for subjective spirit. The feeling will comes to discover that the world is not reducible to its needs and, in fact, resists these needs in many cases. The feeling of the practical ought emerges as a challenge to assert oneself against the indifference of the world. Quoting Hegel, "The 'Ought' (*Sollen*) of practical feeling is the claim of its essential autonomy to control some existing mode of fact."[27] This ought is experienced in different ways, and it is fair to say that the greatest predictor of moral health is how agents contend with this drive to reduce the world to their will. What's more, as we shall see momentarily, emotions can be distinguished in large part by the form of "ought" they instantiate, which is to say, the type of ownership they make on the world. As Hegel makes explicit, "Delight, joy, grief . . . shame, repentance, contentment, etc., are partly only modifications of the formal 'practical feeling' in *general*, but are partly different in the features that give the special tone and character mode to their 'Ought'."[28] The difference between moral emotions and other emotions such as jealousy or lust does not merely reside in their objects, but the actual evaluative experience we have of these objects. We experience our emotional commitments to law and duty, if they are properly cultivated, fundamentally differently than we experience other kinds of emotions; the former we experience largely intellectually rather than corporeally.

In the *Zusatz* to § 472 of the 1830 *Enzyklopädie* Hegel stipulates three levels in which the practical ought expresses its emotive claims. First are those emotions that register what is agreeable or disagreeable. Second are those emotions whose content arises through intuition or representation and that have determine objects, such as pleasure, joy, hope, fear, anguish, and pain. This second class of feelings, as Hegel specifies, has no "immanent" content; these feelings arise in response to situations. Another way of expressing this claim is to say this second class of emotions is largely episodic and bears a somewhat contingent relationship to agents. The final class of emotions, Hegel qualifies in this way: "[T]here is a third kind of feelings (*Gefühlen*) arising when the substantial content of right, morality, ethics, religion, which originates in *thought*, is received into the feeling will."[29] Within this third class of emotions Hegel considers remorse and shame as emblematic. If we translate Hegel's definition into the language of contemporary philosophers of emotion, we can designate this third level of feelings collectively as "emotions of self-assessment."[30]

As Hegel emphasizes repeatedly, the key component of emotions of self-assessment is cognition, which establishes the level of emotional attachment or concern. Only with cognition do emotions gain their "truth" or "authentication" and then lose their contingent character as they are grounded in an objective cultural/conceptual core whose value is explicable in terms of relationships, ideals, and actions. It is here that our emotions encounter an object that cannot be immediately reduced to the concerns and needs of selfhood alone. Consequently, these emotions give the most visceral confirmation to subjective spirit of an objective world of inherent value in which humans participate. Although they may express themselves episodically, these emotions can become part of an agent's sense of identity and self-worth, bringing the motivational core of subjects to completion. Unlike the genius of the self-feeling soul, which functions as the base biological register of disposition or that of personality (§405), assigning character traits contingently, emotions of self-assessment enable agents to determine the merit of their emotive experiences. Consequently, this third class of emotions provides the foundation for a life of moral character. These emotions of self-assessment make one uniquely "at home with oneself" in the world. These emotions are no longer contingent or accidental. They express our deepest choices for ourselves and our commitments. What were once merely personality traits can now become integrated into one's ethical disposition. Following Adriaan Peperzak, we can see why the psychology of the will is the foundation of Hegel's moral philosophy, since it is the psychology that analyzes the fundamental "ought" that remains inseparable from concrete subjectivity.[31]

Hegel charts the final transition into emotional maturity in § 477. He states that the will is now reflective, so it can give itself "specific individuality and actuality. It is now on the standpoint of choosing between inclinations, and is option or choice" (*Willkür*).[32] The greatest confirmation of this integration between thought and emotion at the level of subjective spirit comes with the desire for happiness, where agents confront a world whose independence holds the key to their own sense of personal satisfaction. Thus, the desire to be happy demarcates the most immediate way in which our web of emotional commitments corroborates and affirms a complex environment of mutually referring thoughts and passions. Happiness, then, is the final object in the will's drive for basic integration, and the first in the education of spirit proper.

Once emotions become integrated with the reflexive will, they serve as judgments about the world and our standing in it. Just because agents have reached a basic level of emotional integration, however, does not mean they have reached moral maturity. The desire to mold the world to fit our aims is characteristic of the "practical ought," yet there is no guarantee that this desire will find its proper register in the ethical objectivity of laws, rights, duties, and religious practices. Emotion cannot educate itself, for it generates no criteria of itself. As Peperzak clarifies, feelings are pure forms that can attach to any object, whether the object is rational or not so that the strength of our feelings can also lead to our own undoing.[33] If our emotions find no sense of lasting orientation and durable confirmation in the world of others, positions that only reason can provide, our emotions will turn to feed off the subsequent restlessness that results. This alternative Hegel qualifies as the road toward selfishness and finally evil.[34]

The breadth of Hegel's account of emotion, the integral function this account plays in the concretization of consciousness, and his differentiation of emotion into different types give us a sophisticated theory of emotions. What this theory indicates is that emotions serve an indispensible function in the transformation from the natural soul to the thinking (reflexive) will. Emotions are neither irrational nor "biologically primitive," but an integrative psychical phenomena.[35] Consequently, although emotions arise out of more elemental neurological feedback mechanisms, their involuntary character is mitigated as the will arises and volition becomes the mandate of subjectivity. Along this journey Hegel distinguishes brute sensation from those emotions that develop later at the level of practical feeling. Hegel refines this taxonomy with even more precision by distinguishing emotions of self-assessment from other types. In so doing, Hegel specifies how these emotions underlie moral character and self-worth. The result, as I indicated at the beginning, is an evaluative theory of emotion that stipulates the role emotions play in enabling subjective spirit to know itself in a way that is concrete, individuated and meaningful.

There is much to be praised in Hegel's theory of the emotions. Hegel takes care in delineating the basic features of emotion and in the process provides a basic taxonomy of emotion types. I want to conclude, however, with one potentially serious criticism of Hegel's position. It seems clear that Hegel believes emotions have a physiological basis that helps in distinguishing one emotion from another. This point Hegel makes explicitly in the 1827–28 lectures about the possibility of a "psychical physiology," and it is a point repeated again in the 1830 *Enzyklopädie*.[36] It is reconfirmed in Hegel's underlying thesis that emotions have no justificatory content of their own but are rudimentary forms of sensory organization that receive their truth from thought.[37] Finally, the importance Hegel gives to discussion and rational reflection in treating insanity supports the idea that the affective core of emotions can be separated from their rational contextualization and justification. It is important for Hegel that some measure of physiological individuation remains in all emotions, for this individuation allows us to confidently identify the feeling state and "idealize" or negate it. The more individuated the feeling state, whether this be "in the breast" or "in the pit of the stomach," the more easily one can identify the state, label it, and integrate within a more fluid drive, such as the scope of the reflexive will. If many emotional states turn out to have no clearly identifiable physiological cause, that could create problems for Hegel's account because the requisite individuation needed for the act of appropriation to be successful is threatened. How does one appropriate what has no location or psychic space?

On first glance this criticism appears misplaced. Hegel does repeatedly affirm that feelings gain their justification, and consequently their identity, from the content they are given. Feelings are formal arrangements of physiological processes, which are integrated with content as agents develop. It is this integration that distinguishes the appropriateness and typology of the emotion. Emotions are not separable from reason, but they are a lower grade of rational organization: "[T]here is only one reason, in feeling, volition, and thought."[38] De Vries qualifies Hegel's position by stating that a "coherent explanatory account of our feelings is not logically required to coincide with the causal account of sensory states."[39] I agree, but the problem is that there is ample evidence to suggest Hegel conflates the two accounts, superimposing one level of analysis on another, the sensorial upon the cognitive/interpretive, which threatens the coherency of his approach.[40]

The key problem comes in the pronounced separation Hegel wants to maintain between the form of emotions and their "content." It is not at all clear that one can have distinguishable inner feeling states awaiting content or application without already being individuated, either conceptually or through socialization. Consider for a moment the way Hegel puts the problem. By studying "the bodily form adopted by certain mental modifications, especially the passions or emotions," one could demonstrate why anger and courage are felt in the breast rather than some other locale. What is more, in Hegel's model this mapping might be done with basically all emotions.[41]

Recent science has refuted Hegel's claims here. Decades of psychological research on the physiological causes of emotion have made it abundantly clear that physiology plays little if any role individuating emotion types. The extensive research of Stanley Schachter and Jerome Singer demonstrates that the variety of emotions and moods are by no means matched by an equal variety of visceral patterns. In fact, repeated testing has confirmed that "the same state of physiological arousal could be named 'joy' or 'fury' or 'jealousy' or any of a great diversity of emotional labels," whose differentiation is dependent more on cognitive appraisals of one's situation than anything else.[42] The extensive work on the philosophy of emotion advanced by figures as different as Jean-Paul Sartre, Amélie Rorty, Martha Nussbaum, Ronald de Sousa, and Robert Solomon has come to much the same conclusion.[43]

Hegel writes as if shame or anxiety, examples he develops in the 1827–28 lectures on the *Philosophy of Subjective Spirit*, are naturally occurring and localizable feeling states, which are then integrated with a conceptual drive that determines the appropriateness of the feeling. For Hegel, all emotions have distinguishable physiological arousal states, states that are attached or incorporated by the reflexive will vis-à-vis conceptual maturation and socialization. But this claim seems to miss at least part of the story about emotions. Hegel is confused if he thinks shame, guilt, anger, or any of a host of other emotions have localizable affections that we can use to identify and contend with emotions. On the contrary, quite often we can be confused about the emotions we experience, and we may try to resolve our confusion by referring to the past or conferring with other people. What distinguishes anger from guilt, or remorse from joy, has nothing to do with physiological processes but lies in their respective intentional objects. Hegel explains that all inner feelings arise from the natural soul, so they are internal. They received their differentiation from a passive process of sensorial serialization akin to what happens with our five external senses. Once these inner feelings are differentiated, they are developed by being given a specific content or application. The crucial point is that Hegel strongly implies that this differentiation happens before the reflexive will organizes and indexes the feeling. This is where Hegel appears mistaken, or at least confused. The differentiation of feeling states into identifiable emotions cannot occur without some level of conscious integration. Moral emotions such as shame are not sets of feeling states awaiting an appropriate object. That is what Hegel implies in § 472, where he states that ethical feelings are shaped by the dictates of formal practical feeling in general, that is, that ethical feelings have an identifiable physiological cause, which is colored by thought. One could reply that Hegel is simply differentiating between a necessary and a sufficient condition here, but he is doing more than that. It is one thing to say all emotions are accompanied by states of physiological arousal, itself a debatable point. It is quite another thing to argue that these arousal states come in certain localizable forms that help us identify and appropriate the corresponding emotion.

I have a strong sense that the consequences of Hegel's confusion are considerable. Certainly the issue is more serious than a mistaken belief in animal magnetism or some other psychic phenomena, since such beliefs do not play a central role in Hegel's ontology of subjective spirit, whereas emotions do. Hegel is confident that the reflexive will can determine the proper role of feeling states because these states already exist as differentiated physiological episodes awaiting appropriation. Once this premise is accepted, it is easy to grant the claim that emotions have no independent justificatory content. Much of the current evidence weighs against this interpretation, or at least against the way Hegel presents it. Emotions such as guilt, jealousy, and pride arise through socialization. They do not exist in any meaningful sense beforehand, not even as physiological forms of arousal. This limitation means that decoupling the form of emotion from its content is much trickier than Hegel imagined, because the form or affective pattern our feelings take comes from socialization, which occurs in many cases as early as infancy. Once we become reflective enough to control or amend our emotions, we do not simply realign feeling states with new content, because these feeling states have been infused with some manner of content since their inception. There are few if any "brute emotions" that await the taming influence of the will for their orientation, because emotions are never simply brute and always register more than just bodily disturbances but are "ways of seeing" the world.[44] Repeated research has confirmed, in the words of James Averill, that there is "no invariant core to emotional behavior which remains untouched by socio-cultural influences," and the idea that there is, is the result of prejudice more than anything else.[45] Consequently, our emotional life resists transparency and determination not primarily because of its singular and contingent character, in a word its lingering irrationality, but because of the early psychological investment that goes into emotions.

It is rather ironic that the consummate philosopher of intersubjectivity should come at emotions with such an underlying positivist frame of mind. We can agree with Hegel that the flexibility of emotion helps make cognition possible, without reducing emotion to a blind form awaiting the wisdom of thought for its content and direction. The problem with Hegel's account of emotion in his work on subjective spirit, however, is that despite his prescience in grasping the complexity of emotion, he still ends up portraying emotion as little more than an enabling condition of rationality.

Notes

My thanks to Dr. Rolf Samuels for looking over earlier versions of this chapter.

1. Aspects of the argument provided here were first presented in a much condensed form at the 27th International Hegel Conference on Spirit in September 2008 at the Katholieke Universiteit, Leuven, Belgium. See Jason J. Howard, "The Spirit of Emotions," *Hegel-Jahrbuch* (2010): 198–201.

2. For a clear and brief overview of the major positions on the emotion debate, consult *What Is Emotion: Classical Readings in Philosophical Psychology*, ed. Cheshire Calhoun and Robert Solomon (New York: Oxford University Press, 1984). See the introduction by Calhoun and Solomon, 3–40.

3. LPS. See 110, note 93, which is especially helpful in illuminating the terminological confusion around such terms as *Empfindung* and *Gefühl*.

4. LPS, 110.

5. LPS, 112.

6. Alfredo Ferrarin, *Hegel and Aristotle* (United States: Cambridge University Press, 2001), 268.

7. Enz. (1830), § 402. In all references to this work, I have used PM.

8. Enz. (1830), § 401.

9. Willem De Vries, *Hegel's Theory of Mental Activity: An Introduction to Theoretical Spirit* (New York: Cornell University Press, 1988), 61.

10. Enz. (1830), § 401.

11. LPS, 121; Enz. (1830), § 401.

12. Enz. (1830), § 409.

13. Ferrarin, *Hegel and Aristotle*, 278.

14. Enz. (1830), § 410.

15. See Richard Dien Winfield, "Identity, Difference, and the Unity of Mind," in *Identity and Difference: Studies in Hegel's Logic, Philosophy of Spirit, and Politics*, ed. Philip Grier (New York: State University of New York Press, 2007): 103–27.

16. Winfield, "Identity, Difference, and the Unity of Mind," 113.

17. Winfield, "Identity, Difference, and the Unity of Mind," 113.

18. Enz. (1830), § 410.

19. LPS, 155.

20. LPS, 155.

21. Enz. (1830), § 410.

22. Enz. (1830) § 410.

23. Enz. (1830), § 410 Z. What I take as Hegel's thesis on the origin of emotion through habit is partly confirmed by recent psychological research, which demonstrates that basic emotions emerge very early on in human ontogeny and do not appear to depend directly on higher order thinking or judgments. According to Carroll Izard, a leading figure in the psychology of emotion, "Most theorists agree that basic emotions are few in number, relatively infrequent, and short in duration"

(265). These basic emotions are strongest in infancy and decrease rapidly with "socialization, cognitive development, and social learning," being quickly incorporated into "emotion-schemes," that is, the common dispositional and motivational patterns that account for much of adult emotional life (262). See especially the work of Carroll E. Izard, "Basic Emotions, Natural Kinds, Emotion Schemes, and a New Paradigm," in *Perspectives on Psychological Science* 2, no. 3 (Sept., 2007): 260–80. If Hegel's approach could be shown to support something like a theory of basic emotions, which then develop into "emotion-schemes," it would go a long way in avoiding the criticisms I level at him later in this chapter.

24. Ronald de Sousa, "The Rationality of Emotions," in *Explaining Emotions*, ed. Amélie Rorty (Berkeley: University of California Press, 1980), 137.

25. Enz. (1830), § 444.

26. Enz. (1830), § 471.

27. Enz. (1830), § 472.

28. Enz. (1830), § 472.

29. Enz. (1830), § 472 Z.

30. I borrow the expression "emotions of self-assessment" from Gabriele Taylor, *Pride, Shame and Guilt: Emotions of Self-Assessment* (New York: Clarendon Press, 1985).

31. Adriaan Peperzak, "Hegel über Wille und Affectivität. Ein Kommentar zu Enz §§ 387–92, §§ 468–474, §§ 468–473," in *Psychologie und Athropologie oder Philosophie des Geistes*, ed. Franz Hespe and Burkhard Tuschling (Stuttgart: Frommann-Holzboog, 1991), 367.

32. Enz. (1830), § 477.

33. Adriaan Peperzak, "Hegel über Wille und Affectivität," 388.

34. It is at the level of the "practical ought" that the formal conscience arises, coming to practical fruition in the moment of choice or "resolve." As Giulio Severino points out, however, the roots of conscience reach back to the most elemental levels of spirit, the bare self-assertiveness of subjectivity—the striving of the soul for self-possession. Severino shows how Hegel's growing preoccupation with the unconscious, which becomes evident with the Heidelberg *Encyclopedia*, arises out of his interest in the hidden "dissolving" power of conscience. See Giulio Severino, "*Subjekt und Freiheit in Hegels Denken: Die Einsamkeit des Gewissens und der Schwindel des Bösen*," in *Psychologie und Athropologie oder Philosophie des Geistes*: 396–421.

35. James Averill explains that the idea emotions are "biologically primitive" is based on a value judgment about what we think emotions do, which is a "reification of emotion into a biological given." See James Averill, "Emotion and Anxiety: Sociocultural, Biological, and Psychological Determinants," in *Explaining Emotions*, 37–72.

36. LPS, 121; Enz. (1830), § 401.

37. LPS, 253; Enz. (1830), § 471.

38. Enz. (1830), § 471.

39. De Vries, *Hegel's Theory of Mental Activity*, 82.

40. I admit that bypassing the section on the "Phenomenology" (Enz. (1830), §§ 413–39) that details how the "I" emerges through desire into self-consciousness by confronting an other, leaves out an essential element in the education of desire, and thus, an important part of Hegel's take on emotion. I concede this point, but submit that nothing in the section on the "Phenomenology" deliberately contradicts or cancels out the criticism I am leveling against Hegel's overall approach to emotion.

41. Enz. (1830), § 401.

42. See Stanley Schachter and Jerome Singer, "From Cognitive, Social, and Physiological Determinants of Emotional State," in *What Is Emotion: Classical Readings in Philosophical Psychology*, ed. Cheshire Calhoun and Robert Solomon (New York: Oxford University Press, 1984) 174, 183.

43. Jean-Paul Sartre, *Sketch for a Theory of Emotions*, trans. Philip Mairet (Great Britain: Methuen, 1962); Amélie Rorty, "Explaining Emotions," in *Explaining Emotions*, ed. Amélie Rorty (Berkeley: University of California Press, 1980), 103–126; Martha Nussbaum, *Upheavals of Thought: The Intelligence of Emotions* (New York: Cambridge University Press, 2001); Ronald de Sousa, *The Rationality of Emotion* (Cambridge, MA: MIT Press, 1987); and Robert Solomon, *The Passions: Emotions and the Meaning of Life* (Indianapolis, IN: Hackett, 1993).

44. Nussbaum, *Upheavals of Thought*, 27.

45. Averill, *Emotion and Anxiety: Sociocultural, Biological, and Psychological Determinants*, 57.

Awakening to Madness and Habituation to Death in Hegel's "Anthropology"

Nicholas Mowad

In this chapter I will examine sleeping and waking in Hegel, including madness, which is, I will argue, not just sleeping while awake, but sleeping *in virtue of* the character of the awakening. Thus, the condition of sleeping while awake cannot be corrected through another awakening. Sleep and waking belong to Hegel's discussion of the natural soul in the "Anthropology" section of "Subjective Spirit," the first part of the *Philosophy of Spirit*, volume 3 of the *Encyclopedia*. An examination of sleep and waking must be prefaced, therefore, by a brief explanation of spirit's emergence from nature and the relevant structures from the *Logic*.

Preface: Logic, Nature, and Spirit

Hegel's philosophy of spirit (*Geist*) is an examination of what it is to be human.[1] The human for Hegel is finite spirit, the object of the "Subjective Spirit" section of the *Philosophy of Spirit*. What "spirit" means for Hegel is best understood by relating it to his conception of "nature." Nature for Hegel is essentially parts outside of parts.[2] The human is natural insofar as it is *merely* corporeal, spread out into various parts, each of which is external to the others and internally unrelated to them (though it may enter into relation with them mechanically or even organically while remaining merely natural). That the human is spirit means that the human knows itself, even in its difference from itself, to be identical with itself. Thus, the difference inherent in the human as natural is qualified, and the human is (and knows itself to be) reunited with itself.

Spirit emerges from nature therefore as *the soul*:[3] the ideality of the diversity and mutual indifference of nature. By "the ideality" of nature we mean the unity of nature: nature's connectedness and belonging-together, the omnipresent principle in virtue of which its variations are contextualized as moments, or aspects of one simple totality.[4] The soul is thus to be distinguished from consciousness (*Bewußtsein*), which belongs to a later stage: the soul, unlike consciousness, has not separated itself from nature, its own corporeality; rather, the soul permeates nature such that the soul is present everywhere in nature, identified with every part. Just *how* the soul can be the single and simple principle that is present in any and all of the variations in nature (without these latter ceasing to be variations) is not meant to be clear from the beginning; rather, it is progressively worked out over the course of the anthropology.

The "Anthropology" has three parts: "Natural Soul," "Feeling Soul," and "Actual Soul." To explain these I will use the moments of the concept (*Begriff*) (which are also the terms of the syllogism) that Hegel gives in his *Logic*: universality (*Allgemeinheit*), particularity (*Besonderheit*), and singularity (*Einzelheit*).[5] Hegel's *Logic* is the first part of his *Encyclopedia*, in which he gives the fundamental structures of everything (in spirit and nature, in subject and object, and in their identity). I cannot discuss here the details of the subjective concept (the part of the *Logic* where Hegel discusses judgment and syllogism, the structures I will make use of in this chapter), but the legitimacy of my use of these terms is guaranteed by their ubiquity in the anthropology itself.[6]

Hegel's *Logic* is not a formal logic to be filled in with natural and spiritual content: it is an onto-logic. Judgment and syllogism are not for Hegel forms of thought or language abstracted from but applicable to reality. Rather, they are structures actually constitutive of the things themselves: "all things *are* a judgment."[7] In German "judgment" (*Urteil*) means literally original (*Ur-*) division (*Teilung*). Hegel exploits the etymology of the word to show that judgment, ostensibly simply a union (as "S is P" unites S and P), is also equally a division (since S and P remain distinct even as they are identified).[8] Linguistically, or "logically" (in the formal sense) the subject and predicate are at once linked and separated by the copula. Ontologically, this involves a *real* division within a thing's own identity with itself: when we say, "God is love" or "the human is reason," in each case the two terms are at once distinguished and identified. Likewise, "syllogism" (*Schluß*) can also mean "closing" (from the verb *schließen*): as judgment refers to a thing's difference from itself even as it is identified with itself, syllogism refers to a thing's "closing" with itself, overcoming that gap in its identity with itself and reuniting with itself by the positing of a middle term.[9]

In nature the moments of the idea[10] are presented (initially) as separate and mutually indifferent.[11] Space and time are universals whose singular parts (points and instants respectively) each present themselves as completely self-contained, without reference to the others outside of them or to the whole (the universal: space itself or time itself).[12] The summit of mere nature, the organism, involves singular parts (organs) that cannot be or be understood apart from their relation to other organs and to the whole organism[13]; and the singular organism as a whole which cannot be and cannot be understood apart from its relation to others and to the genus as a whole.[14] This is judgment: the singular *is* human (its genus is its essence); the singular is identified with the genus, but in its immediacy and finitude it is inadequate to the genus (which is not so limited), relating to it as something other in the sexual partner, in which it fulfills its duty to reproduce the genus. Likewise, for the individual animal as the ideality of its singular organs, the inadequacy of the singular to the universal ideality causes the former to relate to the latter as to something other (and operate in a way not conducive to the whole of which it is a part) in the inevitable disease and death of the animal.[15] However, each of these judgments becomes a syllogism (*Schluß*), as the idea closes with itself (*sich mit sich Zusammenschließen*) and spirit emerges from nature.[16]

Syllogism emerges from judgment in the *Logic* by the positing of an "objective particularity" mediating between the singular and the universal.[17] An objective particularity is a determination through which the universal and singular are internally united: it is what *makes* it so that a singular *is* the universal that it is.[18] Thus, the sex relation demonstrates that spirit, the reunion of the terms of the syllogism (the moments of the concept), is the truth of nature (the dispersal of these moments and their mutual indifference). The universal's own reproduction of itself involves a bifurcation into *different* sexes and ultimately produces an *inherently* perishable singular animal (thus the universal is posited as self-particularizing and self-singularizing). The singular animal's death is thus not its falling away from the universal. Natural life itself contains within it the germ of death: mortality (and sexual determinacy) is the objective particular, the middle term reuniting the genus with the singular animals that *are* it—that is, reuniting the concept with itself and constituting spirit's emergence from nature.[19]

Natural Soul

In accordance with this reunion of the universal with the singular, at the beginning of the *Philosophy of Spirit*, soul (as universal) is indeterminately all of nature, the single principle present everywhere in (all the singulars of) nature. The soul is at once universal (pervading all of nature, and not limited to any individual natural body or part) and singular (present in *this particular* natural body or part). The soul will remain so through its culmination as actual soul: the initial determination of soul as both universal and singular is not *wrong*; it is merely indeterminate.

The "Anthropology," the first part of "Subjective Spirit," has for its first part "Natural Soul," the first stage (natural qualities) of which is characterized by the complete interpenetration of the universal and the singular. The human lives in complete sympathy with nature: changes of season and the like determine its disposition, but it is unaware of any causal relation in this influence and does not posit its own "inner" life as distinct from the "outer"' course of nature as a whole.[20] That spirit is determined as "natural soul" here means that it is posited as the ideality of all of nature (which yet remains diverse). The precise relation between spirit's unity and nature's diversity remains to be worked out: the "Anthropology" will be the first step toward a stable relation between the two. Here various ways in which the soul is present in the diverse and even opposing forces in nature are displayed. These phenomena will ultimately be inadequate because they will exhibit only a moment or aspect of spirit, which by itself gives a distorted picture of spirit: for example, natural soul's first part, natural qualities, articulates the immediate sympathy between the human and nature. The syllogism that reunited the moments of the concept at the end of the *Philosophy of Nature* is here expressed as an immediate unity of universal and singular. This union is indeed one aspect of the syllogism that is spirit. But when this union is expressed immediately outside of the context of a mediating particular, it gives a distorted image of spirit (as we will see). In any case, this immediate unity between soul (the universal) and (the diverse singulars of) nature means that the soul *is* a given natural individual. This is posited in the natural soul's second part, natural alternations.

Understanding the transition from natural qualities to natural alterations requires reexamining spirit's emergence from nature. The *Philosophy of Nature* closed with the judgment's transformation into a syllogism in two ways: (1) in the reunion of nature as a whole (as universal) and the (singular) animal; (2) in the reunion of the animal organism (as universal) and its (singular) organs.[21] The beginning of the *Philosophy of Spirit* in natural qualities represents the first syllogism above as an immediate unity in the sympathy between the human and nature. In natural alterations the second syllogism is represented as an immediate unity in its first form, the ages of man,[22] where the individual soul goes through a series of developmental stages. These stages are different but are all of the same human, so the difference does not go beyond the more comprehensive unity. There is an immediate union between the whole human and its various ages insofar as the human is present in each of its ages from childhood to old age. The difference of ages exists but not *for* the human at this stage: the person is absorbed in its determinate age without knowing it as a determinacy from which it is as a universal distinct.[23]

Thus in "natural qualities" soul is determined only as mutual interpenetration of universal and singular. "Natural alterations" witnesses a slightly more adequate articulation of the union of universal and singular. In the ages of man, soul is posited as any given human individual: not simply insofar as the singular human is permeated with soul just like any part of nature (though it is), but also in the sense that this individual *is* soul in a way that what is merely natural is not. The individual human is the ideality of its own natural life (it suffers various changes in its life while remaining the same person), but in this it does not differ from the animal organism, or even the solar system. Yet the human *knows itself* as the ideality of *its own* inner life (its perceptions, feelings, memories, etc.). Thus, it is posited that soul is individualized in different *individual souls*.[24] One and the same individual human being is the singular in the first syllogism, the universal in the second: that is, it is at once a part of nature as a whole, and is itself (and more importantly, it can know itself as) the whole of its inner natural life. Seeing the importance of this step requires forgetting our habitual understanding of the term "individual soul," which seems commonplace and uncomplicated. For Hegel this means that the human being is at once individual *and* that what holds of soul as such[25] (that it is the universal, the ideality of nature) ought to hold as well for the individual human being.

But how can the human being be both an individual and a soul, ideality of nature? An individual is limited by its other, whereas soul is not. Therefore, if an individual truly is soul, its "other" must be its own self—this is the sexual relation. Here the individual soul's individuality comes into conflict with its essence as soul. This is a "real antithesis"[26] in contrast with the ideal antithesis in the ages of man (where the difference of ages is subordinated to the overarching unity of the one life). In the sexual relation, the soul does commune *with itself*, but as something other. It is limited, but that it can *feel* its limitation means it is not merely individual, but rather is soul, and so is always already in its other. As the soul becomes aware of itself in its individuality, it is *awoken*.

The awakening refers to the soul coming to know itself as *this individual*, opposed to its "sleep," the indeterminacy of soul as such. This indeterminacy is called "sleep" because: 1) Hegel understands Aristotle's passive *nous* (which is indeterminate as potentially all things) as "the sleep of the soul";[27] 2) In sleep and dreaming the soul is loosened from its determinate place in nature (it can be instantaneously transported across space or time, and its medley of representations need not obey the laws of nature) such that in sleep the individual soul is the ideality of nature *as a whole*, and *the whole* of nature indifferently stands before it, available to it as material for its dreams.[28]

The awakening is the first inkling of spirit's distinction of itself from its mere being (which will reach is full expression in consciousness). Here however this differentiation is "still burdened with an opposition," to use the apt Hegelian phrase: that is, the soul knows itself in awakening only in opposition to sleep, and thus presupposes sleep, and is only an abstraction from it. This dependence is phenomenally displayed in the production of sleep by its ostensible opposite, the activity of waking life and vice versa.[29]

The soul's sleep is at once called the soul's "mere being"[30] and "its still undifferentiated universality."[31] This may seem contradictory if we take the soul's "mere being" to be its corporeity, its being outside of itself, and its "still undifferentiated universality" to be its essence as soul, for which all distinctions of nature are ideal. However, the soul's "mere being" is not simply its *Sichauseinandersein*: soul as such and soul individualized in the human being are posited as the ideality of nature. There is therefore no pure, that is, no abstract *Sichauseinandersein* for soul.[32] Rather, nature is posited as pervaded throughout by spirit as soul. Therefore, the "mere being" of the soul, its natural life (in which it is absorbed in sleep), is at this stage nothing other than "its still undifferentiated universality."[33] In the awakening this undifferentiated universality of the soul is differentiated from the soul as aware of itself in its individuality, while *both* of these moments remain the soul.

The awakening is a differentiation, therefore, but also a qualification of the radical opposition experienced in the sexual relation insofar as sleeping and waking are alternating states[34] of the same individual. The awoken soul in its individuality has thus appropriated somewhat its indeterminate universality to which it was opposed in the sexual relation.[35] This appropriation is posited in the final stage of natural alterations: sensibility.

In sensibility the soul finds itself adventitiously with contents that are simply "there" and have the status of mere being. The German term for "sensibility" (*Empfindung*) contains within it the verb "to find" (*finden*), indicating that these contents are simply found within the soul.[36] These sensible content-determinacies[37] are immanent for the soul, but have the status of mere being: this latter (in)determination refers to the small extent to which these content determinacies have been idealized. In the "Phenomenology of Spirit" (the section following the "Anthropology") consciousness will develop itself to self-consciousness and reason, at which point the determinations of the subject will be the determinations of the object, and vice versa;[38] but in sensibility the content determinacy is simply present, unsolicited, and not necessarily in agreement with the inner determinacy of the subject (although to express it this way obscures the fact that even the possibility of such a disagreement is not here explicit, insofar as the inner determinacy of the subject comes to light only at the close of the "Anthropology").[39] The discrepancy between the soul and its content (and with it the subject's inner determinacy and the object's "outer" determinacy) emerge only through the soul's immediate identification with the content in feeling.

The Feeling Soul in Its Immediacy and Self-Feeling

Moving from the natural soul to the feeling soul, the second part of the "Anthropology," the course of the natural soul, can now be seen as the gradual individualization of soul as such.[40] The feeling soul's initial definition thus reproduces the original definition of the soul as such, but on the level of the individual: as the soul as such was originally determined as the simple principle present everywhere in the diversity of nature (with no explanation of how this is possible given this original definition), so the (individual) feeling soul is initially determined as the simple ideality of feeling that is present indifferently in each of its many, possibly contradictory feelings (without explanation of how this is possible given here).[41] It is as if Hegel takes the Platonic analogy between the constitution of the individual and on a larger scale of the state,[42] but reverses the direction, stating rather that it will be easier to see in an individual (in subjective spirit) how spirit is the ideality of nature, while reserving for later (in objective spirit) the examination of spirit on the larger scale in the state and history.

As feeling soul reproduces the definition of soul as such on the level of the individual, it is subject to an analogous problem: namely, reconciling the universality of soul with the particularity and exclusivity of its singular feelings. However, we are not simply covering the same ground, but now with soul posited as individual: the course of natural soul leaves us not only with an *individual* soul, but with the soul's indeterminate universality, its mere being, as partially idealized. The soul's indeterminate universality is posited as being in the soul's possession but still a foreign content (as in sensibility). The dream world of the sleeping soul appears here as "an indeterminate mine or pit"[43] in which innumerable feelings lie. This pit is "in" the feeling soul, but the feeling soul is not in control of this content, not yet having undertaken the separation of itself from this content implied by such control.[44] Rather, it is initially immediately identified with each of its many feelings.

The feelings of this indeterminate pit are thus at once the soul itself and other to the soul. The soul's own self is something other to it: this self external to the soul is its genius, lying outside of it, controlling it. Thus, the control the genius exercises over what we might call the passive feeling soul is not a mechanical interaction of two intrinsically unrelated things: it is rather that the different moments of the self appear here as separated spatially.[45] The immediate connection of the feeling self and its content means that when it is sunk in this diseased state it can recall content long ago forgotten, buried deep in the pit.[46] Yet since its feelings remain foreign to it, accessible only problematically, the feeling soul in its immediacy involves a *real* difference that is posited only in the next stage, self-feeling.

In self-feeling the self feels itself in its feeling, identifying with it consciously and investing it with all the importance of its own self: "in this judgment of itself it is always subject: its object is its substance, which is at the same time its predicate."[47] To represent this real judgment linguistically, the feeling self says, "I *am* this feeling." Here the "I" is not the substance, of which the feeling would be an accident that may come to be and pass away while leaving the substance intact. Rather, for the feeling self the selfhood is completely on the side of the feeling, of which it is the accident.[48] Insofar as self-feeling is a judgment, the soul is identified with its feeling only as much as they are already implicitly distinguished. They are already implicitly distinguished, first of all because the soul is universal, absorbed in innumerable feelings, and the singular feeling is one feeling excluding others: that is, they are implicitly distinguished because the soul is broad, and the feeling is narrow. But even without reference to this "broader" nature of the soul (which is present for us, but not for the soul here), they are implicitly distinguished insofar as the feeling for its part is finite and hence limited by and related to its opposite.

Insofar as the soul in self-feeling identifies with the singular feeling in its singularity, not knowing itself as implicitly wider than this feeling, the soul may become fixated on this feeling, which may then usurp the whole life of the soul: this is madness, dreaming while awake.[49] The understanding of madness as sleeping and dreaming while awake is not new,[50] but since "sleep," "waking," and "dreaming" are technical terms for Hegel, we must understand madness in the context of the natural alterations section of the account of the natural soul.

Recall, the feeling soul *is* each of its feelings: it is present as a totality in each one of them. This immediate identification of the universal (soul) and singular (feeling) allows the singular to usurp the place of the universal, to present *itself* as the universal *tout court*. The (actual) soul is properly the substantial ideality of its particular feelings. But in self-feeling this relation is expressed as a judgment, such that the soul *is* this particular feeling (tout court). Now, even the actual soul *is* its feelings: but at that stage the nuanced way in which it "is" its feeling is clear. In self-feeling they are simply united in a judgment. Thus, madness is an inadequate form of spirit not because the soul is simply *not* this singular feeling (rather, it is); instead, madness is inadequate because the soul is *also* its other feelings, which exclude the first one (while remaining the first feeling, which excludes those others). Madness succeeds self-feeling in its immediacy, where the indeterminate universality of the individual soul was indifferently absorbed in any and all of its particular, exclusive feelings. In madness the soul "awakens to its inner judgment":[51] that is, the soul posits the particularity of its feelings, feeling itself as something particular. It is no accident that Hegel here uses the term *"erwachen"* (to awaken). Awakening here does not mean merely becoming aware, but primarily has the technical sense given in the account of the natural soul.[52]

The natural soul begins in natural qualities with a mutual interpenetration of universality and singularity. In natural alterations, we can posit that the soul is *this individual soul* because of this indistinct identification of universal and singular. In the sexual relation the soul feels itself as something limited and opposed to the indeterminate universality of its genus, which it then appropriates in the awakening as its sleep. In the awakening the human being, heretofore both a part of nature and permeated with soul, posits itself as individual *soul*: in appropriating its indeterminate universality as its sleep it asserts *itself in its individuality* as the ideality of nature. Likewise, the feeling soul begins with soul (already posited as individual) in problematic possession of its "undifferentiated universality" or "mere being" as the indistinct mine or pit of its feelings. The feeling soul is a universal that is completely absorbed in each feeling. In self-feeling the soul "awakens" to its "inner judgment," that is, feels itself as particular (it feels itself in its feeling that is posited as particular). Finally, self-feeling is madness because this identification of universal with particular feelings allows one feeling to usurp the status of what is substantial and take over the entire life of the soul. Thus, when Hegel says the mad person is dreaming while awake, he means not that some foreign agent (sleeping, dreaming) has intruded on the soul's waking life, but rather that the structure of the awakening in the natural soul has produced this phenomenon of madness, as waking sleep.

If we recall the two syllogisms operating in the transition from nature to spirit, we can see that the awakening in the natural soul involves the individual (soul) at once *differentiating itself* as individual from its indeterminate universality (which is at once the soul as such and its mere being) and identifying itself with soul insofar as it thenceforth takes the place of the soul as such as the ideality of (what will later be posited as its *particular*) natural life. Moreover, madness involves this shift (with exactly the same ontological structure) in the individual feeling soul: one of its feelings is at once distinguished from the feeling soul (insofar as the soul's *idée fixe* forces out all other feelings, each of which the soul *is* as well), and is identified with the feeling soul insofar as the feeling soul feels itself in this feeling, thus allowing that feeling to present itself as the self *tout court*, usurping the soul's entire life. In both cases the immediate identification of universal and singular has led the singular to usurp the place of the universal.

Madness is thus not simply a collapse back into sleep. If it were, then an awakening would be required, which here would mean that the awakening of the natural soul had failed in its task. However, the possibility of madness cannot be understood without understanding the awakening to have "already occurred."[53] *Prima facie* it would seem that the individual soul's differentiation from the undifferentiated mere being of the soul as such would work *against* madness (dreaming while awake). However, insanity is the immediate identification of singular and universal and the attempt by the singular to stand on its own. Now, the singular *really is* the universal in a way (the individual part of nature *is* the soul; the soul *is* its feeling), but they are not simply identical.[54]

The connection between universal and singular is genuine, but in insanity it is misunderstood as immediate. Insanity is rooted in the awakening because in the awakening the soul is first posited as *this individual* soul. Subsequently in sensation and feeling this individual soul is treated as soul *tout court*, such that what is true of soul as such is also true of this individual soul, without qualifications in recognition of the particularity and exclusivity of this individual soul.

There are in the *Zusätze* many examples of such failures to mediate universal and singular: for example, the lunatic's belief that he is king because a man is king, and he is a man.[55] The lunatic fails to mediate this possibility and himself by his particular circumstances (his station in life, the time in which he lives, etc.). We could also see Hegel's earlier examples of sickness (e.g., how a soul in magnetic somnambulism can know a particular fact it has not experienced or ever been told about[56]) as insanity insofar as the individual would take itself to be soul *tout court* since soul pervades all of nature, and so would suppose that it can see what another soul across the world sees, or that it can sense where water is. We would of course reject the contention that anyone really does know things in this way; and if Hegel thought that people did and called this condition sickness, then we would oppose him in this judgment. Yet we can argue that the illness is the *contention* on the part of the lunatic that he *does* have this power. This interpretation would allow us to rehabilitate much of what Hegel says in paragraphs 405 and 406 (and their *Zusätze*).

Thus the judgment uniting universal and singular immediately is not simply wrong in either case: the soul as such is indeed *this individual* soul, and the feeling soul is indeed *this singular* feeling. Yet neither case is adequate: the individual soul is not in its singularity the soul as such; nor is the singular feeling in its singularity the whole of the soul's natural life. This judgment must be transformed into a syllogism through the positing of a mediating term, the objective particular, which is the corporeity of the particular soul: this is done in habit (the final form of self-feeling) and culminates in the actual soul.

Habit

If habit is becoming accustomed to something previously alien, such as an unfamiliar feeling, then its succession of self feeling appears nonsensical. After all, in self feeling the soul is involved *too much*, not *too little* in its feeling. The self is terrified of the loss of this feeling, as this would be the loss of the soul's own self. The lunatic holds fast to his fixed idea even as the rest of his life falls apart around him. However, illness brings with it the possibility of its supersession, insofar as insanity involves the soul identifying completely with what is essentially contingent, transient, and will almost certainly be lost. In the experience of this loss, habit is cultivated.

Thus, since the feeling is contingent and its object or satisfaction is easily lost, we can see the *negation* of the fixed idea, its *absence* as that experience to which the soul must become habituated. Madness should therefore be understood not merely as the soul's morbid absorption in a singular feeling, but also as the soul's utter lack of acquaintance with the absence of this feeling. The singularity of the fixed idea, its determinacy, entails its relation to its opposite, the absence of such a feeling. As the soul endures this loss, it overcomes illness.[57] What makes self-feeling a susceptibility to illness is the determinacy of this feeling (and its consequent incompatibility in a sense with the soul, its inability to be immediately identified with the soul in a stable way); yet this determinacy also makes the cure in habituation possible. Thus habit succeeds self-feeling: habit grows out of self-feeling naturally, while still solving the problem of insanity.

As an example let us take a madman with an unhealthy fixation on a woman. This fixation is an illness because the madman is completely absorbed in his relationship with this woman. This obsession disrupts the man's family life, friendships, and work. The feeling cannot be integrated into the rest of his life, the other relationships he must maintain. Yet, it would be foolish for this man's friends to exhort him to abandon or even temper his obsession with this woman: this exhortation would belie a failure to understand the structure of self-feeling. In self-feeling the self feels itself in its feeling. The feeling is not an object for the soul; it is a mode in which the soul *is*. To implore the madman to abandon the object of his fixation in the name of "being reasonable" is therefore clearly a hopeless endeavor: nothing could be more unreasonable for the sick soul. The healthy person who fails to grasp the structure of self-feeling may see the sick man's obsession as one aspect of his life, a particularly harmful one that should be curbed or eradicated; but to the sick man, the object of his obsession is quite literally his entire life. The rest of his life and the world are for him only a distraction.

To cure madness, Hegel advocates cultivating in the madman feelings that the actual world, its relationships, and its obligations, have value and are not just an impediment to his (perhaps unrealizable) obsession.[58] An alternate treatment still in keeping with Hegel's understanding of illness and habit as its cure would be that illness is overcome by the experience of the loss of the feeling with which the soul identifies in self-feeling (i.e., the experience of the loss of self).[59] The initial experience of this loss may plunge the madman into the darkest despair. However, that this loss of the self is *experienced* indicates that the self has somehow endured (as that which experiences the loss). The loss of self is integral to habit because this loss is the experience of the *limitations* of the singular feeling (that in it in virtue of which it may not be simply identified with the soul). This limitation is phenomenally revealed in the trauma of the perishing of the singular feeling with which the soul was identified. By "the perishing of the feeling," I mean the bitter frustration and disappointment of the soul that loses that feeling with which it identified. The logical comprehension of this phenomenological experience, however, is that the singular feeling passed into its opposite (thus revealing the singular feeling in its determinacy) while the soul itself persists, and by suffering infinite pain proves itself to be not merely this singular feeling, to be as much the absence of this feeling as its presence. Over time and through these experiences the soul begins to know itself as something distinct from the random, arbitrary singularity of its feelings and identifies instead with what is common to all of them; that is, it identifies with them as a totality, as a *particular* world.[60]

Actual Soul

The particular term that has arisen to mediate between the universal (soul) and the singular (feeling) is the particular body of this individual, ensouled human being. The body determines what the individual soul has in fact experienced, constituting its "particular world." Somnambulism (or the pretension thereto) is a disease because the somnambulist claims to know that which she has never sensibly experienced: she claims that since she is (universal) soul, she can know any (singular) feeling, without mediation of her (particular) body.

Madness, sleeping while awake, is therefore not overcome through a second awakening. The cure for madness is rather the experience of the death of the singular feeling, which is "mortal" because it is contingently received through the body. It happens to be, but need not be, a part of one's particular world. As there is nothing linking the soul to a singular feeling necessarily, but only contingently (the happenstance of what the body experiences), the feeling (and with it the self) can perish—though the self survives this perishing. Likewise, the soul has actual feelings only through its body. Thus corporeity (and the consequent "mortality" of the singular feeling) is the objective particular reuniting soul and its feeling. Once again, the "mortality" of this feeling is not (completely) to be lamented: this experience is what transforms the judgment, feeling soul, into the syllogism, actual soul (soul that knows itself as *particular* in its body, and knows itself to be soul *even in* its particularity).[61]

Both the awakening and natural and spiritual death are connections of universal and singular. However, the awakening is characterized by the outrageous (and frankly, evil)[62] pretension on the part of the singular to be the universal, and to be it *in its immediacy*. The spiritual death that cures madness, on the contrary (like the natural death at the close of the *Philosophy of Nature*), is the universal's lowering of itself: it is not the soul's ceasing to identify with its feeling, but rather its identification with this feeling *even in its perishing*, as it passes into its other. Thus, as spirit emerges from nature in the death of the natural animal, so the "I" of phenomenology emerges from the spiritual death of the feeling.

Notes

1. It may help to recall that what we call "the humanities," the Germans call *"die Geisteswissenschaften,"* the spiritual sciences.

2. Enz. (1830), 7; PN.

3. Enz. (1830), § 391; PM. The deduction in detail of spirit as such from nature is beyond the scope of this chapter, and so I do not present this prefatory material as a genuine deduction of spirit. I openly limit myself to themes *within* the *Philosophy of Spirit's* "Anthropology." In the "Anthropology," the first part of "Subjective Spirit," spirit is determined as "soul [*Seele*]."

4. Enz. (1830), §§ 388–89; PM. Hegel thus means by "soul" something very close to what Aristotle means by *"psyche."*

5. Hegel, Enz. (1830), § 163. English translation: *The Encyclopedia Logic*, trans. T. F. Geraets, W. A. Suchting, and H. S. Harris (Indianapolis: Hackett, 1991).

6. Moreover, insofar as the terms of the syllogism are the very moments of the concept itself, outside of which there is nothing (Enz. [1830] §§ 159 and Remark, 160; *The Encyclopedia Logic*), they *are*, quite literally, everywhere.

7. Enz. (1830), § 167; my emphasis; *The Encyclopedia Logic*. Currently there is a debate about the relevance of Hegel's *Logic* for the rest of his system. For example, Wood claims "Speculative logic is dead, but Hegel's [ethical] thought is not" (Allan Wood, *Hegel's Ethical Thought*, Cambridge: Cambridge University Press, 1990, 4). The pretended independence of the philosophy of spirit from the logic is also echoed by Neuhouser (*Foundations of Hegel's Social Theory*, Cambridge: Harvard University Press, 2000, 134; "On Detaching Hegel's Social Philosophy from His Metaphysics: Reply to My Critics" *The Owl of Minerva* 36, no. 1, 32–33, 35). However, despite these rather extravagant claims, Hegel is quite clear that the *Realphilosophie* presupposes the logic (see Hegel, *Grundlinien der Philosophie des Rechts*. Werke 7. Frankfurt: Suhrkamp Verlag, 1986. § 2 *Anm*. English translation: *Elements of the Philosophy of Right*, trans. Nisbet, New York: Cambridge University Press, 2003. § 2 Remark; see also the *Vorrede* to the *Grundlinien*,

12, and § 7 *Anm*. English translation: Preface to the *Elements of the Philosophy of Right*, 10 and § 7 Remark).

8. This is what Hegel means when he calls judgment "the concept in its particularity" (Enz. [1830] § 166; *The Encyclopedia Logic*): judgment exhibits the moments of the concept (i.e. the terms of the syllogism) in their distinction from each other.

9. Enz. (1830), § 182; *The Encyclopedia Logic*.

10. The idea is the concept as it is realized (Enz. [1830] § 212; *The Encyclopedia Logic*).

11. Enz. (1830), § 247; PN.

12. Enz. (1830), §§254, 257; PN, §§ 254, 257.

13. Enz. (1830) §§ 349–350; PM, §§ 349–350.

14. Enz. (1827), § 368; PN, §368. In the Enz. (1817) and Enz. (1827), this text is in § 368, but in Enz. (1830), it was in § 369.

15. Enz. §§ 371, 374; PN.

16. "The genus is in implicit, simple unity with the singularity of the subject whose concrete substance it is. But the universal is disjunction or judgment [*Urteil*], in order to issue from this its diremption as a *unity for itself*, gives itself an existence as *subjective universality*. This process of its closing with itself [*sich mit sich selbst Zusammenschließen*] contains the negation of the merely inner universality of the genus, and also the negation of the merely immediate singularity in which the living being is still only a natural being." Enz. (1830), § 367; PN.

17. Enz. (1830), § 180; *The Encyclopedia Logic*.

18. Enz. (1830), § 179; *The Encyclopedia Logic*. Hegel gives the example of "having four solid walls" as the objective particularity uniting a singular "this house" with the universal that it is, namely, "[a] good [house]." As stated above, the objective particularity must be an essential determination of the universal as well as a property of the singular.

19. This should show how ludicrous is the old canard according to which Hegel is "too abstract" and has nothing to say to us as we face death (see for example Ernst Breisach, *Introduction to Modern Existentialism* [New York: Grove Press, 1962], 15). It is *because* everything natural dies that the concept is reunited with itself, closes with itself, canceling the gap between its moments which characterizes nature, and therefore is reborn as spirit.

20. Enz. (1830), § 392. The singular human is also said to be in complete sympathy and harmony with his or her "race" at this point. However, race for Hegel is a purely natural division, rooted in the geographical differences of the different continents, the effects of climate, and so on. It does not determine the human being as spirit. The brief mention of race here, and the lamentably racist and frankly un-Hegelian comments attributed to Hegel in the *Vorlesungen* do not constitute the introduction of anything like the social life proper to spirit. G. W. F. Hegel, *Vorlesungen über die Philosophie des Geistes*. Berlin 1827/1828, transcribed by J. E. Erdmann and Ferdinand Walter., *Vorlesungen. Ausgewählte Nachschriften*

und Manuskripte, ed. Franz Hespe and Burkhard Tuschling, vol. 13 (Hamburg: Meiner Verlag, 1994), 41; LPS, 89. This belongs rather to "objective spirit."

21. Hereafter I will refer to these as the first and second syllogisms, respectively.

22. Enz. (1830), § 396; PM. The singulars here are not organs of course, but what I mean by calling the ages of man the syllogism of the animal organism as a whole and its parts expressed as an immediate unity is that in both of them the individual human is the universal ideality of its moments.

23. This knowledge of oneself as universal even if one's determinacy is attained only in sensibility, the last stage of the natural soul.

24. In fact even in the ages of man the human is still only the ideality of its natural life *for us*, but not for itself: it does not have being-for-self, knowledge of itself in its determinacy. However, it is in the ages of man that (*for us* at least) soul is posited as not just *present in* this individual part of nature, but as an individual soul.

25. By "soul as such" I mean soul in its original definition as the ideality of nature in general. This can be distinguished from an individual soul (though the individual does remain "soul" despite this distinction), and it is precisely this distinction and the explanation of how the individual, natural organism can "be" soul, which drives the "Anthropology." The root of this problem is in the transition from nature to spirit, in which the syllogism that is spirit has a dual character, as mentioned above. It is: (1) the reunion of nature as a whole (as a universal) and the (singular) animal; (2) the reunion of the animal organism (as a universal) and its (singular) organs. The first syllogism expresses spirit as what I am calling "soul as such." The second expresses spirit as individual soul.

26. Enz. (1830), § 397; PM.

27. Enz. (1830), § 389; PM.

28. According to Boumann, Hegel says in the addition to § 405 of the *Encyclopedia* that "the human soul in the state of dreaming is not merely filled with *single* affections, but [. . .] more than is commonly the case amid the diversions of the waking soul, it attains to a profound and powerful feeling of the *entirety* of its *individual* nature, of the *complete compass* of its past, present, and future." PSS, 235. Of course we need not suppose that one experiences with regard to the future anything more than fantastical representations thereof.

29. As the individual living in sympathy with nature (which we saw in natural qualities) was a statement of the first syllogism as an immediate unity of universal and singular while the ages of man (in natural alterations) was a statement of the second (similarly as an immediate unity), so here the sexual relation is the immediate unity of natural qualities (from the first syllogism) transformed into a judgment, while the awakening is the immediate unity of the ages of man (from the second syllogism) transformed into a judgment. However, the awakening *must not* be derived simply from the ages of man as its judgment, but rather also from the sexual relation: the "Anthropology" and the *Philosophy of Spirit* generally concern these two syllogisms coming into relation with each other.

30. Enz. (1830), § 398; PM.

31. Enz. (1830), § 398; PM.

32. As Hegel says in the addition to § 377 of the *Encyclopedia*: "For spirit, there is a complete absence of thoroughgoing alterity." PSS, vol. 1,·5.

33. Moreover, being, the first category of the *Logic*, is the most indeterminate of all. Enz. (1830) § 86; *The Encyclopedia Logic*.

34. Enz. (1830), § 399; PM.

35. Insofar as: 1) the sexual relation is the judgment of the first syllogism, and thus concerns the relation between the individual human being and its genus (*Geschlechtsverhältnis* means "sex relation" in the sense of "gender relation," relation between the differentia of the genus, though it does involve a "sex relation" as act of copulation); and 2) in the awakening the individual appropriates this universality as its sleep (without of course having a firm grasp on it)—it can indeed be said that all dreams are of a "sexual" nature.

36. Greene also notes this etymological connection. Murray Greene, *Hegel on the Soul* (The Hague: Nijhoff, 1972), 82.

37. Enz. (1830), § 399; PM.

38. Enz. (1830), §§ 438–39; PM.

39. Thus, insofar as nature is permeated with soul, and therefore in sensibility the soul always knows what is essentially a "psychic" content, a content already at least partly idealized, the indeterminacy of the content-determinacy is indeed reflective of its character as pervaded by soul, insofar as soul itself is still utterly indeterminate.

40. Hegel says: "The soul is in itself the totality of nature: as an individual soul it is a monad: it is itself the posited totality of its particular world" Enz. (1830), § 403 Anm; English translation is my own. Hegel here relates what I have been calling the soul as such with the soul as the individual human. The tension in the "Anthropology" turns on the relation between the identity of and difference between the soul as such (ideality of the totality of nature) and the individual soul (ideality of its particular world).

41. Enz. (1830), § 403; PM. Hegel says here that the individual feeling soul is posited as the totality of its particular world (*besonderen Welt*), but § 403 belongs to the introductory paragraphs to the feeling soul section in general. It is only in the final stage of the feeling soul, habit, that the feeling soul will be so posited.

42. Plato, *Republic*, trans. Allan Bloom (New York: Basic Books, 1968). 368c–369a.

43. "*ein bestimmtlose Schacht.*" Enz. (1830), § 403. I have slightly amended Wallace's translation from PM).

44. Enz. (1830), § 404; PM. In fact Hegel does not say here that this pit is "in" the soul, but rather that the soul *is* this pit: the feeling soul in its immediacy is characterized precisely by this mutual interpenetration of the soul and its feeling(s).

45. Enz. (1830), § 405; PM. Hegel gives as an example the mother and the child in her womb: the child is not only physically dependent, but spiritually dependent, insofar as the one self for both of them is the mother. The child receives impressions as passively as it does fluids, and has no developed character

which would allow it to experience these impressions *as* good or bad, hoped for or dreaded, but rather receives them all indifferently. This also occurs (as a diseased state [Enz. {1830} § 404 Anm.; PM]) in adults (or those who are naturally but not spiritually mature) in the case of "magnetic somnambulism"(Hegel, Enz. [1830], § 406; PM) or what we would call today hypnotism (this is perhaps the only one of the many examples Hegel gives of this genius relationship which we would consider valid today). Though this is properly a diseased state, we might say that it is still a sign of the dignity of spirit that for it this spatial separation is a nullity (see Enz. [1830], § 392; PM).

46. Hegel, PSS, vol. 2, § 406 Z (269, 275, 277).

47. Hegel, Enz. (1830), § 404; PM.

48. Of course, the feeling self here does not "have" its feeling, it *is* its feeling, so it is not really the accident of something other than it: since it *is* its feeling and this feeling is the self, then it is (in a way) the self. It is the self through not being it however, since to be the self properly speaking would be for it to have selfhood in virtue of itself, not through another.

49. Enz. (1830), § 408; PM.

50. This understanding of insanity goes back at least as far as Aristotle, according to whom "the faculty by which, in waking hours, we are subject to illusion when affected by disease, is identical with that which produces illusory effects in sleep." *On Dreams*, 458a26–28. trans. Beare, *Basic Works of Aristotle* (New York: Random House, 1941). Kant also says: "The play of fantasy with the human being in sleep is called dreaming, and it also takes place in a healthy condition; on the other hand if it happens while the human being is awake, it reveals a diseased condition." *Anthropology from a Pragmatic Point of View*, trans. (Louden, New York: Cambridge University Press, 2006), 68.

51. "*zum Urteil in sich zu erwachen*," Hegel, Enz. (1830), § 407. I have slightly amended Wallace's translation from PM).

52. This point has been largely ignored in the scant secondary literature on the "Anthropology." Greene (*Hegel on the Soul*) discusses madness as sleeping while awake without any reference to what these terms mean for Hegel according to his account in natural alterations (114, 119, 126–27, 129). Neither DeVries, *Hegel's Theory of Mental Activity* 9Ithaca: Cornell University Press, 1998), nor Lewis, *Freedom and Tradition in Hegel: Reconsidering Anthropology, Ethics, and Religion* (Notre Dame: University of Notre Dame Press, 2005), discusses sleeping and waking, though the former does discuss madness briefly (77–8). Berthold-Bond, *Hegel's Theory of Madness* (New York: State Univerity of New York Press, 1995), discusses madness as succumbing to the "Lure of a Primordial Unity" (77), arousing expectations of a discussion which recalls sleep (as determined in the natural soul) as just such a sinking into indeterminate universality. But rather than locating this primordial unity where it belongs, in the concept of spirit as it emerges from nature, and in the natural soul as spirit is first determined, he places it in the self-consciousness of the 1807 *Phenomenology*. However, this cannot be right according to Hegel's account in the *Encyclopedia*. Consciousness succeeds habit

and actual soul, where the *particularity* of the individual soul in its corporeity is posited. This positing is the *cure* for madness, and consciousness (as well as self-consciousness) *presupposes* this positing.

53. Of course, Hegel is not giving us a temporal sequence of events, so we can only mean that the awakening has "already occurred" in a metaphorical way: namely, that the insane soul must be understood in the context of its explicit differentiation as this individual soul from its sleep as the undifferentiated ideality of all of nature, and its assertion that it as individual soul is the ideality of natural life.

54. When we say that the singular *really is* the universal (in a way), or that insanity has *some* legitimacy, we mean only that this is indeed a form of spirit, if only an impoverished one that is deceptive in its presentation of spirit. If insanity were *radically* anomalous, if it were utterly devoid of spirit, then it would be incurable, because there would be no trace of rationality in the lunatic that could be nurtured and developed. In fact, natural idiocy (resulting from physical deficiency or deformity) is incurable (Hegel, PSS, vol. 2, § 408 Z [373, 375]); but the sickness of the soul that Hegel is concerned with here is necessarily corrigible because it is only an inadequate form of spirit. Thus, Hegel says that all treatment must presuppose the underlying rationality of the patient (Enz. [1830] § 408; PM), who, we might add, is necessarily therefore never merely a patient, but always also an agent and a collaborator in her recovery.

55. PSS, vol. 2, § 408 Z (343).
56. PSS, vol. 2, § 406 Z (259ff).
57. Thus no insanity is incurable (aside from *natural* idiocy).
58. PSS, vol. 2, § 408 Z (381).
59. It could be that the cultivation of an appreciation for the value of the actual world and its conditions would be easier on the patient and preferable to that extent; however, my purpose is not actually to promote any change in clinical practice, but only to elucidate Hegel's account of illness and what habit does to overcome it.
60. Enz. (1830), § 409; PM.
61. Enz. (1830), § 411; PM.
62. Hegel defines evil as "the negative that does not subsist on its own account, but only *wants* to be on its own account, and is in fact only the absolute *semblance* of inward negativity." G. W. F. Hegel, *Werke in zwanzig Bänden [Theorie Werkausgabe]*, ed. E. Moldenhauer and K. M. Michel (Frankfurt: Suhrkamp, 1970), Band 8. § 35 Z; *The Encyclopedia Logic*. This is precisely what begins in the awakening and leads to madness: the attempt on the part of the singular to present itself as in its immediacy the universal.

Awakening from Madness

The Relationship between Spirit and Nature in Light of Hegel's Account of Madness

MARIO WENNING

Understanding the relationship between spirit and nature has been one of the most perplexing problems of philosophy. Hegel's original idea, or so I want to argue in this chapter, consists in not conceiving of the move from sensing to free thinking as a straightforward progression in which the authority of nature is replaced by that of spirit. Free thinking cannot be understood without a "natural" dimension. This natural dimension cannot be superseded but remains a constitutive background of our mental lives. Kant's philosophy, if Hegel is right, ultimately leads to a form of subjectivism that is incapable of accounting for our mind's natural dimension in treating subjectivity as prior and categorically distinct from natural conditioning. Hegel, however, shows that subjectivity without nature becomes empty, and, in terms of politics, it ushers in the blind revolutionary terror. Only when we find an adequate way of accounting for the "opaque" natural dimension *in* our subjectivity will it be possible to conceive of an embodied form of rational free spirit. By interpreting the discussion of madness in the *Encyclopedia* and the *Lectures on the Philosophy of Spirit* we can see that the prominent characterization of Hegel as an idealist who "disenchants" nature and denigrates it to a mere preparatory stage in the development of spirit needs to be reconsidered.

Hegel addresses madness in his lectures on anthropology. When he presented these lectures in Heidelberg and Berlin, he was fulfilling a basic requirement of a university lecturer in the faculty of philosophy at that time. During his tenure, he lectured 35 times on anthropology and thus much more frequently than on phenomenology or psychology. It was quite common to teach anthropology especially to medical students to provide them with a first overview that should enhance their understanding of the work they were endeavoring to undertake.[1] It is important to keep in mind this audience since we have to assume that Hegel's remarks were intended for (and must have had) practical implications with regard to the professional practice of his students in treating patients diagnosed with mental pathologies.

By "anthropology" Hegel does thus not mean a philosophical discipline that would provide an answer to the question What is man? Under the heading of what could perhaps be translated best as "the logic of the human," he discusses issues ranging from geography, race, temperament, and education to the relationship between the sexes. These topics are discussed with the goal of better understanding the relationship between spirit and nature.

"Anthropology," Hegel introduces the first part of his *Lectures on Subjective Spirit*, "has for its subject matter the soul in its uncultivated natural condition."[2] What does this mean? There are three parts to this definition. First, anthropology addresses the human soul (rather than the physiological developments or geographic conditions for human life). Second, however, it does not just address the human soul, but the soul in its *uncultivated* state, which is, third, designated as a *natural* condition. The study of anthropology presupposes, we can infer, that the soul can also be investigated in its cultured, that is, spiritual state. This will be the topic of the subsequent parts of the system, the philosophy of subjective spirit, including psychology, and, finally, the philosophy of objective and absolute spirit, comprising the cultural manifestations of the most advanced forms of reflective life.

The first part of the *Philosophy of Subjective Spirit*, "Anthropology," is divided into the three sections "Natural Soul," "The Dreaming Soul," and "Actual Soul." The natural soul is a feeling soul or, following Williams' translation, sentient soul (*empfindende Seele*). The more the human soul distances itself from its animal nature, the more it cultivates itself, the freer it becomes. This process of cultivation is one of overcoming and leaving behind particular differences that are attached to natural conditions such as climate, race, and temperaments. The human being is distinguished from the animal in that he is capable of taking a stance with regard to his natural condition.

To sublate one's conditioning by nature through relating to it does not mean to get rid of it, or to surpass it once and for all. Rather, it means to enter into a conscious relationship to it. Only such a conscious life allows the soul to manifest itself as totality. "This," Hegel writes, "is how the human being distinguishes itself from the animal. Much effort has been expended in determining this distinction."[3] This conscious being related to one's natural conditioning can take on the power of a transformation through habit. Our upright posture—"the primary gesture of the human being"—allows us to provide us with an orientation in space, an orientation that "is a matter of its willing." That we are able to gesture and use our faces to express deep emotions is a further determining factor.

The natural state of the soul is said to be at the same time "unnatural" in that it drives to a state beyond the natural, that is, to the spiritual state. Its goal is "liberation from this uncultivated natural condition." Nature and spirit are thus the two poles and potential conditions the human soul can be in. Hegel's anthropology has received little attention because it is, apart from the philosophy of nature, the most empirical and thus, it is commonly argued, the most outdated part of his system. Although the precursors of modern psychology of the eighteenth and early nineteenth centuries from whom Hegel takes his knowledge concerning psychology, figures such as Francois Boissier de Sauvages or Michael Adanson, were very important for the development of their discipline, little of their work is of relevance for contemporary psychology and medicine. Hegel's views on anthropological psychology are said to be outdated not only because current psychological findings contradict what Hegel took for granted. Rather it is Hegel's underlying systematizing methodology that has been criticized. It is difficult to accept Hegel's claim that philosophical anthropology should strive to integrate the empirical findings of psychology into a *systematic* program according to which the development of the soul should increasingly free itself from feeling, which Hegel sees as its merely natural state. Although it is true that Hegel often equates freedom—the being at home with oneself—with a "liberation from desire" by way of "subsuming" and thus "taking possession of one's feelings," it is also the case that Hegel emphasizes the role of emotions as motivating reasons for any action.

Hegel develops his account in accordance with the nature of the human soul as it has been laid out in Aristotle's *De Anima*. By way of using contemporary psychology within a framework of a hierarchy leading from sensation to free thinking along Aristotelian lines, Hegel strives to update inherited accounts of psychic development. The program to combine ancient psychology with recent discoveries in the natural sciences is not revolutionary in that it finds important precursors in Descartes' *Traité de l'homme* (1632), Hobbes' *De homine* (1658), Lamettrie's *L'homme machine* (1747), and Wolffianism.

Hegel goes beyond these accounts in accounting for an unconscious psychological dynamic. By discovering the unconscious mind he anticipates Freud, Jung, and other depth psychologists.[4] He also anticipated important therapeutic applications resulting from his theory of the unconscious. While his engagement with obscure topics such as animal magnetism and somnambulism seems rather outdated to the modern reader, what interests Hegel about the therapeutic ideas of Mesmer, Puységure, and Deleuze is very much in line with hypnosis and cognitive psychology of our day.

Madness is not simply seen as the loss of rationality. Hegel conceives of it as an essential possibility of mental life. It is in madness that "something emerges that is not under the power of our conscious actuality."[5] Although not every individual has to go through stages of madness, madness remains a constant possibility, a possibility of "sinking into nature" that spirit cannot guard itself against once and for all. Hegel's anthropology is a particularly valuable starting point to understand his concept of mental life. Only when we follow Hegel in trying to elaborate how our empirical self is inseparably linked with a natural dimension is it possible to understand various forms of subject-object incongruity, which are thematized in the *Phenomenology of Spirit*.[6] It is surprising that Hegel scholarship, with only few exceptions,[7] has ignored these writings. Other works emphasizing the history of pathologies of the time have remained almost conspicuously silent about Hegel's treatment of mental pathologies and their relationship to his analysis of the necessary conditions of self-determination, the project of a philosophy of spirit.[8]

This lack of engagement is particularly apparent with regard to his treatment of various mental or "spiritual" pathologies ranging from frenzy to madness. Only when we come to understand Hegel's conception of madness can we conceive of the master-slave relationship as one of *necessarily failed recognition*, of the French Revolution's turn to wanton terror after 1789 as resulting out of a false conception of liberation, of the various forms of alienation Hegel lays out for us in other writings on religion, history, art, and even philosophy itself. Hegel uses the term "*Verrücktheit*" to characterize madness as the traditional translation renders the term, or dementia, as Williams suggests. "*Verrücktheit*," contains in its root meaning "*verrückt*." The latter means to be displaced, demented, to be moved out of one's natural place and order, or, as Berthold-Bond following Fialko translates the term to be deranged.[9]

Madness is thus not treated by Hegel as the "other" of reason, but as a special form or dimension of reason that comes to hold when the rational mind has been repositioned, disunited, but at the same time continues to be related to forms of rationality. It is a dimension that remains a possibility and even a subterranean dimension of reason even in its most developed stages.

But why is it that Hegel turns to madness as part of his treatment of the "sensing soul" (*die fühlende Seele*)? He throws a new light on the "normal" life of the soul a hundred years before Freud[10] and a hundred and sixty before Foucault by drawing on madness. Madness is not just one condition of consciousness among many others. Hegel regards derangement as the mirror state of the "normal" soul in that it illuminates what spirit is, even if, or precisely in a distorted fashion. In the additions to § 408 of the *Philosophy of Spirit*, Hegel compares the relationship between sanity and madness to that between ethical life and morality as he introduced it in the *Philosophy of Right*.

As the soul's access to the unconscious, madness is connected to a remembering process that reminds the subject that it emerged out of nature. Hegel writes: "The [unconscious] dimension, which is preserved in memory, can be erased by a blow, etc. Conversely, illnesses can again evoke many things that are outside our [conscious] power, and that otherwise could not be called forth again at will. What is thus in our [unconscious] being we cannot know. One forgets what one learns. Afterwards this is posited in one's being and can be awakened again under special conditions."[11]

Madness is perhaps the only access to the archaic natural past that a rational subject bears inside it. It is a depository that accompanies us to remind us of what we, according to Hegel, had to leave behind in the process of becoming self-authorizing rational animals. It is the echo of nature within the subject. Thus, when elaborating his interpretation of madness, Hegel emphasizes that it is necessary to understand it against the background of the sane "understanding" (*verständige*) consciousness.

Critics of Hegel often claim that he does not do sufficient justice to nature by merely treating it as a preparatory stage, which is subordinated to and ultimately needs to be overcome by spirit. Hegel, the objection goes, too easily equates nature with immediacy, particularity, unfreedom, beginning, something imperfect, while spirit is presented as (self-) mediation, universality, end, freedom, (self-) perfection. Yet Hegel complicates such a simplified developmental picture in his anthropology from the very beginning by claiming that the soul "taken in its natural condition" is also "positing of spirit itself." The "play of spirit whereby it comes to itself" consists precisely in understanding that what appeared as nature is (and, in a rudimentary sense, always was) spirit. We could blame Hegel for not sharpening his thought by using two different terms for what he means by "spirit." In the case of spirit, he refers to a state that replaces nature as that which is free. In the case of spirit, he refers to a faculty that is latently existent and gains an understanding of itself by way of reflecting on itself. That Hegel chooses to use the same term to characterize these rather different conceptions cannot be explained by reference to the speculative concept or identity and difference. Rather, there is a more substantive reason at play here. To refer to nature *as spirit* and nature *qua nature* is meant to point out that these two dimensions of our soul cannot be fundamentally distinguished: "in the soul the unity of the physical and the spiritual is present." Neither of the binaries has a priority that would be granted if one first categorically separated them. By attributing to our soul in its natural condition an underlying natural as well as spiritual dimension, Hegel preserves the possibility to emphasize two processes of cultivation.

First, to become free means to free oneself from arbitrary constraints and conditioning by external nature. Is it then the case that Hegel is an arch-rationalist who denigrates what has been en vogue in recent philosophical debates under the heading of the body and emotion? Is the human being essentially a spiritual being that is in some sense sick if not following her spiritual vocation? Can we assume that Hegel's ideal of humanity is a self-conscious subject, which has authorized its guiding norms and translates them into the adequate affective responses? In short, is Hegel a closet Kantian? Although Hegel's positive vision of ethical life is rather different from Kant's, it can reasonably be argued that they share an common enemy: the standpoint of claims of immediate feelings or inclinations in matters of ethics. According to this interpretation, cultivation means for Hegel a gradual move away from nature by means of suppressing it.

However, cultivation also means what Hegel refers to as an "awakening from slumbering natural life."[12] In the 1827 *Lectures on the Philosophy of Spirit*, the entire middle part of the "Anthropology," the part in which madness is being systematically addressed, is entitled "The Dreaming Soul" (*die träumende Seele*), and not, as three years later, "The Sensing Soul" (*die fühlende Seele*). The metaphor of sleeping and awakening, *Aufwachen*, does not just allude to the rallying cry of the age of enlightenment as an awakening from one's "self-incurred tutelage." To awaken from a slumber was the project inaugurated by Kant's critical philosophy. The purpose of addressing mental derangement as a form of sleep was intended to wake up. Waking up from slumbering life or from nature does not mean to leave it behind once and for all but to enter into a conscious relationship to it.

The dreaming consciousness is one that develops compensation strategies against a "loss or misfortune." It cannot reach satisfaction and cannot restore a relationship to the universal. Derangement is characterized as the "dream within being awake itself." It often starts, Hegel asserts, as absent-mindedness and daydreaming. It occurs when the soul experiences a primary division—an *Urteilung*—that distinguishes itself from itself as a split consciousness and at the same time distinguishes it from recognizing itself in meaningful social structures. Thus, deranged consciousness becomes alienated and fundamentally imprisoned in its own conceptions of reality that do not link with those of the actual world: "[M]isapprehension and foolishness," Hegel states in the additions to § 408, "only become derangement once the person takes his merely subjective beliefs to be presented to him as objective and holds on to them against the opposing actual objectivity."[13] The result is an abstraction from concrete actuality. If I take myself to be a king or a great artist and hold on to this belief even if no one else in the world confirms this self-conception, I become alienated from my environment and retreat into an inward world of abstract possibility. Derangement is thus the result of becoming a prisoner of contingent, merely possible believes, which "move us out" (*herausrücken*) of the center of our actuality, while retaining a rudimentary consciousness of this reality. In Freudian terminology, the deranged consciousness loses its anchor in the reality principle. Hegel conceives of deranged consciousness as a split consciousness that cannot unite a sense of reality and a sense of possibility because it privileges the latter.

It is not only misfortune that leads to dementia, but also too much happiness. Taking oneself too seriously or not taking oneself and one's claims to happiness seriously at all both correspond to states of dementia. The first one is a form of romantic arrogance connected to the cult of the mad genius, which makes one incapable of coping with the world because one is estranged from it. The second form, taking oneself not seriously at all, easily succumbs to melancholy, a condition Hegel attributes to Englishmen. When succumbing to melancholy one becomes incapable of action.

One way to better come to terms with the relationship between madness and its surrounding world is to consider the phenomenon of genius and in particular the mad genius. Genius is, for Hegel, not an achievement of spirit. Rather it is a form of coercive motivation that cannot be avoided even if it leads to doom and disaster. Although not all geniuses are mad, and certainly not all mad people are geniuses, there is a close affinity between the two. Madness is advantageous for geniuses, because it connects them with nature. We have gotten used to thinking of Beethoven, Hölderlin, and Hegel himself as geniuses who compulsively position themselves under a work for whose creation they are a mere arbitrary and thus exchangeable means. To illustrate the way that genius can lead to a loss of one's connection to social norms, Hegel mentions the example of Archimedes, who immersed himself so thoroughly into a problem that he forgot everything else for days, and Newton, who used the finger of a lady to stuff his pipe. While forgetting his social responsibilities, the mad genius also sees himself as being an indispensible mouthpiece for the absolute. This tension between seeing oneself as merely instrumental and as at the same time indispensible corresponds to the tension of sanity and madness.

Hegel was existentially confronted with madness on at least two occasions. Hegel was acutely aware of the chronic illnesses of his sister Christiane. He praises Pinel's plea for a moral treatment of the deranged patient in the latter's *Philosophische-medizinische Abhandlung über Geistesverirrungen oder Manie* (1801) and was a close friend with Friedrich Schelling's brother, Karl Schelling, who was physician known for his mild and humane treatment, which he also applied to Hegel's sister. Hegel was also observing his close friend from the Tübingen Stift, Friedrich Hölderlin. Although Hegel does not mention Hölderlin once in his writings, we can assume that he took madness as seriously as he did, because two of the closest people in his vicinity were suffering kinds of dementia.[14] His knowledge of Hölderlin's case confronted Hegel with a theoretical challenge because Hölderlin at once slipped over into an "abyss of indeterminateness" in which he was "shut up in his own subjectivity," while on the other hand retaining—or we would now even say improving—his creative and rational powers during his derangement. Hölderlin's case reveals how difficult it is to determine clearly where sanity stops and madness begins: "It is difficult to determine its boundaries."[15] Against the Cartesian clear separation of reason from madness, Hegel sees madness and sanity as being a quantitative differences rather than a clear-cut qualitative distinction. Both madness and sanity characterize the dynamic life of the soul.

Conceiving of madness as a dimension of the soul, which is not categorically distinct from sanity, constitutes a break with the kind of systematizing that was prominent in the eighteenth century. Before Hegel, madness was often treated as the "other" of reason, some demonic lapse into a condition that had to be violently attacked, locked away, and rooted out. Rather than developing an encyclopedic etiology, a classificatory scheme along the lines of Linné, Hegel was aware that madness and sanity were two extremes that were at times closely intertwined. The recently translated 1927 lecture notes on the *Philosophy of Spirit* reveal Hegel's skepticism about a final classificatory scheme of madness much clearer than the final discussion in the last version of the *Encyclopedia*.

Today it is difficult to understand the humanizing affect Hegel's account of madness must have had. Rather than simply locking up or otherwise getting rid of the unwanted deranged, Hegel argues for a humane treatment that addresses the conscious and unconscious aspects of the human mind and uses the, at the time, most advanced physiological and psychological means of therapy. Labor is supposed to reawaken a person's loss of focus and fulfilled engagement with the world, a swing is supposed to reverse the distorted inner life to its original form, placebo treatment is supposed to free the deranged from their illusions, and jokes are said to regularly heal foolishness. The main aim of these therapies was to regain the trust (*Vertrauen*) of the mentally deranged, trust in the external world, and, more importantly, in their own ethical power, "because the deranged are after all ethical beings."[16] The task, Hegel continues, should be to "awaken the feeling that there is after all something important and dignified." Although Hegel refers to madness as being a form of evil (*Bösartigkeit*), he, citing Pinel's remark that the most loving spouses and fathers can be found in the soul asylum, emphasizes that "evil"—with regard to madness—is not to be interpreted in a moral sense.

This account of madness had enormous consequences for Hegel's conception of anthropology, which was primarily supposed to lead to practical devices in curing or at least improving the fate of those affected by mental derangement. After identifying the three stages of mental derangement—(1) imbecility (*Blödsinn*), (2) folly (*Narrheit*), and (3) frenzy (*Wahnsinn*)—Hegel places much emphasis on potential therapeutic treatment. If one aims to cure derangement, if one wants to put the mind straight again, it is necessary to appeal to the rational potential that is left within madness. Madness is not a total loss of sanity, but bears a sane moment in it just as any sane mind bears the potential of "regressing" to a state of nature that continues to survive within it.

Madness is a particularly interesting somatic and psychic phenomenon to consider because it is not just a developmental stage that is overcome in processes of increasing formation. This would be empirically unconvincing and logically implausible. Madness is, at least chronologically, often a late stage in life. It is often the culmination of a process rather than an initial stage that could be superseded once and for all. We might think of

Nietzsche and Hölderlin, who serve as the most prominent examples of people spending a large portion of the end of their lives under a state of dementia. Rather than addressing the problem of madness as connected to processes of psychophysical aging (as we tend to address Alzheimer nowadays), Hegel sees it as a uniquely human possibility that accompanies spirit. Only when madness becomes a fixed condition that fully loses touch with reality does it become a truly pathological state.

Following Kant's criticism of the attempt to conceive of the connection between the brain, sense impressions, sensations, and the power of memory in strictly causal terms, Hegel does not think that it is possible to reduce mental illness to some external state in the manner of somatic psychology. In his philosophy of nature, he spends much polemic and argumentative energy to criticize Scot John Brown, who in his *The Elements of Medicine* claimed to have transformed pathology into a subdiscipline of Newton's mechanics. Hegel also refuses to reduce mental illness to a mere spiritual phenomenon as a naïve idealist or the romantics did. Hegel rather admits that "[w]hether the physical or the mental constitutes the beginning is difficult to say, or impossible to determine. Often one finds nothing abnormal in the anatomy of demented people; in other cases many abnormalities are present."[17]

We have seen that Hegel reveals a progressive understanding of madness that breaks with prevailing tendencies of his day to either mystify madness or to reduce it to the other of reason. In contrast to the romantics, Hegel does not go so far as to idealize madness as the mark of a genius. We have stressed that Hegel dismisses clear-cut categorization that situates madness as the "other" of reason. Madness is difficult to situate with regard to sanity in that it remains a constant possibility and mirror image of the rational soul.

However, Hegel remains suspiciously quiet about the historically specific forms of mental pathologies that every reader of Foucault will try to uncover. In spite of being aware of external influences, Hegel refrains from reducing madness to external causes, including sociohistorical ones. The task of the philosopher consists in understanding madness itself, how it is internally structured, how it relates to sanity, and what can be done about it, rather than treating it as a merely contingent historical occurrence. However, in principle there is no reason to assume why Hegel should not have acknowledged historically specific causes of certain forms of madness. The *Phenomenology of Spirit* and the *Philosophy of Right* provide ample evidence of how seriously Hegel took the impact of history on the development of spirit.

In line with the spirit of his philosophy, Hegel might have answered Foucault that any convincing account of madness needs to draw on socially constructed images of what counts as normal that determine our self-conception. Without being recognized and without recognizing, subjects fail to build any internally or externally viable identities. The difference between Foucault and Hegel is not just a difference of emphasis. Neither is it a difference between social constructivism and ontology. Contrary to Foucault, Hegel does hold that madness is a form of pathology, which, Hegel argues, is both spiritual and physical. We should look for potential therapies to address this condition of the soul. Foucault would have automatically identified any form of medical cure or therapy as a form of moral and social correction and reeducation, ultimately a form of violence. Madness, according to Foucault, is not an illness but a way of disenfranchising and marginalizing those who are not taken to fit into inherited standards of reason and rationality.

There is, however, a different aspect with regard to which Hegel, taken on his own terms, owes us an answer. We have seen that Hegel addresses madness not for its own sake, but with the intention of learning more about sanity, the "normal" life of the soul. What we get, however, is a phenomenology of madness. What consequences does Hegel's account have for the self-conception of sane consciousness, of spirit in its most complex forms of self-reflection? Knowing that it constantly can regress to nature, knowing that it does operate parallel to a subterranean "unconscious" dimension, how should the mind relate to this dimension? Can or should the sane mind guard itself against an eruption of the "dark, infernal powers" of nature that Hegel designates as evil? Given his account of madness, he would have to stress that liberated consciousness cannot be a superseding of nature, but one that retains a different relationship to it. Assuming that progress is always connected with a dimension of remembrance and that therapy, in order to be effective, essentially has to be self-therapy, Hegel owes us a story about what it means to be awake after having gone through the experience of madness. What does it mean to acknowledge that awakening is always accompanied by dormant sources that reveal themselves in the form of day dreaming and, we might add, wishful thinking, longing, or mourning, forms of thinking that do not easily translate into rational thought? How can the age of enlightenment acknowledge its own necessary blind spots? Positively stated, what Hegel accomplishes is accounting for the rational mind's vulnerability, a vulnerability which shows that it retains its natural conditionedness as an essential feature.

Notes

1. Concerning the purpose of anthropology and the different schools at Hegel's time, cf. Michael John Petry, "Systematik und Pragmatik in Hegels Behandlung von animalischem Magnetisus und Verrücktheit," in *Psychologie und Anthropologie oder Philosophie des Geistes*, ed. Franz Hespe and Burkhard Tuschling (Stuttgart: Friedrich Frommann Verlag, 1991); Odo Marquard, "Anthropologie," in *Historisches Wörterbuch der Philosophie* (Darmstadt: Schwabe Verlag, 1971), 362–74.

2. LPS, 81.

3. LPS, 160.

4. Cf. Daniel Berthold-Bond, *Hegel's Theory of Madness* (Albany: State University of New York Press 1995).

5. LPS, 141.

6. Williams calls our attention to the similarities between Hegel's account of dementia and the analysis of the beautiful soul in § 658 of the *Phenomenology of Spirit*. Just as the person suffering from dementia is unable to sustain a self-conception that integrates his or her particularity within a larger, meaningful lifeworld, the beautiful soul takes flight from the world and everything in it to its subjectivity, while holding on to an ideal fantasy world, which is allegedly higher than the real world. Both states of consciousness are capable of certain forms of rational deliberation, but fail to translate their aspirations into meaningful action. The result is a merely negative, enclosed freedom that lacks in actuality. Williams suggests that the beautiful soul can be conceived of as a preparatory stage with a high potential of leading to dementia. Cf. footnote 51 in LPS, 16f. Daniel Berthold-Bond emphasizes that it is not just the characterization of the beautiful soul that converges in many respects with the account of madness. Hegel's depiction of skepticism, the law of the heart, virtue, absolute freedom, and terror can also be understood as manifestations of forms of madness.

7. Cf. Daniel Berthold-Bond, *Hegel's Theory of Madness*; Michael John Petry, "Systematik und Pragmatik in Hegels Behandlung von animalischem Magnetisus und Verrücktheit," in *Psychologie und Anthropologie oder Philosophie des Geistes*, ed. Franz Hespe and Burkhard Tuschling (Stuttgart: Friedrich Frommann Verlag, 1991).

8. Cf. Michel Foucault, *Histoire de la Folie* (Paris: Librairie Plon, 1961); *Meladie Mentale et Psychologie* (Paris: Presses Universitaires de France, 1962), *Naissance de la Clinique* (Paris: Presses Universitaires de France, 1963). Whereas Foucault sees madness as ultimately being a social construction, Hegel treats it as the interplay of certain internal and external failures to achieve an appropriate level of self-organization: "Das Verbrechen und die Verrücktheit sind Extreme, welche der Menschengeist überhaupt im Verlauf seiner Entwicklung zu überwinden hat" (crime and derangement are extremes, which humanity needs to surpass in general during the course of its development). See *Enzyklopädie der philosophischen*

Wissenschaften, vol. 3 (Frankfurt: Suhrkamp, 1970), § 408 Z. Madness is a form of "disease," because it undermines the "natural" totality of the feeling soul and fixes it as a particularity which is internally divided and detached from its environment.

9. Daniel Berthold-Bond, *Hegel's Theory of Madness*, 1.

10. Cf. Darrel Christensen, "Hegel's Phenomenological Analysis and Freud's Psychoanalysis," *International Philosophical Quarterly* 8, no. 3 (1968): 356–78. Cf. also H. F. Ellenberger, *The Discovery of the Unconscious: The History and Evolution of Dynamic Psychiatry* (London: Penguin,s 1970).

11. LPS, 141.

12. LPS, 104.

13. Hegel, *Werke* 10, § 480 Z.

14. Alan Olson has argued that "Hegel's silence (concerning the mental deterioration of Hölderlin) "is transparent to his own inordinate fear of madness—and reasonably so, owing to his sister Christiane's chronic mental depression." *Hegel and the Spirit: Philosophy as Pneumatology* (Princeton: Princeton University Press, 1992), 84–106. Since we lack any convincing evidence attesting to such a fear, and it would easily lead to "reducing" Hegel's work to a psychological condition, it has to be treated as an unfounded, although not implausible, stipulation.

15. LPS, 142.

16. Hegel, *Werke* 10, § 480 Z.

17. LPS, 144.

Between Nature and Spirit

Hegel's Account of Habit

Simon Lumsden

Hegel's discussion of habit takes place at two critical junctures in his work. In the *Philosophy of Right* it occurs in a well-known paragraph at the outset of the discussion of ethical life. Habit in this context is used to show the limitations of Kantian autonomy and morality as a model for the kind of freedom possible in a modern society. The second juncture, which has received much less attention and which is the focus of this chapter, is the discussion of habit in the subjective spirit. In the *Encyclopedia* Hegel makes a strong claim for the importance of habit in the development of spirit, describing it as "what is most essential to the existence of all spirituality within the individual subject."[1] There he argues habit is critical to the emergence of consciousness and is the key bridge between nature and spirit.[2] What I argue in this chapter is that habit is more than just a transition point, dissolving itself and nature with it in the move from nature to spirit. The way Hegel conceives habit, particularly his characterization of it as second nature, challenges the dualism of nature and spirit.

One of the recurring issues that emerge in the wake of Kant's critical philosophy is just how successfully he was able to reconcile the dualism of mind and world. The critical philosophy tries to bridge the competing epistemologies of rationalism and empiricism, each of which took truth to reside in either mind or world. Kant attempts to overturn this opposition by taking receptivity (the passively delivered empirical content) and spontaneity (the distinctively human capacity for self-determined thought and action) to be distinct arms of a single unified knowledge. What is significant for our purposes, in this context, is not the details of Kant's critical project but the way in which this core distinction between concept and intuition comes to structure much subsequent philosophy. One of the defining questions for post-Kantian thought was judging just how successful Kant was in overcoming the dualism of mind and world. Certainly his immediate successors and many of his contemporaries were not convinced he managed to achieve this, and few in contemporary philosophy would probably think it was an approach that was wholly convincing. Despite the ongoing debate and dissatisfaction with Kant's approach, the terms of the debate for understanding the relation between mind and world or spirit and nature have tended to be structured by Kant's receptivity-spontaneity distinction. For example John McDowell attempts to resolve the apparent dualism of mind and world, which he takes to plague analytic philosophy, by drawing on Hegel, particularly his notion of second nature. By arguing for the unboundedness of the conceptual, McDowell hopes to reenchant nature[3] in such a way that spontaneity, and hence mind, cannot be isolated from nature.

What I want to argue here is that the way Hegel conceives habit is not straightforwardly able to be identified with spontaneity (if we take spontaneity as McDowell seems to as necessarily within the space of reasons) but neither is it purely receptive or natural.[4] Hegel's account of second nature challenges the dualism of the "space of reasons" and the "space of causes," a conceptual division that animates much contemporary philosophy. Hegel does, however, reconcile the two in a manner different to McDowell.[5] The account of second nature that McDowell presents is much more akin to *Bildung* than to second nature as Hegel describes it. McDowell's second nature invests second nature with more spontaneity than Hegel wants to give it. Habit is a domain of lived experience that is between discursivity and receptivity that we do not transcend.

The Spirit-Nature Division

There is a broad spectrum of thinkers who largely conceive the world in terms of the space of reasons/space of causes division. There are those like bald naturalists who conceive the world in causal terms and others like Kant who take both these two spheres to represent the essential way in which the world should be considered—a causal nature (which includes animals) and a domain of spontaneous human beings. Spontaneous subjects are free by virtue of their capacity to authorize and instantiate norms. In the case of the reading of Hegel offered by Brandom and Pinkard the freedom of the spontaneous subject involves elaborate processes of giving and asking for reasons. This space of reasons as Pinkard represents it, which Hegelian freedom both presupposes and realizes itself in, incorporates discursivity in general as well as the complex ways in which norms are authorized and legitimated through dynamic (distinctly modern) social and political institutions. Hegelian spirit on this view should be considered to be a reflective and rational sphere by which our values, norms, and morals should be considered self-determined achievements. The origin and determination of norms are on this view overwhelmingly portrayed as Kantian autonomy writ large,[6] that is, equated with the public space of reasons.

The pervasiveness of the mind-world division that we see in diverse figures such as Korsgaard, Habermas, and Brandom conceive norms, ethics, and morality largely as explicit, shareable, and "ownable" rational commitments. What this effectively Kantian view ignores or underplays is that there might in fact be a source of practices, norms, and values that one cannot understand as self-consciously authorized (owned) *or* natural and yet *are part of human identity*. Most contemporary discussion of the determination of norms concentrates on the reflective, intersubjectively negotiated and rational determination of norms.[7] Such theorists downplay or neglect why so many of our values and practices appear to have a different origin to rational discourse, practices of giving and asking for reasons, explicit commitments, and so on. Moreover, it leaves unexplained why many of these norms, values, and practices, which make up much of our everyday life and culture, remain overwhelmingly uncontested in rational debates and are for the most part isolated from our explicit commitments.

The neat dividing of the world between a reflective self-determined domain and a mechanistic purely causal nature has been challenged on a number of fronts. Indeed the desire to muddy this distinction and to show the limitations of it for understanding humanity, animality, and the world is perhaps one of the few unifying themes in what has come to be called continental philosophy. Figures as diverse as Heidegger, Gadamer, Dewey, Bourdieu, Foucault, Merleau-Ponty, Taylor, and Dreyfus all hold there are sense-making practices (historical, habitual, political, and everyday coping strategies) that are normative, understood in the widest sense, that are not conceivable as reflective acts of cognition by autonomous subjects. All these figures try to show the limitations of a straightforwardly rationalistic approach to the determination of norms and values.

Hegel's account of habit is a precursor to this tradition. In his objective spirit habit plays a central role in the cultivation of ethical life, where the norms of our communal life have a rationality that is inscribed in cultural life itself, rather than being authorized and legitimated by a single autonomous agent. These norms permeate into conduct, protocols, and customs and operate as a "second nature." Given the right institutions and individuals attuned to the correct sensibility, which is cultivated through a "good" family life and education, then the norms of daily life can govern our lives rationally without having to be at every opportunity reflected upon in a conscious act of authorization and validation. There is a clear rationale for appealing to habit in this context. Habit functions as a quasinatural mode of behavior in the sense of being something that happens without requiring the kind of attention that Kantian self-determined freedom would seem to require.[8] Habit has its place in this context because its resilience, its hardness as Hegel likes to describe it, is structured by the ethical education inculcated by family and culture but without this pedagogy, and the good customs it creates, as well as the dynamic institutions of civil society, habit is limited. Habit is only something *vital* if the norms, values and institutions within which habits are situated are also vital. If practices are continued simply out of tradition and custom, then culture is without spirit. Even understood in this thoroughly socialized context, habit does not fit neatly into the standard dualism of causal nature and reflective rationality. It is a central aspect of human life that hovers between spirit and nature, a space incidentally we share with animals.

The limits of this rigid nature-spirit division are at issue in Hegel's explicit discussion of habit in the subjective spirit. Hegel's account of habit in the subjective spirit undermines the dualism of nature and reflective subjectivity. Habit challenges the exclusivity of the spirit-nature divide in three ways that will be examined below. First, positing transforms nature into habit; second, the will makes a distinct form of self-identity that is both natural and spiritual; third, second nature establishes habit as an immediate corporeal necessity.

Self-positing

In the discussion of self-feeling, which immediately precedes habit in the subjective spirit, we see the emergence of being-for-self in a sentient form.[9] Feeling provides the basis of selfhood; the soul (the early form of selfhood in the subjective spirit) identifies itself with its feeling.[10] Self-feeling is an organizational totality. It has some kind of awareness that its feelings are its own and that those feelings are organized into a coherent totality. In self-feeling, mental life and feelings are combined. The immediacy of mental life and corporeality is unbroken. Self-feeling provides a co-coordinating and active self that is self-aware but only in an immediate way. It is difficult to conceive what such an immediate self-awareness is, since it is preconceptual and is certainly not autonomous. Nevertheless, the self-awareness at issue here, despite it not being able to be conceived as anything other than a feeling, is capable of recognizing and overcoming conflicting feelings. Its self-awareness lies in its relation to the determinateness of those feelings. Self-feeling realizes that it is not identical to its particular sensations and that it is also not determined by its particular feelings. It is, however, immersed in particularity. The various mental pathologies that Hegel presents in his own fairly colorful way in this section show that the organizational activities of this subject are in need of a consistent, better organized, and coordinated self-relation; this is what habit provides. The path to spirit and a higher expression of consciousness than the soul requires the emergence of thinking. It will be argued here that habit is both a transition to conceptual thought and also a distinct feature of self-identity that does not disappear in the move to more adequate expressions of the Idea.

The transition to habit in the subjective spirit involves overcoming the division of the soul that emerges in derangement/insanity (*Verrücktheit/Wahnsinn*). The insane soul is plagued by a contradiction between "objective consciousness and its fixed idea" (*Vorstellung*). In response to this contradiction the soul strives to "restore its inner harmony [*Harmonie*] of spirit" and so to make the soul at home with itself.[11] The unsettling contradiction that emerges out of self-feeling, in its mentally unstable form, is a tension between a unified self-awareness and the identification of itself at a corporeal level with one of the particular ideas or presentations (*Vorstellungen*) that emerge in this unstable mind. The madman is torn between the unified self-awareness of his self-feeling and some particular idea that he takes to be true of the objective world and from which he appears unable to attain any reflective distance. This tension produces an inner division that self-feeling itself is unable to resolve.

Habit brings self-feeling to fulfillment by separating mental life from its immediate identity with corporeity. In self-feeling the self is present but the character of its self-relation is one of immersion in the particular. Nevertheless, at least minimally, self-feeling must be able to distinguish itself from particularity, since it is in truth "in itself a simple self-relation of ideality, a formal [*formelle*] universal, and this is the truth of these particularities."

In order to realize itself the self must "be posited in it, and made appear in this life of feeling," in such a way that it can be distinguished from the particularity of its feelings and in so doing realize itself as a universal.[12] Particular feelings, sensations, and the satisfaction of desires do not in themselves allow the stable self-relation that is itself the very condition of selfhood and that would allow these feelings to be more than fleeting and transient. What is needed is a simple self-relation that allows the being-for-self to break free from the particularity of its corporeity. Habit is able to respond to this challenge:

> Habit is there not only as a particular momentary satisfaction; rather I am this habit. It is my universal mode of being—what I am is the totality of my habits. I can do nothing else, I am this. In my individual feelings, I make it so one time, and another time not so. *Then I do not say that I am so but I am so in a general feeling that belongs to my self as such, as simple self-relating unity. Such habit is something posited by me.* Through this self-positing, habits are distinguished from natural qualities to which I have attributed nothing.[13]

Self-positing is the critical notion here in understanding how habit breaks with nature, though as we will see, that break with nature does not leave nature behind. Habit operates in the space between reason and nature. Hegel distinguishes habits from nature because despite being a form of self-relation that is not discursive it does not have a *purely natural origin*. As Hegel puts it in his typically Fichtean language in the above passage: "habit *is something posited by me.*" It has already been indicated that the self of self-feeing is implicitly more than any of the particular feelings with which it successively identifies. In habit the first genuinely stable form of self emerges in which it shows itself to be not simply identical to its particular feelings. There is minimal indication of what this abstract being-for-self is. In habit this implicit being-for-self, or consciousness of self, becomes present to itself and it is self-positing that is critical to this.

The positing that is at issue here in habit is more than just a transitional point on the way to full-blown spirit, it also represents a distinct form of self-other relation that is neither natural nor spiritual, and yet it is both. Self-positing is realized in habit through the subject relating its feelings to itself as its own determinations. On the surface this positing appears to take place in a seemingly very passive way. The soul is described as being "indifferent" (*gleichgültig*) to these feelings, but indifference ought not be interpreted as passivity.[14] Rather the soul "posits" its indifference to the feelings, which means they do not determine its identity as it were heteronymously; it stands in a relationship to these feelings "neither distinguishing itself from nor being immersed within them."[15] This indifference marks its capacity to take possession of those feelings and make them its own (I will have something more to say about the importance of this appropriative feat of the will later).

The appropriation of the particular transforms it into a universal. Repetition achieves this remarkable feat by the subject recognizing that the individual units of sensation have a unity. Hegel comments: "The reducing of the external multiplicity of sensing to its unity being one and the same as the positing of this abstract unity."[16] Importantly, this recognition of the unity is something posited by the subject. Not only does repetition allow it to unify particulars, the critical issue is that the recognition of the repetition enables the subject to habituate that feeling, sensation or action and thereby make it part of its identity, something it could then be *indifferent* to. The further step of making this particular a universal is making it ideal.

"In passion the human being is immersed in a particularity, and so is not at home with itself. This Self-feeling comes to itself by making its particulars ideal."[17] Ideality is the distinctive feature of spirit: "The concept of spirit, stated abstractly, is that spirit is free, and freedom means that all determinations of spirit may be posited as something only ideal, as something spirit negates so that spirit is the self-relating pure light."[18] This passage shows that this idealization of the particular is an important transition to thinking, which is the real home of spirit. We need to make sense of just how habit makes this critical step. Something is made ideal through the sublation of otherness; this idealization is the incipient self-determination of spirit, which as we see in this passage, is spirit's freedom.[19]

> The point of transition [to the I and consciousness] is the simple determination that the soul is not merely a being, an affirmative relation, but rather that the soul is relation to self through negation and *rendering the immediate ideal*. It is therefore negative relation to itself (it is infinite); it is the simple self-relating negativity.[20]

Habit effects this critical transition from self-feeling to being an I by making the immediate sensation ideal. In so doing it cancels otherness and so therefore represents spirit's self-determination and freedom.

Habit and Self-identity

In his subjective spirit Hegel gives a compelling account of why taking possession of feelings, desires, and our skilful practice has a central place in our self-identity. The self habituates its urges, instincts, and feelings by *appropriating* them. Habit organizes and structures the contingent array of fleeting particular feelings. Habit has a natural origin, but once particular feelings are infused with the will, Hegel describes this as a "liberation" from nature,[21] since the will makes the feelings its own. However, it would be a mistake to jump to the conclusion that what Hegel means by liberation here is that nature is thereby left behind and that we have now kicked the ladder from nature to spirit away from us once and for all. While nature may be an inadequate expression of the Idea, and in a very real sense habit is no longer purely natural, nevertheless habit does not mark "the death of nature" as some commentators have argued.[22] But before discussing second nature, which undercuts the absoluteness of any liberation from nature, I want first to examine a little further why Hegel considers us to be fundamentally at home or with ourselves in habit.

Habits are ways of repeating behaviors, desires, and so on that are already our own. They are already our own because as we have seen, the will liberates them from nature, and the satisfaction of them is something under one's control (bad habits are clearly to the contrary). "Habit implies that the satisfaction is already mine, something that has become part of my self-feeling."[23] The language of giving and asking for reasons, autonomy, explicit normative commitments, and causal nature are not adequate ways of capturing habit. Habits are practices, feelings, and sensations that *belong* to the being of our habituated self and that are determinative of the way we experience the world, the way we act, judge, and so on. The way in which we are at home with ourselves as habit *is not an autonomous act*. Habits are part of who we are and how we relate to the world in a way that cannot be conceived in terms of the nature/reason division that we have seen above.

Dewey, who has perhaps the most detailed account of habit in modern philosophy, stresses the centrality of habit in human life and identity:

> [Habit] overrides our formal resolutions, our conscious decisions. When we are honest with ourselves we acknowledge that a habit has this power because it is intimately a part of ourselves. It has a *hold upon us because we are the habit*.[24]

Habit is more than something that has a "hold on us"; it is an essential part of us. While habit in the subjective spirit is conceived primarily as practices and skills by which our bodily comportments and desires are controlled, it can also be conceived as operative in our norms and in cultural life more generally, as it is in the *Philosophy of Right*. There the customary norms are presented as determinative of our identity, but they are not commitments that we authorize by *rationally* and explicitly *standing behind* them in the Kantian sense. As habituated we act on them not as explicit affirmations but in some sense as if they were reality itself.[25] The sedimentation of norms in customs, habits, and self-identity makes them far more rigid than much social and political theory has recognized.

The social mediation of norms in our habits and practices (and that our identity could be strongly invested in them) does not fit easily into the space of reasons/causes division. When the normativity of practices is made explicit, that is shown to be normative and not a given feature of reality or abstract rationality, they are still extraordinarily difficult to change.[26] A retrospective rational justification of these practices may be possible, but their origin is of another order than rational deliberation (habit), and this means that these habituated norms/values and our habituated self-identity can come into conflict with rational reflection and argument. As we will see shortly what Hegel has to say about habit as second nature explains why habit has to be seen as a second nature and not purely spirit. This helps explain why habits can be very difficult to change.

The division between the "space of reasons," which is the exclusive preserve of humans (our free, socially mediated, and self-determined nature) and a "space of causes" or the realm of law (nature) is a division that does not capture our habitual life and by implication the experiential life of ourselves and of animal life more broadly. Self-determination is for the most part conceived exclusively on the model of self-legislative autonomy. As we have seen habit can be considered self-determined, something self-owned, *but it is not an act of a reflective and self-determined*, rational, autonomous subject.[27] Hegelian habit shares much with Bourdieu's idea of *habitus*. Habitus is used by Bourdieu to show how social and practical norms are embodied in habits that are at the heart of our relation to the world and ourselves, as well as our sense-making practices. On this view habits are "systems of dispositions" through which

> [t]he world is comprehensible, . . . , because the body, . . . has the capacity to be present to what is outside itself, in the

> world, and to be impressed and durably modified by it, has been protractedly exposed to it. Having acquired from this exposure a system of dispositions attuned to these regularities, it is inclined and able to anticipate them practically in behaviors which engage a corporeal knowledge that provides a practical comprehension of the world quite different from the *intentional acts of conscious decoding that [are] normally designated by the idea of comprehension.*[28]

As with Hegel's account of habit, habitus collapses the distinction between mechanism and idealism. While habitus does not negate the spontaneity of the subject, nevertheless it points to a different kind of active subject, who engages with the world on the basis of an *already* "socialized body,"[29] through which norms of appropriate conduct and principles of action are incorporated and habituated into the subject through the history of its social experiences. What habitus produces are patterns of behavior and rule following that are neither autonomous self-legislative acts of a free subject nor can they be considered causal. Habitus is an ordering of body and mind that takes place through a kind of osmosis of the social order. This exposure produces *dispositions* that incline us to respond in appropriate and essentially predetermined ways to the social world that has *already* ordered our dispositions in line with it. These dispositions and responses allow us to inhabit the world with an immediate familiarity. Bourdieu describes the reason for this familiarity in a decidedly Hegelian turn of phrase: "[H]e feels at home in this world because the world is also at home in him, in the form of habitus."[30] In this case our self-relation is mediated through practices and norms, which from the perspective of the social space of reasons cannot be seen as appropriated through autonomous acts of a rational subject.

The discussion of habit in the subjective spirit does not conceive habit in the complex socially, pedagogically, and culturally embodied form that Hegel does in objective spirit or in the comprehensive way that for Bourdieu describes it. Nevertheless, unlike the very brief discussion of it in *Sittlichkeit* the discussion of second nature in the *Subjective Spirit* provides a focused and precise challenge to the spirit-nature division.

Second Nature

As we have seen, habit "liberates" the soul from nature by allowing the subject to control and order its sensations and feelings, which produces a subject no longer simply immersed in particularity. Making sense of how habit determines itself in a distinctive way requires unpacking the central claim of habit: "[H]abit is a [second cultivated] nature, it is a being—I am thus—this is my habit. This latter quality preserves this aspect of natural immediacy in itself."[31] The critical feature of habit is that it is a "necessity" created by the will.[32] The necessity here is not a necessity in the manner of natural law or Kantian self-legislative rationality. Despite being an act of the will, habit is described as second nature because the will operates here not as a reflective act of an autonomous self-legislating subject, but is used to create a skill, control a drive, inure the self to heat or cold, and so on. While Hegel uses the language of the will and spirit to describe habit, these terms have to be understood in the most exiguous of senses. Spirit might have begun to rear its head, and the will is certainly how habit controls its drives and breaks free from its immersion in immediate feelings, but we are not in a sphere of self-legislated freedom. The will that invests itself in sensations transforms them into universals at a wholly corporeal level; that is, they are not reflective acts. The appeal Hegel is making to the will and its very conscious alignment with the term "second nature" gives a strong hint that habit is not a break with nature.

There is something of a Rousseauian touch to the way Hegel conceives habit here. While the habituated soul must be considered natural, it does not have an identity and self-awareness that is identical to its passions, drives, and desires, but rather it must forge for itself a character, which it does in its habits. *Its activity* makes it what it is by reducing the particular feelings, drives, and so on to determinations of its being in such a way that they are part of it as something it possesses. The habituated soul does not distinguish itself from sensations and feelings, as a rational self over and against natural sensation; nevertheless, selfhood is not subsumed by sensation. Habit thereby allows the self to have a world, since the practices and skills that are acquired in habit allow attention to be relinquished to other activities that can in turn become new habits, which no longer need concerted concentration. Habit is in this sense a precursor to *Bildung* and ethical life, but in the subjective spirit, it is not values, norms, and ethics that are being taken up into the disposition of the subject as it were through the ether of culture and pedagogy as it is in ethical life; here it is much more *direct* and practical relation to sensation.

This "second nature" habit is "an immediacy created by the soul."[33] The soul makes feelings attributes of itself through repetition and idealization as we have seen. The will molds feelings and sensation and transforms them into corporeal regularity. By so doing they become not external determinations of the subject in the way that instincts are, but as "second nature" they are constituent features of the being of the subject *as its own*. It is in them, once they have been appropriated. Habits are intimately part of who we are; indeed as with Bourdieu's habitus, they might be said to be more part of us than our conscious choices since they are *hardened pathways* in which *and* through which we live our lives. When these hardened habituated pathways are challenged, the challenge is not simply at the level of rational argument but is *experienced* as a threat to self, as a conflict between a habituated self, which in some sense we take to be reality and rational reflection. In his discussion of habit in the subjective spirit Hegel gives only the barest of accounts of how the sedimentation of habits in our identity takes place. Bourdieu's habitus gives a far more sustained and broad account of this. Nevertheless, both Hegel and Bourdieu see habit as a realm of human life that determines us but that cannot be seen as only either natural or rational.[34]

Hegel's aside on monkish attempts to free oneself from drives is instructive here. He remarks, "Monkish renunciation and violence [*Gewaltsamkeit*] are not a liberation from them and neither are they rational."[35] The monkish attitude to desires and drives is that one ought to train oneself to suppress the drives. The practice of self-control is designed to deny their hold on the subject. The drives are in us, and they are natural, but they must be struggled against and repudiated. In Hegel's case natural feelings and sensations are controlled not through denial and abstention but through the satisfaction itself. Either by controlling how, when, and if we satisfy that desire or by developing other habits that diffuse a destructive desire, for example exercising when one craves a cigarette and so on. The general point is one ought not strive to deny the sensations, drives, and so on. We should indeed recognize they are us even though we are not controlled by them. The vitalism of life has its origin in these natural forces and the conflict they cause in us.[36] While habit itself can annul the particular ways in which these life forces are instantianated such that they become routinized and stagnant,[37] in the case of the abstemious monks the denial of the life force of drives and sensations is a fundamental denial of who we are.

The most detailed example Hegel uses in various versions of the *Subjective Spirit* to illustrate just how enmeshed nature and the will are in second nature is the upright posture of the human being. In this example he shows how the will appropriates a feeling or disposition and establishes a new hardened pathway through which the self lives in such a way that it is at home with itself:

> The form of habit includes all kinds and stages of spiritual activity. The individual's standing upright is its most external, its spatial determination, and is made habitual by its will, . . . Man stands only because and insofar as he has the will to, and only as long as this will is unconscious.[38]

He takes this even further a little later in the text describing man's upright posture as:

> his absolute gesture, he alone is capable of it . . . Man is not naturally, not originally erect; he raises himself through the energy of his will, and although once it has become habitual the posture no longer requires any strenuous volitional activity, it has always to be pervaded by our will or we collapse instantly.[39]

We have a natural disposition to uprightness, but it is merely a physical possibility. It only becomes our defining spatiotemporal feature by virtue of our will. In being upright the will does not have to be consciously employed on every occasion. Through habituation we do not have to comport ourselves through a reflective act; nevertheless, the will is still present in our standing. This very act itself "means that this unity becomes itself inwardly posited, becomes posited in the self, so that the self takes possession of its feeling. Only insofar as it has taken possession of its feeling is it at home with itself."[40]

This taking possession cannot be achieved just through my individual act of will, by for example deciding that I am not going to get annoyed by the cold, a light that comes into my room at night when I am trying to sleep, the loud chirping of cicadas in summer, the smell of old dog in a damp house, or whatever it may be. The will alone cannot habituate you to those sensations and dispositions. The sensation must becomes an *immediate part* of oneself in a way such that: "the self-feeling as such, consciousness, reflection, and any other purpose *are no longer involved* [*verwickelt*] *with it.*"[41]

Habit is in this sense Hegel says "a mode of natural existence," and accordingly "a person of habit is not free."[42] In habit there is a change to the way in which I inhabit my world. The responses to drives, urges, annoyances, and so on are in habit transformed into a way of experiencing the world that is an immediate, as it were, natural existence even though it is only posited as such by the will. While Hegel stresses the importance of this, he does not have a lot to say as to how this takes place. He characterizes it as a *"hardening of the disposition [Anlage]."*⁴³ This way of describing second nature and how it is immediately taken possession in the body is markedly distinct from Kantian self-legislation. Through practice or acclimatizing, through exposure to the feeling of cold for example, the feelings and so on are no longer as it were external determinations of the subject but are brought under our control, through the recognition of the repetition of the feeling, which allows them to be seen as universal modes of action with which we can be at home.⁴⁴

Habit does not mark the ascent into an exclusively spiritual domain but is the way in which human beings can be at home with nature, such that its reflective abilities do not have to be employed at every turn, but more importantly than that, this subject can be at home with nature because habit makes nature immediately part of it; yes it is infused with spontaneity in some minimal sense through the will and positing by which the natural is transformed into a second nature, but in so doing it is does not leave the natural behind.⁴⁵

Habit conceived as second nature is designed to capture a fundamental aspect of our identity. The will as we have seen transforms the natural into this second nature in which a conscious subject can be at home with nature and itself. Habit is not, however, a discursive sphere, even if it makes the discursive possible. It does not establish habits through a process of normative authorization in the manner of the space of reasons. In Hegel's example we can't think of standing upright as something we are persuaded to do through the giving and asking for reasons. Similarly if an accepted practice, such as for example meat eating is recognized as just a habit, not a given fact of reality, but something that needs to be justified, that is it requires good reasons for its continuance, the demand to give reasons can be unsettling, not necessarily because it is in itself unjustified, but because it is an *unrecognized* norm or value that we are invested in and that is intimately bound through habit to our sense of self. Practices like these are nothing necessary; they are not given features of reality but are instead normative, and thereby requiring justification. Nevertheless, when these habituated norms are challenged, they pose a threat to ourselves, and this threat is felt as a challenge to the world and to our identity.

But what is being threatened in such cases? Not a rationally authorized norm and not our causal nature. These kinds of practices are sedimented in very complex ways in our culture and practices such that we take them to be of an almost natural order. They are illustrative of what Hegel is trying to capture with habit, namely, that much of our identity is sedimented in habit, not in rationally deliberated and self-determined actions and values. These kinds of practices operate with a necessity that is self-imposed in a thoroughly corporeal way and in this sense is hardened into our second nature.

Notes

Paul Redding and Heikki Ikäheimo read an earlier draft of this chapter. Their detailed comments were particularly helpful.

1. PSS, §410.
2. Here "the soul becomes master of its natural individuality, of its bodily nature, reducing this to subservient [gehorchenden] means and projects from itself as an objective world that content of its substantial totality which does not belong to its bodily nature. Reaching this goal, the soul appears in the abstract freedom of the I and thus becomes consciousness." PM, 402 Z.
3. John McDowell, *Mind and World* (Cambridge, Mass.: Harvard University Press, 1994), 83.
4. See McDowell, *Mind and World*, 84.
5. On this issue of the similarity between second nature and *Bildung*, see the papers by Axel Honneth and Rübiger Bubner in *Reading McDowell: On Mind and World*, ed. Nicholas Smith (London: Routledge, 2002).
6. Terry Pinkard does think that Hegel takes the Kantian view of autonomy to be problematic; indeed Hegel's response to what he calls the Kantian paradox (an unresolved tension in Kant's view of autonomy) largely defines Hegel's philosophical project. Nevertheless, the way Pinkard equates spirit and freedom with the space of reasons conceives it too strongly in terms of Kantian self-legislative freedom. See his *German Philosophy: 1760–1860* (Cambridge: Cambridge University Press, 2002).
7. See Christine Korsgaard's discussion in *The Sources of Normativity* (Cambridge: Cambridge University Press, 1996).
8. See G. W. F. Hegel, *Elements of the Philosophy of Right*, trans. H. B. Nisbett (Cambridge: Cambridge University Press, 1991), § 151 and Z.
9. LPS, 140; VPG, 109.
10. Soul is the animating feature of human corporeality; it is a pathway to spirit; it inhabits the natural but it represents a transitional organising force between nature and spirit; it "forms the bond between [spirit and corporeity]." See *The Encyclopaedia Logic: Part One of the Encyclopaedia of the Philosophical Sciences* trans. T. F. Garaets, W. A. Suchting, and H. S. Harris (Indianapolis: Hackett, 1991). In the preface to the second edition of this same work Hegel comments that it is the lowest stage of consciousness that we share with animals (12).
11. PM, § 410 Z.

12. PM, § 409 Z, trans. revised.
13. LPS, 153/VPG, 124; my emphasis.
14. PM, § 410.
15. PSS, § 410.
16. PSS, § 410.
17. LPS, 152; VPG, 123.
18. LPS, 73; VPG, 21; See also PM, § 381 Z.
19. See Willem de Vries' discussion of this in *Hegel's Theory of Mental Activity* (Ithaca, Cornell University Press, 1988), 49.
20. LPS, 163; VPG, 136–37; my emphasis.
21. LPS, 154; VPG, 125; PM, § 410.
22. John McCumber, "Hegel on Habit," *The Owl of Minerva* 21, no. 2 (1990): 161.
23. LPS, 155; VPG, 127.
24. John Dewey, *Human Nature and Conduct* (New York: Henry Holt, 1922), 24; my emphasis.
25. For an interesting discussion of this issue, "the ritual basis of self-identity," see John Russon, *Reading Hegel's Phenomenology* (Bloomington: Indiana University Press, 2004), especially 173–77.
26. Western attitudes toward the eating of meat represent an exemplary instance of this. Within the public space of reasons we have extraordinarily diverse reasons for not eating meat, but even in the most intellectual of circles, these reasons do little to change conventions, attitudes, and habits.
27. But precisely because these norms are established through the embodiment of established social structures that are not explicitly rationally and reflectively determined, they also, despite our being at home in them, have great potential for injustice, because they can transcribe onto habit inequalities and "irrational" practices that because they are habituated are unreflectively and stubbornly part of our identity. The reverse can also be true, which is what Hegel tries to capture with the notion of ethical life; there can be rational structures that are habituated but that we have not adopted and affirmed consciously and reflectively.
28. Pierre Bourdieu, *Pascalian Meditations* (Cambridge: Polity Press, 2000), 135; my emphasis.
29. Pierre Bourdieu, *The Logic of Practice*, trans. R. Nice (Cambridge: Cambridge University Press, 1990), 53.
30. Bourdieu, *Pascalian Meditations*, 143.
31. LPS, 154; VPG, 125.
32. PM, § 410. See also LPS, 154; VPG, 125: "in reference to the will habit is a necessity."
33. PM, § 410.
34. There are more parallels here with the suffering that can be effected at the level of habitus, where injustice is socially mediated and inscribed in habit that injustice can express itself as pathologies.
35. PM, § 410.

36. See LPS, 157; VPG, 130.

37. "The natural death of the national spirit may take the form of political stagnation, or what we call habit. The clock is wound up and runs on automatically. Habit is an activity with nothing to oppose it; it retains only the formal property of temporal continuity, and the depth and richness of its ends need no longer be expressed. It is, so speak, a superficial and sensuous kind of existence whose profounder significance has been forgotten . . . [T]heir existence is devoid of life and interest, because the needs which have created them have been satisfied, and nothing remains but political stagnation and boredom." Hegel, *Introduction to the Lectures on the Philosophy of World History*, trans. T. M. Knox and A. V. Miller (Oxford: Oxford University Press, 1985), 59.

38. PSS, § 410.

39. PSS, § 411 Z. In LPS, 160; VPG, 133, he uses the same example.

40. LPS, 154; VPG, 126.

41. PM, § 410; my trans., my emphasis.

42. PSS, § 410.

43. LPS, 154; VPG, 126.

44. See PM, § 410 Z. Interestingly Hegel clearly takes this recognition of repetition to form the basis for more advanced rule following.

45. While I have some difficulties with the Christoph Halbig's conception of Hegel as a metaphysical monist, his account of how nature is preserved in Hegel's system is compelling. See his "Varieties of Nature in Hegel and McDowell," *European Journal of Philosophy* 14, no. 2 (2006): 222–41.

The "Struggle for Recognition" and the Thematization of Intersubjectivity

MARINA F. BYKOVA

Although Hegel's concept of recognition and its significance for the account of intersubjectivity became a central topic for many recent publications of Hegel scholars, there is a noticeable deficiency in literature discussing this problematic on the material of Hegel's *Philosophy of Spirit*. In contrast to the vast amount of publications on Hegel's *Phenomenology of Spirit* of 1807, a good portion of which deals exclusively with questions of intersubjectivity and recognition, there are only a few—mostly dating back to 80th–90th—investigations into the conceptual role of intersubjectivity in the mature *Philosophy of Subjective Spirit*. Furthermore, the authors of those publications are in a serious disagreement about the conceptual status of Hegel's account of intersubjectivity as well as the role of the latter in the constitution of an individual human subjectivity in the theory of subjective spirit. For commentators the most troublesome and puzzling appears the dense section of the *Encyclopedia* "Phenomenology," especially its subsection on self-consciousness (§§ 424–37) where Hegel formulates his positive account of mutual recognition. The existing confusion among commentators concerns the significance of the "Phenomenology" section in the *Philosophy of Subjective Spirit* and the real function of the concept of recognition in the thematization of intersubjectivity. Perhaps the most negative interpretation of the role of recognition and intersubjectivity in Hegel's late system is offered by Axel Honneth. He identifies a real potentiality of Hegel's concept of recognition for developing what he calls "a formal conception of ethical life," but maintains that all the promising insights about intersubjectivity and recognition that Hegel has date back to his early Jena period, still prior to the 1807 *Phenomenology of Spirit*. They are, however, completely lost in his system of a "monologically self-developing spirit"[1] where intersubjectivity becomes reduced to a temporal subordinate episode of the spirit formation. This position is echoed in Jürgen Habermas' interpretation of the role of intersubjectivity in Hegel's system. According to Habermas, Hegel's intersubjective intuitions visible in his early works are fatally harmed by the peculiar subjectivism of his later philosophy centered around the concept of the "ego" or "absolute self-consciousness," which is unfolded in the *Logic*. As a result, "[i]ntersubjectivity is repressed by subjectivity, leaving no presence in the presentation of the absolute idea."[2]

In general agreement with Honneth and Habermas are also some prominent Hegel scholars. For example, Vittorio Hösle maintains that "the thematization of intersubjectivity does not assume any vital role in Hegel's system." He further notices that due to "the fundamental limits of his [Hegel's] philosophy, [i.e.] his inability to categorically distinguish between subject-subject and subject-object relations,"[3] Hegel cannot really grasp the intersubjective or subject-subject relation effectively. The reading that reduces Hegel's account of recognition to a single-subject theory is also offered by Adriaan Peperzak who claims that "the entire sense of the 'struggle for recognition' in the *Encyclopedia* phenomenology is not at all consisting in the thematization of intersubjectivity [. . .], but only in a process through which the immediate or abstract self-consciousness must become another for itself in order to be able to identify with itself."[4] It should be said, in all fairness, that there are commentators who hold contrary views on significance of intersubjectivity in late Hegel, emphasizing intersubjective character of self-consciousness and considering mutual recognition as a foundation for the constitution of the subject in Hegel.[5] However, those commentators are dramatically outnumbered and not always consistent in their views. For example, Hermann Drüe, who points to the intersubjective character of recognition in Hegel, yet believes that Hegel's account of self-consciousness is not thought of as the actual development of consciousness, but is rather a pure logical and historic-fictional conceptual construction.[6]

In the light of such a critical disagreement and real confusion in understanding the role of recognition and intersubjectivity in Hegel's late system it is crucial to take a closer look at *Encyclopedia Philosophy of Subjective Spirit*, especially at its section on the phenomenology of spirit, where, in my opinion, Hegel lays out his concept of intersubjective recognition and develops it as a condition of self. This reading of the section is largely supported by the 1827–28 *Lectures on the Philosophy of Spirit*[7] and Hegel's remarks concerning recognition and "Philosophy of Spirit" in general that are provided there. Thus the further delving into *Encyclopedia* "Phenomenology" should be supplemented by discussion of Hegel's *Lectures* that can shed light on the issue under consideration.

The goal of this chapter is to uncover a real function of the ("Phenomenology") section on self-consciousness within Hegel's *Philosophy of Spirit* and discuss it as a positive account of intersubjectivity that is formulated in terms of the "struggle for recognition." Thus the main focus will be on the subsection on self-consciousness (§§ 424–37) where the theme of mediation of consciousness in recognition of and by other consciousness becomes an important element in the unfolding of the full structure of consciousness.

I

The organization and systematization of the *Philosophy of Subjective Spirit* remain controversial issues for Hegel scholars. If one adheres to the traditional linear approach where the *Philosophy of Spirit* is interpreted as a kind of a *genetic* development of spirit then the role and function of many of its subsections and systematical parts become questionable. This is especially true about the "Phenomenology" section, which does not fit well a pure genetic model of spirit development.[8] Another theoretical difficulty concerning *Encyclopedia* "Phenomenology," which should not be ignored, is that it appears to be a successor of the *Phenomenology* of 1807, and not only in title, but what is more important, in its general structure and execution. The overall systematization and the most important stages of the "pathway of consciousness" of the *Phenomenology* of 1807, though slightly or sometimes substantially modified, are reproduced in the *Encyclopedia* "Phenomenology." Both of the issues mentioned above, the systematization of *Philosophy of Subjective Spirit* and relation between the two versions of the *Phenomenology*, have been the subject of several studies[9] and cannot be further analyzed here. Yet, for our topic, it is important to recognize that by all respect to conceptual similarities of the two texts of the *Phenomenology*, there are essential differences in their aims and functions. The *Phenomenology* of 1807 was intended to be an introduction to Hegel's "System of Science" and as such was supposed to provide a solid epistemological foundation for the future system. It thus appears as a kind of "genealogy" of knowledge from pure immediacy and sense certainty to conceptual (absolute) knowing. The aim of the *Encyclopedia* "Phenomenology" is more modest and systematically less profound; it is largely determined by the purpose of the philosophy of spirit within mature Hegel's system. The latter is the deduction of the concept of spirit, which is laid down as the process of achieving the unity of self-consciousness.[10]

The aim of the "Phenomenology" within the *Encyclopedia* system is to examine perhaps the most crucial stage of this development, namely, the transformation of consciousness from the natural immediacy (the abstract I = I) into self-consciousness and then by the means of reciprocal recognition into universal self-consciousness as an intersubjectively mediated result. As Robert Williams points out, "The Phenomenology is supposed to show the development from the I in its immediacy, wherein it takes itself to be a bare, abstract, self-seeking particular, through the struggle for recognition and master/slave, to the I through which reciprocal recognition has become a universal consciousness, a 'We'."[11] Self-unfolding of spirit in phenomenology does not appear as a linear progression. It is an intricate multistep process that is animated and driven by the dialectic of difference, opposition, and overcoming of this opposition at the next, more complex level of the spirit's development. This development coincides with the development of the I, the individual self, which is a real agent acting in the world. A real function of the *Encyclopedia* "Phenomenology" should be thus understood in terms of the requirements for the self-constitution and self-realization of the I and conditions for meeting those requirements. A systematic examination of those requirements is approximately represented in the main division of the "Phenomenology" section into "Consciousness" (§§ 418–23), "Self-consciousness" (§§ 424–37), and "Reason" (§§ 438–39). The main question of the subsection on consciousness is the question of how the I is able to identify itself as a conscious individual, capable of reflection and propositional attitude. This is a question about the condition of our awareness of the world. In the subsection on self-consciousness the main focus is shifted to the inquiry into self and the self-awareness that should be established and discovered in the context of our essential interdependence and intersubjective interrelation. The realization of universality of the I and its necessary mediation with the world (including other individuals) becomes then the main topic of the subsection on reason. All of these inquiries are essential to Hegel's central concern, the nature and development of (human) freedom that is understood as a process of establishing real autonomy, self-positing, and self-organizing activity of individual toward the totality of being for itself and at home in its own world. In the "Phenomenology" this liberation is not yet complete, but it undergoes a significant stage, where the I breaks from its natural immediacy and "atomic" individuality, and by the means of the struggle of recognition achieves the level of universality and community (the development of universal self-consciousness and social reason).

The task of the "Phenomenology" within the *Philosophy of Subjective Spirit* is thus to show intersubjecive character of this liberation and the necessity of intersubjective relation for self-realization of the I, for the very possibility of selfhood. The details of intersubjective liberation Hegel provides in the subsection on self-consciousness.

II

Hegel's starting point is that the I as self-consciousness is a creature of desire. Desire reveals a fundamental lack and emptiness in the self that must be filled through the overcoming of separateness and independence of external objects. This is how Hegel clarifies this point in the *Lectures*: "The lack in me appears as an external object. The latter is only something that is not an end in itself and has no absolute independence. The object has thus proven itself to be without independence in self-consciousness. This is the standpoint of desire."[12] Hence desire makes me realize that I am missing something to be complete and makes me aware of my difference from the object, the not-I. Behind all types of desire a deep dialectic at work: embodied human life depends for survival on the external world and, as a result, part of the self is always outside itself and the otherness of objecthood is already launched in self. Thus the two realms (of the self-consciousness and of the external objects) which appear in desire as opposing to each other are not distinct and must be conceived as one integrated world. The unity resulting from the subject's "desiring" relation to the object sustains life itself. This is the idea that one's self-certainty can be achieved only if one's real unity with the external world is established. By reconciling what is subjective and what is objective, Hegel contends that this unity is nothing else but revealing of *freedom* itself, "the free self . . . that remains in its identity with itself."[13] Yet at first this freedom is "completely abstract" and "formal freedom, because [actual] freedom . . . comes to be through and out of consciousness, [. . . .] through another, which is its condition."[14] The two important moments should be noticed here. First, the reconciliation that Hegel has in mind here is not a momentary act; it is a long and complex process. Freedom is a practical achievement; it occurs within the time of, and on the basis of, the living world. Second, the actual freedom is not achievable at a pure individual level. For consciousness to be able to distinguish itself from the external world and at the same time be aware of both world and itself, it has to be mediated in and by other consciousness. This mediation becomes a means of overcoming of purely "atomic" individuality and attaining of actual freedom. Here Hegel is clearly departing from a view of the I as a closed and monological (atomic) entity. The I's "openness" to the world is the condition of the full self-realization of (self) consciousness and formation of the individual self-identity.

For Hegel, the self is created in its continuous struggle to overcome the foreignness of the other. The immediate self suffers from the delusion of self-sufficiency under which the difference from others is absolute and must be negated through the arrogation of absolute sovereignty. The other is treated as inferior and inessential, of lesser value and importance than self.[15] This "negative relation" of self-consciousness to its object is an integral part of the self's desire for self-certainty, for its self-identity. A difficulty arises from the fact that, in pursuing desire, the self tends to destroy (negate) its object (e.g., by consuming it), even though so doing thwarts the sense of self-certainty. Indeed, the first reaction of the desiring self when faced with the other is to seek immediate satisfaction and heal the split between subject and object by negating the object. The desire for food, for instance, negates the otherness of the food itself by eating it. But even after hunger is satisfied, the self retains its partiality: the only result of this very act is self's *illusory* self-identity, which does not differentiate humans from animals. Furthermore, in the act of desire self-consciousness is caught in particular bind. The object, which self-consciousness took to be a pure nothing, gains the character of independence precisely in the movement of self-consciousness to negate and destroy it. Nevertheless, it *must* continue to supersede and thus negate the object, for self-consciousness must realize itself as the unity underlying the difference between itself and the apparent otherness. Self-consciousness remains stuck in a vicious circle of desire, destruction, and the resurgence of desire. True satisfaction eludes it, and its unity with itself *in the other* cannot be made explicit. Thus Hegel can say that "it is in fact something other than self-consciousness that is the essence of desire," because the living object, now independent, is a stubborn unity only *for* self-consciousness and not *for itself*. Human desire is thus addressed not by an object, but by the other self-consciousness. Hence the next step for the self is to accept its dependence on the other but to keep the relation between self and other external. The force of this necessary requirement ushers in a new stage in Hegel's phenomenological reflection, and it marks the beginning of true self-consciousness in the process of leaving behind the sensuous world. The desire that self-consciousness has and needs to satisfy in order to get a sense of its existence as an independent subject is a desire to be desired by others, that is, a desire for *recognition*:

> There is a self-consciousness for a self-consciousness, at first *immediately*, as one thing for *another*. In the other as I, I immediately behold my own self, but I also behold in it an immediately real object, another I absolutely independent in face of myself. The sublation of the *individuality* of self-consciousness was the first sublation; self-consciousness is thereby determined as *particular*.—This contradiction supplies the urge to show itself as a free self, and to be there as a free self for the other,—the process of *recognition*.[16]

We can already see that for Hegel all self-conscious desire is ultimately desire of self. Since the unity of self-consciousness is the true unity underlying the apparent difference between self and sensuous world, the negation of the apparent difference through a negation of the immediate object constitutes the attempted realization of self-consciousness' unity. As such, all "desire for the immediate object" is truly a *self-conscious* desire for the unity of self-consciousness.

At the beginning stage of the recognition, however, the two consciousnesses know they need the other's desire and recognition, yet believe that they can forgo or force it through the exclusion, marginalization, or suppression of the other. Here desire is totally narcissistic; the other is only the foil in a quest for unreciprocated prestige, typically evident in the relationship between master and slave. In this "one-side" relation, the other is accepted in its difference, but not in its identity with the self, that is, not as a free independent subject. Thus, there must be established a special relation between myself and another self that exists on one's own terms, as an independent I seeking its own self-identity and self-certainty. This requirement of self-certainty cannot be satisfied by simple intellectual identification of other persons who acknowledge my intellectual capability; they have to recognize me as a free individual who is conscious of his own freedom for self-determination (self-actualization). But this recognition must be reciprocal. My freedom remains a simple abstraction unless it is not challenged and eventually "approved" by other individuals who at the same time also seek my recognition of their freedom. "The freedom of every individual exists only insofar as he is recognized as free by the others, and the others have in him the consciousness of their own legitimacy . . ."[17] Thus, mutual recognition is the third step, which completes and overcomes the first two. Now the other is accepted both in her identity and in her difference from self and, as a result, self discovers itself as integrally related to the other. The other's recognition and desire allows self to see itself reflected in another self and create a nexus of links and dependencies that affect all aspects of both selves. Recognition works if it is mutual. I must be recognized by someone I recognize as human: I must reciprocally know myself in another. Yet, mutuality of recognition is not a mere fusion; mutual recognition necessarily acknowledges the difference of the two independent selves and dissymmetry in their relation to each other. When full mutual recognition operates, the two selves stand in a relationship in which the self-understanding of each passes through the other, and the relationship of each to the other depends on the self's self-relation. It is possible only if each of these two selves maintains its independence and potential self-identity (free agency) as a person.

Hegel's account of mutual recognition is thoroughly normative. This normativity is not posited as an ideal, which ought to be (yet may be not inevitably) achieved, but rather as a necessary condition for individual freedom. Hegel argues that individual freedom is possible and justified only on the basis of reciprocal acceptance of mutual obligations to acknowledge and respect others' free individual agency and rights to freedom.

Recognition is both an essential characteristic of phenomenology of identity and an integral element of a theory of knowledge. I can only become a certain type of person, if I recognize in the other the characteristics of that type which are then reflected back onto me. I cannot change myself therefore without changing the other and changes in the other who stands in recognition of me change the self too. As epistemological phenomenon, recognition, by assuming the object to be another subject, turns knowledge into a process of cultural mutuality and exchange, and self-knowledge into self-exploration and self-control through the understanding (and appreciation) of the other. It is worth noticing though that in contrast to the *Phenomenology* of 1807, in *Philosophy of Spirit* recognition is to a lesser extent a pure theoretic-epistemological concept. Here Hegel moves from theoretic-epistemological to the life-world sense of recognition, which is discussed in terms of the intersubjective interactions between individuals.

The mutual recognition culminates for Hegel in "the affirmative awareness of oneself in the other self."[18] This is the stage, when self achieves its real (and not anymore illusory) and complete self-identity. As full self-consciousness, self is now the "unity of oneself in one's other being." Identity embraces both being for oneself and being for another and is achieved by accepting self as the "identity of identity and non-identity."[19] The self-conscious individual, created through the other's desire, retains the separation from the other as one part of his identity and recognizes himself both in the other and in his difference from her. In this sense, self-consciousness both negates the split between self and other and preserves it. At the same time, the self can never be *absolutely* self-identical: it is a dialectical combination of self and otherness, of sameness and difference. Identity is therefore dynamic, always on the move. It is ongoing dialogue and interaction with others, which keeps changing the image others have of myself and redrawing my own self-image. The *relation* between self and other, one's reciprocally concerned engagement with another conscious individual, is the essence of the phenomena Hegel calls the *universal self-consciousness*. It should not be understood as an absolute ideal, neither as a "third self-consciousness" emerging from the relation between self and other. Rather these are *intersubjective* ties that are manifest through recognition. These ties are a realization of communal (social) drive[20] that the self-consciousness has and that is essential in shaping personality. For Hegel, the relationship between self and the other is crucial for the construction of both self and community. The self is not a simple, stable entity fully identical with itself that, once formed, then goes into the world and build relation with others from a position of self-sufficiency. While Descartes and Kant had presented consciousness as a solitary entity confronting the outside world, Hegel insists that self is constituted reflexively and is radically dependent on the action of others. The struggle for recognition is the key social relationship, and as such is the main form of practical intersubjectivity. In this sense, recognition is a mode of socialization. But the other's recognition of my identity makes me also aware of my specificity and difference from all others and thus helps my individuation. Hence Hegel believes that individual self is created in and through struggles amongst people for the reciprocal recognition of their identity.

Hegel's insight here is that I become an actual individual only through a *universal* self-consciousness. My (unconditional) freedom is possible only as the *universal* freedom, a common freedom that we all share. There is no free self without other individuals: others and their freedom become a constitutive moment of myself and my own freedom. "Freedom [as unconditioned] . . . comes to be through another, which is its condition."[21] The other becomes thus an indispensable condition for the self-consciousness and the actualization of my own freedom. Despite the resemblance between Hegel's and Kant and Fichte's treatments of the self as well as the similarities in used terminology, Hegel's account of intersubjectivity differs from all previous interpretations. He derives the principle of intersubjectivity as a fundamental practical principle that is grounded in the concept of self-consciousness and thus is essential to the structure and development of the self. Contrary to Kant and Fichte, for Hegel, recognition is not an outward requirement,[22] but rather the very condition of self-consciousness that can be satisfied by engagement in (intersubjective) interactions with other free individuals.

In this sense, significance of the section "Self-consciousness" within the *Philosophy of Subjective Spirit* is that it shows *the necessity* of overcoming a pure individual level of subjectivity (the stage of isolated solitary individuality) and of manifesting universality of the self.[23] Hegel hints on this issue in the *Encyclopedia*,[24] but it is more clearly articulated in the *Lectures*. Consider the following remark:

> ... [T]the self-consciousness must be for another self-consciousness, and the individual must come into relation to another. This has been called a social drive, but in fact it is reason, the unity of self-consciousness.
>
> The fundamental point is that this unity must be realized, and it can be realized only in the self-consciousness of other individuals. The material, in which the I, freedom, can be realized, can only be another self-consciousness. The latter is the reality, the objectivity, and the externality of the first.[25]

The intersubjective interaction is thus not an arbitrary act. It is rather necessitated by the very concept of self-consciousness. The latter is possible *only* in relation to other self-consciousness and *only* as intersubjective.[2] No (self)-actualization and no (self)-realization of the I are achievable without the mediation by another. Only through the mediation and the following suspension of this mediation the universality is possible.

Even though at the stage of self-consciousness Hegel mainly deals with the individual particularity, the structures of the *"universal self-consciousness"* appear as the essential elements of individual consciousness in its striving for self-certainty.[27] Hegel makes it clear that developing of real individual (actual self) is a concrete universal process in which each of us necessarily participates and through which we become aware of ourselves and the external world. This process can occur only if an individual interacts with other individuals collectively pursuing their own goals. Hence self can acquire its real individuality (its sense of self-certainty and true freedom) only in and through its own activity, activity that is not only directed towards the world, but is also mediated through reciprocal relations and interactions with other people.

In the *Lectures* Hegel clarifies his positive concept of recognition further. Here it becomes clear that his account of self-consciousness is not a logical construction or a historical fiction (Drüe) or a kind of "monological" theory that has a limited (internal) use (Peperzak). The process of recognition is for Hegel not just a means for achieving the level of universal self-consciousness or reason (Hösle).[28] Instead, this is a real process of intersubjective interaction only by and through which one's self-awareness is possible. The agents of this interaction are not abstract concepts, but real individuals who live and act in the actual world.

> There are two real, independent beings confronting each other. [...] They are both personally, absolutely independent, and nevertheless they are for each other. This I know that the other is an I, but in it appearance it confronts me like a thing, like something completely external to me. This is the highest contradiction—the most perfect indifference towards each other, and [yet] perfect unity and identity. The suspension of the contradiction—for it cannot remain a contradiction—is the process of recognition.[29]

Recognition comes about through a dramatic struggle that arises from the encounter of two self-consciousnesses. Hegel describes this life and death struggle in terms of the dynamic master-slave relationship. The ultimate lesson of the master-slave dialectic is that the realization of our capacities as individuals in the world requires the mutual recognition of ourselves as members of a community.

Here Hegel indicates an essential feature of human self, that its reality lies not in solitary existence but in interaction with other selves. This is an interaction that is mediated not only by "externality" (the objective world), but also by others and is "an infinite relation of myself to myself ... *in the being of other persons.*"[30] But this being is not just a disinterested coexistence. For Hegel, a man acquires the characteristics of self only in the *fact of him being recognized* by other free practical agents. A question may be raised of how then we can act freely and autonomously if we are so dependent on the recognition by the others and thus are ultimately interdependent beings. The point that Hegel makes clear in the *Encyclopedia* and then, based on the broad social material, further explicates in the *Philosophy of Right* is that our free agency is possible only as a result of recognition of fundamental conditionality of our fundamental freedom upon intersubjective interactions and interrelations. Yet this recognition is not an abstract act of acknowledging of our sociality and dependence on social institutions. This is also recognition of our mutual interdependence, which is normative for manifesting our individual free agency. Thus, the very phenomenon of recognition is for Hegel the most important means for becoming the actual self, a "fully fledged person" that freely determines itself. Hegel shows that in order for the recognition to take place, self must define itself in relation to *others* who are not only distinct from, but are also opposed to self. The process of recognition is thus a dialectical progression toward the unity of conflicting entities in which the otherness of what is opposed is not simply consumed, but rather is appropriated in a way that allows development to higher stages of consciousness.

III

The key theme of Hegel's discussion of a struggle for recognition is that the development of an individual is impossible without an actual engagement with other people in the world. This involves recognizing a very basic feature of our mutual interdependence, even as thinkers, namely, our intersubjectivity. Hegel is confident that subjectivity and individuality are always intersubjectivity and communality, because individual self is necessarily mediated through its relations with others. In *Lectures* he writes:

> Self-consciousness thus reaches beyond itself; it continues in another self-consciousness so that there are no longer two self-seeking individuals opposed to each other; rather there is a single self-consciousness, and thus it is a universal self-consciousness . . . The substance of this self-consciousness is the universality of a self-knowledge that leaves behind self-seeking [particularity] and that continues itself in union with the other.[31]

The specifics of mutual interdependence lie in the fact that, although it results from our individual activity, it necessarily has fundamental universal elements in it. This universality is determined by the very character of communal (social) connections. Although intersubjective relations are heterogeneous, they always have something in common, namely, similar ways of behaving, both bodily and linguistically, without which interaction among individuals cannot take place. What is common in each of us and without which our life would be impossible is our communal and social nature. This is what Hegel designates here as "universal self-consciousness" and later on—in the next section—"social reason."

In the later chapters of the *Philosophy of Spirit*, Hegel further explains the idea of intersubjectivity by highlighting its centrality to human social life in the various forms of its appearance. By examining social dimensions of human individuals, including customs, practices, and institutions within which individuals become who they are, he shows that individuals and social institutions are mutually interdependent; neither exists nor has the character it does without its proper complement. Yet already in the "Phenomenology" section, and especially its subsection on self-consciousness, Hegel shapes and underlines the whole concept of the theoretical principle of intersubjectivity.[32] Hegel makes it clear that the coexistence of free agents and their interaction presuppose as an a priori condition the idea of *community* of individuals that is, not historically, but transcendentally, prior to these individuals. A "we" grounds the "I"; it is not only that my freedom is possible only because my agency is acknowledged by others, but the very concept of individuality is a reciprocal concept and can be thought only in relation to another self. Making recognition a crucial element of the progression of the self toward its sheer self-awareness, Hegel demonstrates that individuals are conscious of themselves only as "universal" individuals, participants in collective values (and institutions), not as the atomic individuals, bearers of independent selfhood of their own. Unlike Descartes or Fichte, whose approaches to subject and subjectivity can be described in terms of "atomistic individualism," Hegel develops a position may be called "moderate universalism."[33] According to his view, epistemic and ontological justifications cannot depend simply on the single individual subject. Each ontological and epistemic principle must be developed in a justificatory process that must obtain not merely individual but collective validity. It is not sufficient to assess someone's judgment individually; it requires mutual assessment of many rational individuals. Thus, although individual autonomy and the epistemic and ontological conditions of the individual subject are necessary for rational justification and real affirmation, only collective ("universal") autonomy can fully achieve such a justification. The same point holds true regarding the social practices and principles that govern communal life, which likewise can be justified only in and through interrelations among individuals.

In contrast to Fichte, who also stresses the importance of intersubjective relations for the self's development, but for whom intersubjectivity is an arbitrary notion, Hegel contends that intersubjectivity is a necessary active engagement with concrete communal and social life. He views intersubjectivity as a crucial element of the life of any individual. The self-awareness and the sense of individuality of any person are mediated by relation to other people. If one's free agency is not acknowledged by other (rational) subjects, one cannot become properly conscious of oneself and one's freedom. The relations between self and others are fundamental to human awareness and activity. The otherness that consciousness first experiences as a barrier to its goals is the (apparent) external reality of the natural and social world. This apparent externality blocks individual freedom and independence. Yet this otherness cannot be destroyed without destroying oneself; thus, there must be a state of reconciliation between the other and the self so that consciousness grasps itself through the other. This stage of reconciliation involves and requires reciprocal recognition.[34] Through acknowledging the other as another and likewise as a self, one comes to recognize oneself as a free and conscious being. One's self-consciousness or self-awareness is possible only through mutual recognition by other subjects; this justifies our collective and ultimately social nature. This is why the intersubjective activity that animates our spiritual, that is, our communal life takes place in a broad context of social reality and is a crucial part of the process of enculturating the self.[35] The mechanisms of this enculturation as well as the ways we express ourselves collectively and culturally Hegel illuminates in the further sections of the philosophy of subjective, objective, and absolute spirit.

Notes

1. Axel Honneth, *The Struggle for Recognition: The Moral Grammar of Social Conflicts*, trans. J. Anderson (Cambridge, Mass.: Polity Press, 1995), 61.

2. Jürgen Habermas, "From Kant to Hegel and Back—The Move towards Detranscendentalization," *European Journal of Philosophy* 7, no. 2 (1999): 149.

3. Vittorio Hösle, *Hegels System. Der Idealism der Subjectivität und das Problem der Intersubjektivität*, 2 vols. (Hamburg: Felix Meiner, 1987), 370, 379.

4. Adriaan Peperzak, *Selbsterkenntnis des Absoluten. Grundlinien der Hegelschen Philosophie des Geistes* (Stuttgart: Frommann-Holzboog, 1987), 40.

5. See, for example, arguments developed by Franz Hespe in "System und Funktion der Philosophie des subjektiven Geistes," in *Psychologie und Anthropologie oder Philosophie des Geistes*, ed. Hespe und Tuschling (Stuttgart-Bad Cannstatt: Frommann-Holzboog, 1991), 490–521, as well as in "Hegels Philosophie des subjektiven Geistes im enzyklopädischen System," in *Hegels enzyklopädisches System der Philosophie*, ed. Hans-Christian Lucas, Burkhard Tuschling und Ulrich Vogel (Stuttgart-Bad Cannstatt: Frommann-Holzboog, 2004), 221–68. Another passionate advocate for this reading of Hegel's *Philosophy of Subjective Spirit* is Robert Williams. See his *Hegel's Ethics of Recognition* (Berkley: University of California Press, 1998). This interpretation is especially emphasized in the translator's introduction

to G. W. F. Hegel, *Lectures on the Philosophy of Spirit*, trans. and intro. Robert Williams (New York: Oxford University Press, 2007). See also Heikki Ikäheimo, *Self-Consciousness and Intersubjectivity: A Study of Hegel's Encyclopedia Philosophy of Subjective Spirit (1830)* (Jyväskylä, Finland: University of Jyväskylä Publications in Philosophy 67, 2000).

6. See: Hermann Drüe, "Philosophie des Geistes (§§ 377–577)," *Hegels Enzyklopädie der philosophischen Wissenchaften (1830). Ein Kommentar zum Systemgrundriß*, ed. Herbert Schnädelbach (Frankfurt: Suhrkamp, 2000), 260–61.

7. See VPG; first English translation appeared in 2007, as LPS.

8. Hegel himself greatly contributed to such a suspicion toward phenomenology by not even mentioning it in the title of his lectures on philosophy of subjective spirit. In the official lecture announcement, the course was listed under the title *Anthropologie und Psychologie oder Philosophie des Geistes*. See *Briefe von und an Hegel in 4 Bände*, Bd. 4, ed. Johannes Hoffmeister, Friedhelm Nicolin (Hamburg: Felix Meiner Verlag, 1977), 122.

9. See, for example, Hespe, "Hegels Philosophie des subjektiven Geistes"; Burkhard Tuschling, "Die Idee in Hegels Philosophie des subjektiven Geistes," *Psychologie und Anthropologie*, 522–75; Burkhard Tuschling, "Von der Monade zum subjektiven Geist: Leibniz, Hegel," in *Geist und Willensfreiheit. Klassische Theorien von der Antike bis zur Moderne*, ed. Edith und Klaus Düsing, Hans-Dieter Klein (Würzburg: Königshausen and Neumann, 2006), 83–106. These topics are also touched upon in VPG (1827–28): xii–xv.

10. VPG, xxivff.

11. LPS, 19.

12. LPS, 185.

13. LPS, 185.

14. LPS, 183. See also PM, § 424.

15. "The things are null in themselves." LPS, 185.

16. PM, §430.

17. LPS, 194.

18. PM, § 436.

19. Hegel, *Phenomenology of the Spirit*, trans. A. V. Miller (Oxford: Oxford University Press, 1977), 140. (G. W. F. Hegel, *Phänomenologie des Geistes*, ed. Wolfgang Bonsiepen und Reinhard Heede, *Gesammelte Werke*, vol. 9 [Hamburg: Felix Meiner, 1980], 197).

20. LPS, 190.

21. LPS, 183.

22. Both Kant and Fichte treat recognition as a necessary requirement for and condition of morality.

23. While Hegel extensively discussed the I in the *Phenomenology* of 1807, at that time he had not yet developed a sophisticated conception of the universal subjectivity that was completed only in *Logic*. In the *Encyclopedia* system, subjectivity is already conceptualized as a principle or essence of spirit. It now appears as a nonempirical universality (cf. PM, § 412) which realizes itself as the I or

(individual) spirit. This apparent dichotomy is nothing else but differentiation of the individual moments and tenets of spirit. They are moments of one and the same reality though, and they are united in the concept of all-encompassing subjectivity (cf. PM, § 215 A).

24. PM, §§ 428–29.
25. LPS, 190.
26. The same point makes Hespe when he states that the "reference to intersubjective conditions of possibility of self-consciousness is not to be understood just as an expression of empirical fact, but rather articulates what self-consciousness *is* according to its concept." Hespe, "System und Funktion der Philosophie des subjektiven Geistes," 511.
27. PM, § 436–37; LPS, 185, 19ff.
28. Hösle, *Hegels System*, 379.
29. LPS, 187.
30. PM, §490.
31. LPS, 194.
32. To avoid a misunderstanding, it is important to distinguish between intersubjectivity as a theoretical principle deduced from the requirement for self-consciousness and intersubjectivity as a practical principle that appears as a requirement for morality and communal life in general. In *Encyclopedia* "Phenomenology" Hegel *sketches* the concept and also *derives* intersubjectivity as a theoretical principle. At the same time, Hegel only *explains* here the concept of intersubjectivity as a practical principle, while still setting the stage for a "real performance": a proof that this concept is true of us human being. This proof is outlined in the philosophy of objective spirit (the deduction of the concept of right). The further details, by bringing more factual historical material, are given in the *Philosophy of Right*. In the *Philosophy of Right* Hegel develops his proof for intersubjectivity in terms of the concept of a community of free agents. This community is not just association based on reciprocal recognition, but requires a kind of supraindividual identity that is distinct from and logically prior to the individuals. This supraindividual identity is warranted by intersubjective relations. In the case of a more abstract community of right (at the beginning of the *Philosophy of Right*) that exponent of subjectivity is right itself as the universal substance of the will of the individuals.
33. Here I follow Kenneth Westphal who calls Hegel's unique social ontology "moderate collectivism." See Kenneth R. Westphal, "Spirit," in *The Dictionary of Continental Philosophy*, ed. J. Protevi (New Haven, CT: Yale University Press, 2006), 555–56.
34. "This [condition of self-externality, of being beyond oneself] is the condition of being recognized. In an ethical totality such as family or a state, all are recognized. Thus the struggle for recognition has disappeared." LPS, 194.
35. LPS, 190, 193.

Freedom as Correlation

Recognition and Self-Actualization in Hegel's Philosophy of Spirit

ROBERT R. WILLIAMS

In a recent essay, Robert Pippin asks, "What is the question for which Hegel's Theory of Recognition is the answer?"[1] His answer to this question is that recognition is bound up with the issue of the nature and possibility of freedom and that Hegel's later writings are extensions, not repudiations, of his earlier Jena view. Pippin's claims about the systematic connection between recognition and freedom, as well as the continuity between Hegel's early and mature position are I believe correct. However, understanding the systematic connection between recognition and freedom does not, in Pippin's estimation, require understanding recognition as a theory of self-consciousness or of intersubjectivity. Instead Pippin claims that the "question for which recognition is the answer" narrows to the question, why does Hegel think that a subject cannot be free alone? In answering this question, Pippin presents an account of Hegel that is historicist and constructivist. According to Pippin, it is his radical historicism and constructivism that leads Hegel to recognition.[2]

The question is, how can Pippin's antisubstantialist, constructivist, left-Hegelian interpretation of recognition ground the normative aspects present in Hegel's mature account of ethical life? Pippin concedes that his reconstruction is too constructivist and relativist to do justice to the historical Hegel or to the normative issue.[3] It is not clear how one moves from a formal constructivist reading of reciprocal recognition to Hegel's mature, nonformal theory of ethical life.[4] Pippin observes,

> Once Hegel's anti-dualism about Geist, and a radical anti-realism or constructivism about norms is conceded, and some version of Hegel's critique of formalism is accepted, then there is just nothing left to 'counting as a norm' other than being taken to be one . . . Without a possible Aristotelian appeal to the realization of natural capacities in order to establish when one is really acting in a practically rational way (realizing one's natural potential) . . . this turns out to be the only criterion left: one is an agent in being recognized as, responded to as, an agent; one can be so recognized if the justifying norms appealed to in the practice of treating each other as agents can actually function within that community as justifying.[5]

This is circular and inadequate as Pippin concedes. This circularity betokens a formal, nonteleological, and nonholistic view of mutual recognition. Pippin treats normative questions by appeal to preestablished community practices that are broader than and external to recognition. Instead of grounding community and norms, recognition presupposes these.

In his *Die Logik des Absoluten*, Stefan Majetschak claims that recognition is connected not so much with the nature and possibility of freedom as with self-actualization.[6] Majetschak observes that for Hegel, the actuality (*Wirklichkeit*) of being-for-self (*Fürsichsein*) consists in "being recognized by the other, of counting absolutely for the other."[7] The self becomes objective, that is, actual, in the recognition of others. Thus, finding oneself in another's recognition is part of what self-actualization means. As Hegel frequently asserts, freedom means being at home with oneself in another (*bei sich im anderen zu sein*). Here is a straightforward answer to Pippin's question, Why does Hegel think that a human being cannot be free alone? Moreover, if mutual recognition is a condition of self-actualization, then mutual recognition cannot be void of normative significance, for a cognitively and socially isolated subject could not be free or actual in any significant sense.

Given his programmatic thesis concerning self-actualization in recognition, it comes as a disappointment that Majetschak fails to make explicit the connection between recognition, freedom, and self-actualization. I want to explore that connection. Freedom for Hegel is being at home with oneself in an other. Freedom is actual only in relation, not apart from relation.[8] But a relational freedom is not absolute. It is a mediated autonomy. A mediated autonomy is a vulnerable, fragile autonomy. Its self-actualization can be prevented, and if it does become actual, its self-actualization is a mediated one.

The normative significance of mutual recognition—what is at stake— becomes clear principally in the negations and distortions of recognition that undermine, prevent, or harm the self in its mediated actualization. Misrecognition not only prevents the I from becoming a We, it also prevents the achievement of proper independence within relationship and full participation in ethical life.[9] This, rather than the practices of any specific community, constitutes the normative significance of recognition. Recognition is a condition of self-actualization in this sense: it establishes the fundamental intersubjective pattern of self-actualization immanent in the normative institutions ethical life; these institutions are both extensions and conditions of mediated free self-actualization.

In what follows we will focus principally on Hegel's *Lectures on the Philosophy of Spirit* in 1822–25 and 1827. These lectures have only recently become available, and they are not widely known or appreciated. They constitute the oral elaboration Hegel himself deemed necessary for understanding the compressed paragraph outline of his *Encyclopedia Philosophy of Spirit*.

First we will clarify the meaning of the term "self-actualization" by examining Hegel's appropriation and transformation of Aristotle from an 1825 introduction. Next we will examine some texts from Hegel's *Philosophy of Spirit* 1825 and 1827 that clarify mediated self-actualization through recognition. Mediated self-actualization is an alternative to criticisms that Hegel collapses the other into self-relation and favors unity and identity over difference. Mediated self-actualization also constitutes a reply to criticisms that Hegel reduces the self-relation to the interiorization of preestablished community practices. We shall examine how Hegel understands the self as a correlation of relations, that is, how he understands the self-relation as conditioning possible relations to other, and how relation to other conditions and shapes the self-relation. We shall explore this correlational selfhood as it develops into Spirit as a totality, and as providing the concept of ethical life. Finally we turn to an examination of misrecognition, tragic self-contradiction, which constitutes a "tragic proof" of the vulnerability of mediated freedom and of the normative character of the recognitive solidarities and institutions of freedom constitutive of ethical life.

Hegel's Transformation of Aristotle

Like Aristotle, Hegel presents a teleological, self-actualization account of freedom; unlike Aristotle, Hegel's account of self-actualization includes recognition by other. Aristotle's well-known view of self-actualization as the realization of a natural potential does not define, much less exhaust, Hegel's concept of freedom, because Aristotle has no account of the other, otherness, or negation.[10] Hegel's understanding of the end or telos of human activity is not the Aristotelian *eudaimonia* and good life, but rather a freedom that is fully actual not in abstract isolated individuals but in community membership and participation.[11]

Hegel understands the human being roughly in Aristotelian terms as self-actualizing, but not as following an end prescribed by nature. Rather, human being must liberate itself from nature and natural determination. A suggestive text is found in Hegel's introduction to his 1822–25 *Lectures on the Philosophy of Spirit*, which I shall quote at length.

> Although the Greek has as his portion that which is human, that is, the free spirit, this free spirit has not yet appreciated its infinity. What would be poured forth over the Greek world and what the Greek might gain knowledge of, is not the absolute, holy spirit. Rather it is man as *free within nature*, as retaining in nature the organ of his consciousness as remaining restricted within nature, however, and while undoubtedly progressing into pure thought only in philosophy, not in religion, being unable to free himself from the abstraction, an entanglement corresponding to immediacy in thought, and not able to come to the concept of spirit itself . . . .
>
> At the same time the task [of knowing spirit] presents itself to us in a manner which is different in many respects, for it is precisely through the raising of our consciousness to the consciousness of infinite spirit—a raising which began in religion—that our general standpoint is a higher one. It is through this standpoint that the absolute spirit has confronted the spirit which used to be understood as the human spirit, and through this comparison the latter has been reduced to a finitude, i.e., to a limited natural spirit. On the other hand, it is through that very relation which comes into effect with that comparison, that *the human being has gained a wholly free foundation in himself, and established for himself a different relation to nature, namely, a relation of independence*.[12]

Hegel regards Greek spirit as limited in its consciousness of freedom, or as spirit in its immediacy.[13] The infinity of spirit was not yet appreciated; here freedom meant realizing ends prescribed and predetermined by nature. Spirit comes to a deeper, more profound sense of itself in Judaeo-Christian religion, which draws a distinction between God and world. In light of this distinction, the earlier Greek view of freedom is relativized, reduced to a freedom within nature.

According to Hegel, the raising of consciousness to spirit's proper infinity begins in religion; in religion absolute spirit confronts the human spirit. In comparison with infinite spirit, human spirit becomes mortal finitude. In the same relation that limits it to mortal finitude, spirit also discovers a foundation within itself by virtue of which it can become independent of nature.[14] Freedom is now understood as liberation of spirit from its immersion in nature and natural ends. Spirit's infinity consists in its capacity to be self-grounding and self-determining. The life and death struggle for recognition is the beginning of the liberation of spirit from subordination to nature. In the life and death struggle, self and other place their natural existence at risk. This struggle shows that human spirit is not restricted to realizing ends prescribed by nature. The human being has a natural origin, but in this condition it is not yet what it ought to be. The human being must transcend nature and complete itself through freedom, namely recognition, and this is part of what self-actualization means.

Hegel's text continues:

> The spirit which we are considering here is thus placed as a middle between the two extremes, nature and God—between a point of departure and a final purpose and goal. The question what is spirit, contains two questions, namely, whence does spirit come and whither is it going! . . . Where does it come from? It comes from nature. Whither is it going? It tends towards its freedom. What spirit is is just this movement of liberating itself from nature. This [movement] is its very substance, so that it is not permissible to speak of it as a fixed subject which does this or brings about that . . . [T]*he activity of spirit is its substantiality, its being is actuosity* [*Actuosität*].[15]

The human spirit is a middle between nature on the one hand and God on the other. Precisely because the human being has to liberate itself in order to become itself, the human being has no fixed or given nature, but is restless activity.[16] Nevertheless, it has a goal or vocation. While it is self-determining, the human being is not absolutely self-creating; rather, it is both dependent in relation to God and independent in relation to the world and others. The latter independence *vis à vis* the world is grounded in the former relation of dependence on God: "Generally speaking, the highest independence of man is to know himself as totally determined by the absolute Idea; this is the consciousness and attitude that Spinoza calls *amor intellectualis Dei*."[17] This dependence does not suppress, but rather grounds, freedom and summons the human being to its task and vocation. The human being completes itself in freedom by creating a realm of substantial, actualized freedom, a cultural world of spirit produced from within spirit itself as a second nature.[18]

Recognition as Negation of Negation: Counting for Something

The starting point of Hegel's analysis of recognition is the collision between self and other, the zero point of their mediation. The account of recognition begins at a preethical level of indeterminacy and mutual externality in which each regards the other merely as a finite obstacle to be eliminated. The process of recognition proceeds through the life and death struggle, the halfway house of master and slave, and is consummated in mutual recognition. Each phase or *Stufe* of the process of recognition has ethical significance, ranging from the preethical violence of the life and death struggle of the state of nature, to relations of domination—mastery and servitude—founded on coercion, to the mutual realization of freedom as a social infinite in mutual recognition. Mutual recognition is the consummation of the process, because only in it do "I find myself in another person; for this other I count for something, who in turn counts for me."[19]

Hegel begins with an account of the doubling of self-consciousness. This doubling (*Verdoppelung*) is both an *intrasubjective* doubling within consciousness and an *intersubjective* doubling "between" consciousnesses. These must be distinguished, yet they are not separate. They are tied together in correlation. On the one hand, self-relation is more than a simple internalization of the other-relation. The self's understanding of itself and its way of relating to itself also conditions and shapes the way in which it relates to others. On the other hand, the self in its own self-relation is not absolutely autonomous, but it is open to, shaped by, and dependent on other.

The open, mediated self-relation means that the self is vulnerable to misrecognition.[20] For example, the initial encounter with the other divides the self. This division is experienced as self-alteration and self-loss. The altered, divided self seeks to reconstitute itself as a whole. But it can do so only if the problem created by the presence of the other and the problem of doubling/self-diremption can be overcome.

The presence of the other reveals the self to be not only a particular, but a particular in opposition to another particular. Prior to encounter, the self is indeterminate, potentially universal, and yet parochial and exclusive. In the encounter its parochialism becomes explicit. The other, by his mere presence, constitutes an unmediated opposition; this opposition effects a transition of the self from abstract, immediate indeterminacy to determinacy. To be determinate is to be limited by and dependent on another. This has been negatively expressed by Sartre in a classical formulation: The other means that my transcendence is transcended. I am no longer master of the situation. Through the presence of other, I come to realize that I am a transcendence that has been transcended, that I am my body, that through the other I "fall" into the world as an object among other objects.[21] This situation is intolerable. It is an existential contradiction, and, as Hegel notes, contradiction "moves the world."[22]

According to Hegel, there are three possible types of "solution" to the "problem" of the other. 1) Eliminate the other, thereby restoring the self to its original immediacy and subjective certainty. But to eliminate the other means not only that I must risk my own life, but also that the other is taken to be only a negative limit to my freedom and not its condition. To eliminate the other is self-defeating because the self needs and depends on the other's recognition. This "solution" is obviously prerecognitive and preethical. 2) Assimilate and dominate the other. This implies asymmetry, for example, one is recognized but does not recognize in return, for example, master, while the other recognizes but is not recognized in turn, that is, slave. The slave fears death; in thrall to his existence and desperate to preserve it, the slave surrenders his claim to recognition. He preserves his life, but in the mode of thinghood, of being a mere receptacle for the ends and wishes of the master. The master preserves his independence, but it is an independence tied to coercion and domination.

Neither elimination of the other nor its assimilation solves the problem of the other, because what is needed is the other's free uncoerced recognition, and both 1 and 2 make such recognition impossible. In both cases desire remains an exclusive, self-seeking particular. Although master and slave constitute a relation, owning to its asymmetry, it has to be founded on coercion and the threat of death. In spite of their relation, they remain external. They fall into and perpetuate the false infinity of domination.

There is an alternative, 3) let the other be. This is not indifference. Rather, letting be is the beginning of a noncoercive affirmative mutuality in which both are dependent and yet independent within this dependence. Each limits, conditions, and recognizes the other, such that together they constitute a free whole or totality. This opens the way to an affirmative mutuality in which the I becomes a We. Only here does the other count, that is, possess affirmative and normative significance as both a condition of and limit to my freedom. This conditioning has to be reciprocal; dependence is not the antithesis of freedom but its condition. Freedom assumes the shape of union, mutual participation, and membership, that is, ethical life.

Mutual Recognition as Ethical Self-Actualization: The 1825 Lectures

The 1807 *Phenomenology* presents variations on the theme of master and slave. But master and slave do not constitute, much less exhaust, the possibilities of recognition. Hegel develops the affirmative possibilities of recognition in his *Encyclopedia Philosophy of Spirit* and the *Philosophy of Right*. However, the most explicit account of these affirmative possibilities is found in the virtually unknown 1825 *Lectures on the Philosophy of Spirit*.[23]

We noted above that the intrasubjective self-relation conditions the intersubjective relation to other, and the relation to other conditions the self's relation to itself. The *intrasubjective* self-relation and the *intersubjective* relation to other are correlative. How the self understands itself conditions its relations to others: "The unfree man . . . makes slaves of others. The man who is inherently free lets the others be free."[24] Conversely, the relation to other shapes and conditions self-identity and self-relation. For example, the slave's self-identity and its world are shaken and dissolve under the threat of death, the absolute master. That dissolution is why the mentality of the slave becomes a receptacle for and interiorizes the views and values of the master. The truth of mastery and coercion is seen in the false consciousness of the slave. The self's relation to itself stands in correlation to the recognition, or the misrecognition, it receives from the other. This correlation breaks down any abstract separation between "inner" and "outer." The self is a relation of these relations.

Hegel's 1825 *Lectures on the Philosophy of Spirit* are important for clarifying these correlations.[25] First, there are logical conditions of mutual recognition: Hegel shows that until the self is capable of grasping the contrast between universal and particular, it is trapped in an either/or posture, is incapable of mutual recognition, and cannot forge an affirmative relation to other. Second, the text contrasts the reciprocal recognition constitutive of ethical life with the unequal coercive recognition constitutive of master and slave. Master/slave does not exhaust the meaning of recognition or exhibit its normative actualization. For Hegel the truth of intersubjectivity is not conflict, but mutual recognition and freedom: being at home with oneself in one's other. Third, the text shows how Hegel understands self-recognition in other to be mediated self-actualization. This mediated self-actualization clarifies in turn the concept of spirit as universal consciousness.

Hegel begins by noting that in the account of the life and death struggle and master/slave, the selves conceive themselves and the other as immediate, exclusive singularities: "[A]ll of this lacks the determination and condition of universality and remains in the form of immediate singularity. At this level of self-understanding it is still the case that if I recognize another as free, I lose my freedom."[26] When the self thinks of itself as an immediate singularity—as the "I am I"—recognizing the other as an external singular appears to be a loss of freedom. Hegel notes that under the conditions of immediacy, "Desire relates itself only to itself . . ."[27] In desire, "the immediate singularity of my self-consciousness and my freedom are not yet separated. Consequently I am unable to surrender anything of my particularity without giving up my independence . . . I have not yet renounced this [purely self-regarding, self-seeking] particularity, I have not yet distinguished it from myself, not yet discarded it, have not yet raised the self-consciousness of my freedom to universal self-consciousness."[28] In desire, consciousness has not yet distinguished its particularity and universality, but remains on the pre- or subethical level.[29]

Hegel observes that "the self-consciousness here is still immediate and singular, for it has not yet abstracted from its own singularity; here desire still rules, and the property others possess is taken by the self-consciousness to be a limitation on its freedom . . . [T]he standpoint is that as a self I am still an immediate singular that has not yet renounced its particularity and thus I determine myself according to my desire . . . which refers only to itself."[30] Consequently, under these conditions and presuppositions, "there can be no recognition of the one by the other. Both assert their [unqualified] independence. What is more, each is unwilling to recognize *the other in itself* on account of its own parochial freedom and it cannot be recognized by the others on account of the way in which it is for the others."[31] As long as the selves understand themselves in this narrow, immediate way, mutual recognition cannot occur. Mutual recognition requires that this immediacy be negated, mediated, and articulated. Through the process of recognition, the self raises itself to the universal and becomes capable of being a member of an ethical community and totality.

To sort out the complexity of freedom, recognition, and self-actualization in the *Philosophy of Spirit*, we turn to Ludwig Siep's analysis. Siep notes that Hegel's conception of freedom is characterized by four basic features: *autonomy, union with other, self-overcoming, Freigabe*.[32] Autonomy signifies the independence of the will from external influence and coercion; it is self-generated self-determination. The basic question is, how can such self-generating, negative autonomy be mediated?[33] How can autonomy, which seems to be negative and exclusive, be conditioned by and dependent on an other? How can the self, which in the Cartesian idealist tradition appears to be wholly self-contained and self-sufficient if not solipsistic, nevertheless, be dependent for its actualization on what appear to be external contingencies such as another and its recognition?[34] My thesis is that Hegel breaks with idealism and its one-sided primacy of the subject when he writes that "Self-consciousness is in and for itself when and through the fact that it is in and for itself for another; that is, it exists only as recognized."[35] As Sartre noted, "Hegel's brilliant intuition is to make me depend on the Other in my being. I am, he said, a being-for-itself which is for-itself only through another. Therefore the other penetrates me to the heart . . . Thus solipsism seems to be put out of the picture once and for all . . . and instead of holding that my being-for-self is opposed to my being-for-others, I find that being-for-others appears as a necessary condition for my being-for-myself."[36]

Hegel's concept of autonomy differs significantly from views like Kant's because he holds that autonomy requires relation to other, in order to be actual. True freedom for Hegel consists in union and identification with the other, not in abstract isolation or exclusion of the other. Autonomy is not simply formal and negative, but also affirmative; as affirmative it is realized in relation to and union with other. *Pace* Fichte, not everything posited by the subject is for that reason relative to or dependent on the subject.[37] Autonomy does not exclude relation or community, but requires these.[38]

The second feature of freedom, *union with other*, signifies a breaking through the limits of individuality that separate individuals from others. True freedom signifies not separation from, but rather union with, other. Fichte grasped the other chiefly as a limit to freedom and ended up with a negative view of community. Fichte's understanding of freedom is inadequate, because he assumes that freedom is and remains indeterminate and negative. From this point of view, to become a member of a community is to become determinate, but Fichte treats such determinacy as utterly external and alien. On this view, community is simply tyranny. On the contrary, Hegel holds that "the community of a person with others must not be regarded as a limitation of true freedom of the individual, but essentially as its enlargement. Highest community is the highest freedom."[39] In community, negative, abstract, indeterminate freedom is transformed, and the other is willed affirmatively as included in the self's own end. Since in the union each is reciprocally an end for the other, their relation is also willed as something affirmative, as an end in itself. Thus in community freedom is realized as being at home with self in another.

Such a community is a free space of appearance. This free space constitutes the interpersonal sphere. Hegel claims that in union with other, "I give myself a determinate existence, not in an external object, but in a present counterpart (*Gegenstand*) who is a consciousness. The consciousness of the other is now the ground, the soil, the material, the space, in which I realize myself."[40] The other's recognition is the space of my self-actualization, and the freedom that I actualize there is a determinate, mediated freedom, that is, a dependent independence.

Hegel develops these ideas further in his 1827 *Lectures on the Philosophy of Spirit*. There he points out that union with other cancels and removes the restriction or limit of natural desire and self-seeking. The determinate negation of desire has affirmative significance.

> I lose my self-consciousness in an other, but I also know myself affirmatively precisely in the other. Here the limit or restriction [of self-seeking] that previously was immanent in desire and self-seeking is canceled. Self-consciousness thus reaches beyond itself; it continues in another self-consciousness so that there are no longer two self-seeking individuals opposed to each other, but rather there is a single self-consciousness, and thus it is a universal self-consciousness. Insofar as it is a particular, it is separate from the other. These abstract determinations are present in much more concrete forms. The substance of this self-consciousness is the universality—of a self-knowledge that leaves behind self-seeking [particularity] and that continues itself in union with the other.
>
> This condition is found in love . . . I am no longer a self-seeking I, but a free self-consciousness that knows itself in an other . . .

All the virtues have this foundation, as does love . . . But precisely [in] this condition of self-externality [*Ausserlichkeit*], of being beyond the limits of one's individuality, one gains one's substantial self-consciousness. This [condition of self-externality, of being beyond oneself] is the condition of being recognized.[41]

The third feature of freedom is self-overcoming. Self-overcoming presupposes that the self has a certain internal complexity. We have already noted that the logical contrast between particular and universal is a precondition of distinguishing ethical freedom from desire. Prior to the emergence of the contrast between universal and particular, the self exists in immediacy as self-seeking desire. This is a self-understanding that has to be overcome, as Hegel explains:

The standpoint is that of my still being immediately singular as a self, my particularity has not yet renounced itself—its determination of itself in accordance with its desire. However, the demand of my recognition is that I should count as free and independent in the consciousness of the other . . . at the universal level need is the realization, the counting for something for another.[42]

Self-overcoming is achieved in union with other, which breaks through the limits of narrow self-seeking particularity. Self-overcoming names the process in which the self opens itself to and is enlarged by the perspective of the other, and the need and well-being of the other are included in the self's own end. Self-overcoming is the achievement of a larger inclusive mentality, the genesis of spirit.

The fourth feature of freedom makes explicit its intersubjective mediation and dimension. This feature is *Freigabe*, release, or allowing the other to be. *Freigabe* means to cease attempting to control or possess the other. This qualifies the intersubjective space of recognition as a free space of appearance. *Freigabe* presupposes self-overcoming; that is, each self has to overcome its narrow, exclusive self-seeking desire as a limit that divides it from the other and that makes coercion appear desirable and necessary. When the limitations of that exclusive and narrow form of individuality are broken through and overcome, *Freigabe* clarifies the nature of the union with other; it is a union in which individuals are affirmatively free in relation to each other. *Freigabe* thus clarifies that the union is not a fusion, not a suppression of freedom and autonomy, but rather the intersubjective mutual grounding of freedom and autonomy, whereby these become objective and actual. *Freigabe* makes explicit that freedom is not "located" simply "in the individual," but rather in the "between." The individuals view themselves as partners or members within the relationship. The self-realization of freedom is bound up with the mutual accomplishment of a certain sort of community or "we."[43]

> If we speak of right, ethical life and love, we know that when we recognize others I recognize their complete personal independence. We know too that I do not suffer when I recognize others, but rather that I come to count as free. We know that when the others have rights, I also have rights, or that my right is essentially included in the right of others; i.e., that I am a free person and that this is essentially the same as others also being persons with rights. In benevolence and love, my personality is not undermined or destroyed . . . In relations based on justice, I know that if I respect the property of others, that respect does not only not cause me harm, but also that in the right [of property] my own right is included, for I have renounced all claim to the property of others.[44]

Hegel reflects Aristotle's belief that justice is the right of the other. Hence when the other has rights, my right is included. Hegel points out that "in the civilized condition, especially the family, civil society and the state, I recognize and am recognized by everyone without any struggle [*ganz ohne Kampf*]. There ethical and legal relations are already present."[45] In such community, the other and relation to the other are not only not threatening to individual freedom, but are rather conditions of universal freedom. True freedom *"consists in my identity with the other. I am only truly free when the other is also free and is recognized by me as free."*[46] In the *1827 Lectures* Hegel put it thus:

> This [condition of self-externality, of being beyond oneself] is the condition of being recognized. In an ethical totality such as a family or a state, all are recognized. Thus the struggle for recognition has disappeared . . . In society all citizens are recognized and count as free. The freedom of every individual exists only insofar as he is recognized as free by the others, and the others have in him the consciousness of their own legitimacy. They count for him. In a rightful situation, every person counts,

because he allows everyone else to count as free. I am free, insofar as the others are free, and I let them count as free just as they let me count as free. In love and friendship this [counting] is more at the emotional level, but in civil society I count as an abstract person without regard to my subjective peculiarities.

Spirit: The Universal Recognitive Pattern and Substance of Ethical Life

In spirit, the universal consciousness, freedom is both actual and objective. This constitutes Hegel's "deduction" of the concept of objective spirit. This self-consciousness is objective and has its universal validity in the recognition of others. Hegel locates its affirmativity, its "real universality" (*Reelle Allgemeinheit*), in mutuality (*Gegenseitigkeit*) or reciprocal recognition. The universal consciousness is an affirmative self-recognition in other. It achieves its objectivity when being-for-other is co-constitutive of and united with being-for-self: in knowing the other I also know myself. Hegel puts it this way:

> The universal consciousness is the *affirmative knowing* of itself in another self. Each self has absolute independence as a free singularity, but, by virtue of the negation of its immediacy or desire, does not distinguish itself from the other. *Each is therefore universal and objective, and possesses the real universality (die reelle Allgemeinheit) as mutuality (Gegenseitigkeit)* in that it knows itself to be recognized by its free counterpart, and knows that it knows this insofar as it recognizes the other and knows it to be free.[47]

Real universality and freedom consist in the affirmative knowing of oneself in another self. This is the universal consciousness of membership. In such membership, being for self (self-relation) and being for other are both distinct and yet coincide. Self-consciousness is now objective to itself as the universal consciousness shared by its members. In the *1827 Lectures* he puts it this way:

> *This is the realization of consciousness as self-consciousness* . . . the realization of immediate self-consciousness as universal consciousness, namely, that I as I absolutely exist as free, not according

to my self-seeking, but according to my universal nature. My knowledge of my universality is realized, since I know the other as free, not only in the comparison my self-consciousness has in others, but in the other I know myself, and in the other I have my self-consciousness concretely. *This is the self-consciousness that is objective, the universality existing in and for itself.* There is a mediation, but one that has suspended what was [previously] one-sided in the mediation . . . [T]he other self-consciousness is no longer other . . . for in the other I know myself.[48]

Hegel calls this universal recognitive consciousness in which freedom is actual and objective, "the *substantial form* of every essential spirituality—the family, fatherland, the state, as well as all the *virtues*, love, friendship, courage, honor."[49] These texts undermine Habermas's claim that Hegel abandoned recognition and intersubjectivity in his mature conception of ethical life. Much closer to the truth is Iring Fetscher, one of the few interpreters who has discerned the significance of the above passage, and who explains it thus:

> Reciprocal recognition . . . is the *Urform*, the fundamental phenomenon, of the reason realizing itself in human experience. This universal consciousness is the fundamental form, the structure of *both* the social consciousness (*Gesellschaftsbewusstsein* or We consciousness) *and of the individual consciousness that knows itself to be universally valid and rational.* This universal consciousness constitutes the foundation, the substance of any essential spirituality (institution) . . . Consequently *the universal self-consciousness is not only the human phenomenal form of the ontological principle*, (Idea)—the idea is the true in and for itself, the absolute unity of concept and objectivity—*but also the foundation and substance of ethical life.*[50]

This substantial form is the intersubjective pattern and the substantial, normative core of ethical life. It constitutes substantial freedom or the substantial interest of freedom. This universal consciousness or We includes the I as recognized in its universal validity as end. As objective spirit, the We is actual in its members as their ethical substance, their common ground and substance constitutive of ethical life.

The universal consciousness is clearly intersubjective: "In the condition of this universal freedom, when I am reflected into myself I am immediately reflected into the other, and conversely, when I relate to others I am immediately related to myself."[51] Here the self-relation and relation to other are not just in correlation, but appear to coincide in maximal freedom that involves both dependence on others, and yet within this dependence there is independence. In the universal self-consciousness of freedom both individuals and community come to free self-actualization in and through each other. The universal recognitive consciousness is the concrete universal, objective spirit, the "realm of actualized freedom, the world of spirit produced from within itself as a second nature."[52] This is the intersubjective, social-ontological core of Hegel's mature account of ethical life. As freedom objective to itself in other, the universal consciousness is objective spirit, the foundation of right presupposed by the *Philosophy of Right*.[53]

The further elaboration of the concept of ethical life articulates and clarifies its determinate recognitive unities, that is, the institutions of substantial or objective freedom. These social institutions are required by freedom, and in their determinate shapes they constitute the ethical substance of a people. Participation in these institutions is experienced both as duty and as liberation. In the *Philosophy of Right* Hegel describes liberation as free, mediated self-actualization:

> The individual . . . finds his liberation in duty. On the one hand he is liberated from his dependence on mere natural drives and from the burden he labors under as a particular subject in his moral reflections on obligation and desire; and on the other hand he is liberated from that indeterminate subjectivity which does not attain existence (*Dasein*) or the objective determinacy of action but remains within itself and has no actuality. In duty the individual liberates himself so as to attain substantial freedom.[54]

Pippin's Question Reconsidered

Pippin struggles to find a satisfactory answer to his question, reframed as, Why does Hegel think that subjects cannot be free alone, unless recognized by others?[55] It seems obvious that individuals exist and are free apart from others and community. Hegel diagnosed the "obviousness" of this assumption as reflecting the way the understanding (*Verstand*) misunderstands relations. The understanding, owing to its dependence on sense, believes that everything is external to everything else; the understanding universalizes this view and turns it into a metaphysical prejudice: atomism and mechanism. Recognition challenges this prejudice—as Pippin indicates. But recognition can also be distorted by this prejudice.

Such a distortion of recognition is exhibited in Fichte's account: individuals are on the one hand related, yet they remain abstractly independent, isolated, and separated. Fichte writes, "Both recognize each other in their inner being, but they are isolated, as before."[56] Fichte's view is apparently that in spite of mutually recognizing each other, persons remain as isolated and separate as they were before. Fichte conceives reciprocal recognition as a merely formal reciprocity and as a relation that remains external to its terms. Fichte's account of mutual recognition reinstates the mutual isolation and externality that were supposedly overcome. There is no *Aufhebung* or transformation of individuals into a union or a "We."

Hegel believes that Fichte's treatment of recognition and relation exhibits the metaphysical prejudices of the understanding. In the *Logic* of essence, Hegel identifies one such prejudice as a self-contradictory view of relations. On the one hand, each term is taken in isolation to be independent of every other, while on the other hand, all the terms are given a sense that makes them relative and thus mutually dependent.[57] The understanding fails to resolve this contradiction. Failing to resolve the contradiction, the understanding perpetuates it. Elsewhere, Hegel criticizes the "understanding, whose relations always leave the multiplicity of related terms *as a multiplicity*, and whose unity is always a unity of opposites *left as opposites*."[58] Within reciprocal recognition *as the understanding conceives it*, everything remains independent and unaffected *in spite of being related*.

Hegel believes the understanding's view is inadequate because individuals are only externally related, and their relation, as external, leaves them unaffected and untransformed.[59] The multiplicity of *related* terms is *left* as a *multiplicity*, and the opposites supposedly united are *left as opposites*. This view of relation constitutes the spurious or leveled infinity.[60] In the spurious or "leveled infinite" view, the We or the community remains an ought, an ideal, which falls short of actuality. But in fact no We results, and individuals remain separate. But if they remain separate, then they can be united only by compulsion.[61] Such an external holism of compulsion is "mechanism." Hegel observes that no free institutions are possible with this mechanistic concept of freedom and recognition.[62] Such an external view of mutual recognition and of the state as a mechanism for deterring crime, implies a failure to connect freedom and recognition, dependence and independence, and to comprehend either recognition or spirit.[63]

To be sure, Pippin realizes that recognition is not merely external. Still, his account of recognition appears more like Fichte's than Hegel's in that it yields no "We" and no *Geist*. By Pippin's own admission, something other than recognition is necessary to make sense of recognition claims: "Without such a broader appeal to ethical life as a whole, without understanding these norms as posited within and by an ethical community, the status of coming to recognise each other as rights-bearers . . . or as moral equals in any sense will look opaque."[64] Pippin introduces these considerations of community and ethical life independently of and apart from recognition, as if dropped "from heaven."[65] Instead of grounding the we—the practices and institutions of ethical life—recognition presupposes these. Nevertheless, if the institutions of ethical life are not grounded in mutual recognition but rather imposed on it, this creates a problem, to wit, that recognition is merely formal and that such institutions and ethical life itself may be heteronomous, enforceable only through compulsion as in Fichte's case.

In contrast, Hegel points to recognition as mediated self-actualization in his account of the political disposition—patriotism. Social rationality is a consequence of the institutions within the state (rights) and is actually present. Rationality also receives its practical application through action in conformity with those institutions (duties). This disposition, Hegel tells us, "is the consciousness that my substantial and particular interest is preserved and contained in the interest and end of an other (the state) and in the latter's relation to me as an individual. As a result, this other immediately ceases to be an other for me, and in my consciousness of this, I am free."[66]

Hegel's Antiformalism: Tragic Misrecognition

To summarize, we have focused on freedom as a mediated self-actualization. The texts show that according to Hegel, self-actualization is achieved through a series of mediations that enlarges the self-relation by a progressive incorporation of the perspective of the other. This transformation of the I into a We enlarges and enriches the meaning of self-realization to self-realization in other. Autonomous freedom is not an immediate given, but achieved only in a reciprocal, mutual relationship. Affirmative reciprocities correspond to a progressively mediated and enlarged self-relation and self-realization. Thus the I becomes a We, and the We constitutes spirit as universal consciousness and totality. In this totality, self-relation and being-for-other are not merely correlative, but are mutually mediating and coincide in their differences. These points of coincidence in difference form the substantial interests and institutions of freedom and ethical life.

Participation in these institutions involves not only an enlarged mentality and expanded self-identity, it also liberates the individual from asymmetrical dependence on his merely natural drives, from the burdens of abstract formal moral reflection, and from the indeterminate subjectivity of beautiful souls that fail to become actual.

The requirements and above all the equilibrium of the substantial interests of freedom are violated only at one's peril. To conclude, I should like to illustrate this point by reference to Hegel's treatment of tragedy as an instance of misrecognition that prevents self-actualization. Misrecognition reveals what is at stake in recognition. Recall that Hegel defines tragic conflict as a conflict between the substantial interests and institutions of ethical life. These interests are one-sidedly embodied by noble tragic heroes and are brought into conflict by their action. Tragic conflict is different from moral conflict because it is not a conflict of right against wrong, but a conflict of right against right, of one substantial interest against another. According to Hegel,

> the essence of tragedy is a conflict between parties, each of which, taken by itself, has ethical justification, while each can establish the positive content of its own aim and character only by infringing upon the equally justified position of the other. The consequence is that *in its ethical life, and because of it,* each is guilty—a tragic guilt, not moral guilt.[67]

Tragic guilt differs from moral guilt, because it is incurred by having to do what is right and thereby necessarily infringing another right. This substantial conflict threatens not just individuals but also ethical life with destruction.

Tragic conflict not only is a collision between legitimate substantial interests, it also plunges the characters themselves into self-contradiction. For example, recall Hegel's favorite tragedy, Sophocles' *Antigone*. Antigone and Creon are unwilling to recognize each other and the other in themselves. Antigone sees in Creon's edict against burying rebels who take up arms against the city only an illegitimate act. Creon sees in Antigone's burial of her brother Polynices only a stubborn, irrational woman out to undermine his authority. Each character, by single-mindedly pursuing one legitimate substantial interest, collides with and violates another. Thus each is ensnared by the power which s/he refuses to recognize.

Hegel points out that Antigone and Creon are caught in the power of what they are resisting and fighting. He observes that *they violate what, if they were true to their own values and Sittlichkeit, they should be honoring.* Antigone is the daughter of a king, living under the reign of another king, so she should obey the royal command. Creon is also a father and husband, and thus he should have respected the family tie that is Antigone's pathos, and not ordered anything that would prevent its observance. "So there is something immanent in both Antigone and Creon, which they attack, so that *they are gripped and shattered by something intrinsic to their own actual being.*"[68] By attacking the other, each also plunges into substantial self-contradiction: s/he repudiates a "part of himself" that s/he should recognize and honor. Each contradicts himself/herself as well as the other, and in this reciprocal contradiction they bring their downfall upon themselves. Their conflict threatens their city and culture with division and dissolution, for a whole divided against itself cannot stand.

Yet the family values represented by Antigone and the state values represented by Creon are not a priori contradictory, but equally legitimate, indispensable substantial interests of freedom, both necessary dimensions of recognition and self-actualization. For Hegel the "tragic proof" of this proposition is that those who fail to recognize these substantial interests threaten to disrupt their equilibrium and thereby plunge not only themselves but also their world into self-destructive tragic conflict, a conflict that eventually destroyed classical ethical life. If recognition were merely formal and external, in no way bound up with and mediating free self-actualization, that should not have happened.

Notes

1. Robert B. Pippin, "What Is the Question for which Hegel's Theory of Recognition Is the Answer?" *European Journal of Philosophy* 8, no. 2 (2000): 155–72.

2. Pippin, 162. Pippin claims that being spiritual in Hegel's sense is "an historical achievement of certain animals, not the manifestation of an immaterial or divine substance. The left Hegelians were right."

3. Pippin, 162. Pippin believes that Hegel means to appeal to an inescapable, binding form of human dependence which, when properly acknowledged, becomes the means for the achievement of a collective form of independence. But what this means remains obscure.

4. Pippin, 164.

5. Pippin, 163.

6. Stefan Majetschak, *Die Logik des Absoluten* (Berlin: Akademie Verlag 1992). Majetschak criticizes Jürgen Habermas, who in his *Philosophical Discourse of Modernity* maintains that Hegel later abandoned this intersubjective concept of

spirit in favor of a monosubjectival philosophy of the subject. On the contrary, Majetschak maintains that the later Hegel not only retains the intersubjective conception of spirit, but also that the turn to objective spirit reinforces intersubjectivity.

7. Majetschak, 194, citing Hegel, *Jena Schriften* vol. 3, 202–03.

8. But a relation must have two terms; a one-sided, one-term relation is not only impossible but practically useless, because what is supposed to happen can only come about through both. Hegel, *Phänomenologie des Geistes*, Hrsg. G, Lasson, (Hamburg: Meiner, 1952) 142; hereafter PhG; translation: *Phenomenology of Spirit*, tr. A. V. Miller (Oxford: Oxford University Press 1977), § 182; hereafter PhS.

9. See Axel Honneth, *The Struggle for Recognition*, tr. Joel Anderson (Cambridge: MIT Press, 1996).

10. Even Ferrarin concedes that there is no equivalent for the modern notion of will in Aristotle. See Alfredo Ferrarin, *Hegel and Aristotle* (Cambridge: Cambridge University Press, 2000).

11. Ferrarin, 330. See Hegel, *Philosophy of Right* § 57R, tr. Nisbet, ed. A. Wood (Cambridge: Cambridge University Press, 1991).

12. Hegel, "A Fragment on the Philosophy of Spirit (1822/5)," ed. F. Nicolin, *Hegel Studien*, vol. 1, 1961, 10–48, reprinted in PSS. This is Hegel's introduction to a separate volume on the *Philosophy of Spirit* that he intended to publish as a parallel volume to his *Philosophy of Right*. He never fulfilled this intention, but brought out an expanded edition of his *Encyclopedia* in 1827.

13. For Hegel the deficiency of Greek spirit consists in its not yet being fully *für sich*, for itself. This immaturity is evident in the coexistence of freedom with slavery in Greek culture, in the dependence on oracles or divining the significance of animal entrails as guides in decision making, and above all in the tragic death of Socrates, which is at once his personal tragedy and the tragedy of Athens. Athenian democracy was not prepared to recognize the right of subjective freedom and individual self-determination, the right to determine truth from oneself, that Socrates asserted.

14. "When the human being thinks for himself and explores the depth of his spirit, he knows that his freedom is something far superior to all the creations and products of nature. Through his freedom the human being knows that he is more sublime. The human being knows his freedom, his spirit, justly as something divine in a far higher sense than anything natural . . . In everything human there is included the infinite stamp of spirit, [namely] freedom." VPG; LPS.

15. Hegel, "A Fragment on the Philosophy of Spirit (1822/5)," PSS, 93; my italics.

16. Hegel, *Enzyklopädie: Philosophie des Geistes*, § 378 *Zusatz*, *Werke* (Theorie Werkausgabe, Frankfurt: Suhrkamp, 1970); hereafter EPhG.

17. Hegel, *The Encyclopedia Logic*, trans. Geraets, Suchting (Harris, Indianapolis: Hackett, 1991), § 158 Z; this is part 1 of Hegel's *Enzylopädie der philosophischen Wissenschaften 1830*, *Werke*, Theorie Ausgabe (Frankfurt: Suhrhamp Verlag, 1970), Bd. 8; hereafter cited as EL § 158 Z.

18. Hegel, *Philosophy of Right*, ed. A Wood, tr. H. Nisbet (Cambridge: Cambridge University Press, 1991), § 4.

19. Hegel, *Philosophy of Right*, § 158 Z.

20. According to Stephen Houlgate, Hegel does not privilege identity over difference as is frequently maintained. "Far from arguing that everything absorbs (or tries to absorb) what is external and other into itself Hegel maintains that everything within itself is open to the outside." Houlgate, *The Opening of Hegel's Logic* (West Lafayette: Purdue University Press, 2006), 350. "For Hegel being other-related and and open to the influence of others is built logically into the structure of something (*Etwas*) as such." 354.

21. See Jean-Paul Sartre, *Being and Nothingness*, tr. Hazel Barnes (Philosophical Library: New York, 1956).

22. EL, § 119 Z 2.

23. This is the Griesheim transcription of Hegel's 1825 *Lectures on Philosophy of Spirit*. It has been reprinted and translated by M. J. Petry in *Hegel's Philosophy of Spirit*, vol. 3 appendix, and also as a separate text, *G. W. F. Hegel: The Berlin Phenomenology* (Dordrecht: D. Reidel 1981). All references are to the Berlin Phenomenology. Hereafter cited as BPhG.

24. VPG, 136; LPS, 163.

25. BPhG. I have corrected the translation. On the concept of correlation, cf. Erroll E. Harris, *An Interpretation of the Logic of Hegel* (University Press of America, 1983), 184ff.

26. BPhG, 74–77.

27. BPhG, 76–77.

28. BPhG, 76–77.

29. The practices of comporting oneself "universally," that is, acting out of mutual acknowledgment and recognition of others, and claiming rights for oneself only insofar as these can be claimed by any other and vice-versa, have not yet been imagined, much less achieved.

30. BPhG, 78–77.

31. BPhG, 80–81; my italics. The self in its immediacy, as pure I=I, is immediate and abstract self-relation. Inability to recognize the other in oneself is also a feature of tragic blindness. Hegel employs this feature in his discussion of Antigone; Antigone and Creon do not recognize the claims each makes on behalf of the family and state, with tragic results.

32. Ludwig Siep, "Der Freiheitsbegriff der praktische Philosophie Hegels in Jena," in *Praktische Philosophie im Deutschen Idealismus* (Frankfurt am Main: Suhrkamp, 1992), 159–71.

33. This is Pippin's question, Why can't I be free unless I am recognized in a certain way? It should also be noted that in Hegel' view, Kant's concept of autonomy is formal. Formalism abstracts from all content and makes morality a matter of the pure form of willing. But a purely formal autonomy has no content and thus never gets to that which possesses worth in and for itself. *Philosophy of*

Right, §§ 133–40. This separation of the form of autonomy from content implies further a separation of autonomy from community and from mediation by other.

34. Idealism invokes transcendental subjectivity as condition of possibility of any object and makes all objectivity dependent on subjectivity.

35. Hegel, PhG, 141; PhS, § 178.

36. Jean-Paul Sartre, 237–38.

37. Fichte, *Grundriss der Eigethümliche der Wissenschaftslehre*, 1795, Fichtes Werke, hrsg. I. H. Fichte (Berlin: Walter de Gruyter, 1971), vol. 1, 331–35.

38. This means that community for Hegel cannot be herd-community in Nietzsche's sense, in which individuals are reduced to mere social or herd functions. See *Philosophy of Right*, § 260: "Concrete freedom requires that individuality and its particular interests gain recognition of their right . . . [Conversely] the universal does not attain validity or fulfillment without the interest, knowledge and volition of the particular."

39. See Hegel, *Difference between Fichte's and Schelling's System of Philosophy*, tr. H. S. Harris (Albany: State University of New York Press, 1977), 145.

40. BPhG, 74–75.

41. VPG, 174; LPS, 194. Cf. the following: "Self-consciousness finds its satisfaction only in another self-consciousness." PhG, 139.

42. BPhG, 76–79. Hegel observes that the selves in their immediacy reject this: "But this [demand] contradicts self-consciousness at this standpoint and it must resist recognizing another as a free being, just as each must concern itself with eliciting recognition in the other's self-consciousness, of being posited as an independent being.—We have here merely individual self-consciousnesses opposed to each other, which could allow one another to go without disturbance and rest peacefully together in an ideal and idyllic manner. But the desire to dominate (*Herrschbegierde*) is an evil drive, whatever its origin. The true relation [at this level] is that neither individual can bear to have the other oppose him as independent, and so they must necessarily fall into a struggle." BPhG, 76–79.

43. I hasten to add that identifying and distinguishing these features of freedom constitute no ontological guarantee of mutual recognition. They are intended solely to articulate the complex ontological conditions of Hegel's organic concept of freedom and self-actualization. They are necessary moments or aspects of self-actualization, but self-actualization is not automatic.

44. BPhG, 78–79.

45. BPhG, 78–79; cf. EPhG, § 432 Z: "The struggle for recognition can only occur in the state of nature where men exist as only as single, isolated individuals; but it is absent in civil society and the state because here the recognition for which the combatants fought already exists. Although the state may originate in violence, it does not rest upon violence."

46. EPG, § 431 Z; italics mine.

47. EPG, § 436; italics mine. Such affirmative self-knowledge in other and universal consciousness cannot exist in master and slave, because the slave's self

is suspended in fear and terror, and the slave, not permitted to be a self of his own, serves the alien will of the master as its instrument. Conversely, "the master confronted by his slave is not yet truly free, because he is not able to intuit himself in the other." EPG, § 436 Z. No universal consciousness in Hegel's sense can arise here.

48. VPG, 175; LPS, 194; italics mine.

49. EPG, § 436R. Here Hegel identifies the pattern of mutual recognition as the intersubjective structure of ethical life, which allows him to retrieve Aristotle's account of virtues and vices as determinate modes and shapes of that basic intersubjective pattern.

50. Fetscher, *Hegels Lehre vom Menschen* (Stuttgart: Frommann, 1970), 120; italics mine.

51. Fetscher, 120.

52. *Philosophy of Right*, § 4.

53. *Philosophy of Right*, § 2.

54. *Philosophy of Right*, § 149. Note that what Hegel means by duty here is a recognitively mediated determination of a substantial interest of freedom. A theory of duties is for Hegel the development of those recognitive relations that are required by the idea of freedom and are actual within the state. *Philosophy of Right*, §§ 142–48.

55. Pippin, 156.

56. Fichte, *Foundations of Natural Right*, trans. M. Baur (Cambridge University Press, 2000), 79.

57. EL, § 114R. See Harris 157.

58. Hegel, *Early Theological Writings*, trans. T. M. Knox (University of Chicago Press, 1948), 304; my italics. For a similar statement, cf. Hegel, *Lectures on the Philosophy of Religion*, ed. and trans. Peter C. Hodgson (University of California Press, 1984), vol. 3, 192–93.

59. EL, § 117: "In diversity, the different things are each individually what they are, and unaffected by the relation in which they stand . . . This relation is therefore external to them."

60. EL, §§ 94–95. Cf. § 119. The question of how spirit can be both self-generating and bound to and dependent on what it generates cannot be resolved because the understanding excludes the *Aufhebung*.

61. Hegel criticizes Fichte's notorious attempt to ground right in coercion in *Natural Right*, FNR, §§ 8–14. Hegel sensed and was among the first to criticize this external quasitotalitarian *Machtstaat* in Fichte. The compulsory union of externally related individuals makes ethical life impossible. See Hegel, *Natural Law*, trans. T. M. Knox (Philadelphia: University of Pennsylvania Press, 1975), 84–85.

62. Hegel, *Natural Law*, 84–85; see also Hegel, *Philosophy of Right*, § 5 Z.

63. *Philosophy of Right*, §§ 7R, 158 Z.

64. Pippin, 165.

65. Rolf-Peter Horstmann makes a similar observation that the claim that giving and accepting reasons are abstract general features of social rationality and

praxis is developed independently of Hegel, phenomenology, and recognition. See "Substance, Subject and Infinity," in *Hegel: New Directions*, ed. K. Deligiori (Montreal: McGill University Press 2006), 69.

66. *Philosophy of Right*, § 268.

67. Hegel *Aesthetics*, vol. 2, trans. T. M. Knox (Oxford: Oxford University Press, 1975), 1196; my italics.

68. Hegel, *Aesthetics*, vol. 2, 1215–16; my italics.

Hegel's Linguistic Thought in the *Philosophy of Subjective Spirit*

Between Kant and the "Metacritics"

JERE O'NEILL SURBER

> The power of Spirit is only as great as its expression, its depth only as deep as it dares to spread out and lose itself in its exposition.
> —Hegel, preface to the *Phenomenology of Spirit*

Introduction

Hegel's only systematic treatment of linguistic issues occurs within the division of the *Philosophy of Subjective Spirit* entitled "Representation," itself a subdivivion of "Psychology." In the course of this discussion, Hegel specifically refers to Herder's *Metacritique* and its linguistic attack on Kantian philosophy. This passage is worth quoting in full:

> However, knowledge means that I have the word before me and proceed mindfully in words. Herder has many declamations to the effect that philosophizing is a making and combining of words. By doing this one thinks that one has the thing itself while one proceeds through words, and that this movement through words is only an illusion in which we believe we have the thing itself before us. Cf. Herder's *Ideen zur Geschichte der Menschheit*,

and his *Metacritique*, where he attacks the Kantian philosophy in this way. Names are conditions of thought itself: thinking is consciousness, and so must have an objective [reality] in itself. The content that we possess with the name is what we call the sense (we do not need the image) of which we are conscious, and which we have entirely before us.[1]

This is a curious text. On the one hand, it seems as if Hegel is siding with Herder and the Metacritics against Kant in maintaining that "names are conditions of thought itself," something that Kant seemed explicitly to deny and certainly never mentioned in his own treatments of representation and thought. On the other hand, it is clear from Hegel's preceding discussion of intuition and subsequent treatment of thought (and perhaps also from the somewhat polemical tone of his reference to Herder here) that Hegel could never subscribe to the wholesale "linguistic deconstruction" of Kantian (or, more generally, speculative) philosophy practiced by Herder and his circle. One reading that suggests itself here is that Hegel views signification and language as playing a far more important, even essential, role in human cognition and philosophical reflection than Kant recognized, but that he regarded the metacritical attack on Kantian philosophy as overinflating this role in support of a universal skepticism about all philosophical discourse. Put more simply, Hegel's view might be fairly read as holding that while Kant gave too little credit to language in the general texture of human cognition and thought, Herder and the Metacritics accorded it far too great a scope.

In this chapter, I wish to expand this insight into a more detailed consideration of how Hegel's systematic treatment of language in the *Philosophy of Subjective Spirit* both fills a conspicuous void in Kant's transcendental approach and delimits and counters the universal metacritical skepticism about the possibility of systematic philosophy. Viewed from this perspective, I will suggest that Hegel's linguistic reflections in this text offer an original and positive account of certain features of language needed by Kant and his successors (including Hegel himself) in order to counter the metacritical and other later linguistic assaults on systematic philosophy. I will conclude by considering to what degree Hegel's linguistic views in the present text succeed in this task and what issues remain open.

Kant and the Metacritics

Kant was acquainted, both personally and professionally, with Herder and Hamann (that other "sage of Koenigsberg"), was familiar with the lengthy debate concerning the so-called *'Ursprungsfrage"* initiated by Herder's "Prize Essay" of 1772, and had at least some passing knowledge of British and French empirical and philosophical investigations concerning language.[2] He was therefore well aware that language was emerging as a significant area of empirical and philosophical inquiry when he began the composition of the works that make up his *Critical Philosophy*. However, in a telling passage in the *Prolegomena*, he declared very firmly that the study of language offered nothing of interest to the transcendental philosopher, since, on his view, all linguistic questions were "merely empirical" matters distinct from the necessary and universal principles explored in the Critical Philosophy.[3] True to this principle of exclusion, linguistic issues played no role whatever in that enterprise, even at points like the first (A) version of the Transcendental Deduction, where, given the "transcendental psychological approach" there adopted, one would most expect linguistic considerations to arise.

Kant's own flat rejection of linguistic matters as unworthy of the attention of the critical philosopher immediately opened his project to criticism on precisely those grounds. About the same time as the first edition of the *Critique of Pure Reason* appeared, Hamann drafted a document whose title, "Metakritik," would come to serve as the name of an entire line of linguistic-based criticism directed against Kant's Critical Philosophy and its transcendental approach to philosophical issues.[4] This "metacritical movement," at first more a general attitude than a well-formulated philosophical critique, achieved a fully elaborated form in Herder's *Sprache und Vernunft* of 1799, part 2 of which bore the title "*Eine Metakritik der Kritik der reinen Vernunft.*"[5] Typical of his style at this point of his career, Herder's *Metakritik* was a lengthy, convoluted, often repetitive, and decidedly polemical attack on the Critical Philosophy. Still, several important points emerge quite clearly. In its contours, Herder's critique involved both a broad thesis about philosophical discourse in general and several more specific points directly aimed at Kant's Critical Philosophy.

The more general point, clearly inspired by Hamann's earlier writings, was that any philosophy that presumed to annunciate universal or logically necessary "truths" or "principles" must itself be articulated employing the available resources borrowed from what we would today call a "natural language." However, since natural languages are subject to the vicissitudes and limitations imposed by their own historical and cultural contexts, as well as by the more specific human experiences in conjunction with which languages develop and change, any philosophical language derived from them will be infected by this same contingency and historicity and hence will be incapable of expressing any genuinely universal or necessary "truths" or "principles." At best, philosophical discourse will be merely a restatement of (mostly empirical) generalities already more clearly and forcefully expressed in the natural language from which it is derived; at worst, it will serve to confuse and corrupt the basic soundness of language already well functioning in its "natural contexts." In a way that clearly anticipates later 20th-century developments, Herder's general conclusion was that all sound philosophy can only be *Sprachkritik*, entailing a generalized skepticism about philosophical discourse itself.

More specifically, Herder leveled a whole volley of charges against various aspects of Kant's Critical Philosophy (and that of such practitioners of his "transcendental approach" as Fichte)[6] by way of demonstrating not only that the Kantian transcendental project could not be carried off without reference to linguistic issues but also that it had already begun corrupting the "sound human reason" embodied in the "natural" German language. Among the myriad points that Herder makes in the course of his rather heavy-handed and occasionally confused discussions of Kant's texts, three are worth noting for purposes of the present essay. First, Herder attempts to show that, in his discussion of intuition, Kant failed to realize that the notions of space and time are themselves abstractions based on such "naturally occurring" elements of language as words designating positions and directions relative to the speaker, adverbs and tensed features of verbs, counting words, and so on. Second, on Herder's account, Kant's "transcendental faculties" of imagination and reproduction, rather than being a priori capacities of human cognition, are, in fact, abstract names for such well-known features of natural languages as metaphor and metonymy, reiteration, and even the syntax of complex sentences. While Herder himself does occasionally invoke the "psychological laws of association" already well canvassed by the empiricists, his main point is that, even on such accounts, any description of such processes must involve the intervention of linguistic elements at every point. Finally, Herder argues that Kantian Reason and thought itself rely entirely on words and their combinations. As Hegel quite accurately describes Herder's view in the passage cited earlier, "Philosophizing is a making and combining of words."

In summary, then, Metacritique, especially as developed by Herder, both faults Kant for completely failing to recognize the crucial and ubiquitous role that language plays at every stage of human cognition and further suggests that any philosophy that does the same will end up, like Kant's, merely producing a mass of abstract verbiage that, in Hegel's words, "is only an illusion in which we believe we have the thing itself before us." While the metacritics were surely right in pointing out the unfortunate results of Kant's wholesale dismissal of the role played by language in human cognition and thought, their own "panlinguistic" approach led to a thoroughgoing skepticism regarding any possibility of philosophical thought that ventured beyond the severely limited project of a *Sprachkritik*. Clearly, what was required both to preserve the possibility of the sort of philosophical project commenced by Kant and to counter the skeptical metacritical challenge to it was a view of language that could account for its crucial role in human cognition and thought by elucidating the specific connections among language, cognition, and philosophical reflection, though without going on to collapse all experience and thought into a linguistic "daylight in which all cows are white." This, I suggest, was precisely what Hegel attempted to provide in his own systematic discussion of language.

The Limits of Language in the *Philosophy of Subjective Spirit*

In his short essay, which inaugurated and christened the *Metacritique*, Hamann wrote, taking aim at Kant's "pure forms of intuition": "Sounds and letters are thus pure forms *a priori*, in which there is nothing which belongs to the perception or concept of an object, and they are the true 'aesthetic' elements of all human knowledge and reason."[7]

Almost two decades later, Herder expanded Hamann's insight into a thoroughgoing and detailed analysis of the dependence of all the Kantian "cognitive faculties" on language and concluded, "Reason itself is and is called language."[8] In fact, one of the central *Leitmotiven* of Herder's work was that Kant had introduced a fatal confusion into philosophical discourse with the term *"a priori"*; viewed correctly (that is, from the point of view of the *Metacritique*), Kant *should* have asserted, rather, that language was the true a priori of all human faculties of cognition and thought.[9] On the metacritical view, all human cognition, from bare sensation, through the forms of mental representation, up to Reason itself, presupposed and could be differentiated and elucidated only on the assumption of an already existing natural language as the very ground of their possibility.

Herder's general position, as well as his attempts to demonstrate it in detail (a project that made up the bulk of his *Metakritik*), must have struck Hegel, as it probably does most of us today, as paradoxical and unconvincing, since it left Herder claiming that the cognitive faculties presuppose the existence of natural language at the same time as attempting to account for the origin of natural language on the basis of human sense organs and the cognitive faculties based upon them. Still, the metacritical view was, if exaggerated and paradox-ridden, at least a provocative response to Kant's complete disregard of the role played by language in the overall texture of human cognition and thought. If one rejected their account, then the initial question was to determine where the metacritics had overstated their case, that is, where the limits of the role played by language in human cognition were to be located.

Hegel addresses this issue primarily through the systematic location that he assigns to his discussion of linguistic issues. In the *Philosophy of Subjective Spirit*, Hegel's linguistic considerations occur almost exclusively in the second section of "Psychology" dealing with "Representation." Prior to that, he had discussed the physiological constitution of human being ("Anthropology") and had shown how consciousness emerges from bodily being and develops up to the point of (abstract) Reason ("Phenomenology"). "Psychology" commences when Reason assumes the individuated and embodied form of "Intelligence," the capacity of a living human being to know "objective truth" and appropriate it as its own possession. The first moment of "Psychology," "Theoretical Spirit," then commences with a discussion of "Intuition."

What is important to note is that, over the course of this entire discussion, from the physiological constitution of human being through intuition, language makes no appearance as an operative element or specific theme, even in the "Phenomenology" section where a reader of the Jena *Phenomenology* might well have expected it. Rather, in the Berlin system, Hegel had clearly come to view linguistic issues exclusively as a theme of that part of psychology concerned with the theory of representation. In relation to Kant and his metacritical opponents, Hegel's exclusion of linguistic matters from intuition was reinforced by the fact that, unlike Kant (at least in his theoretical philosophy) and more in line with the metacritics, Hegel tended to treat feeling (*Gefühl*) as a part of intuition. However, unlike Herder, who regarded even feeling as linguistically formed and determined, Hegel specifically notes, in his only reference to language in his discussion of intuition, that "what is true in feeling is the rational" and it is only this that can be expressed in language—in other words, that feeling, taken simply "in itself" and apart from any "rational content" that it may possess, requires no linguistic "medium of expression."[10]

Hegel's treatment in the "Intuition" section of the more familiar Kantian themes of space and time remains consistent with this view. Whereas

Herder went to great lengths to demonstrate that space and time were abstract philosophical concepts based upon certain features of embodied human experience already formed and determined by natural language, Hegel's discussion emphasizes, with Kant, that they are "nondiscursive" and hence, so to speak, "prelinguistic." As Hegel states, "Space and time are the forms of the sensible, forms of intuition. They are not the real [element] in intuition, i.e. determinations of feeling."[11]

Similarly, in the section entitled "Thought" that immediately follows "Representation," linguistic issues no longer explicitly appear and cease to be a thematic concern. Because, as we will later see, Hegel regards signification and language as essential elements of representation, which itself is the necessary foundation of thought, thought will always presuppose and contain an irreducibly linguistic element. This much Hegel grants to the metacritics, as the passage quoted earlier clearly indicates. However, where the metacritics argued that it is in the realm of thought that language and its contingencies are most problematic and intrusive, Hegel's position seems to be that once signification and language have been properly understood as essential elements of representation, linguistic issues no longer intervene in any significant way at the level of thought.

To summarize, then, in the *Philosophy of Subjective Spirit*, Hegel presents signification and language as operative elements exclusively within an account of representation. Clearly, this is a significant departure from Kant's own dismissive view of language as a "merely empirical matter" having no role to play in a proper transcendental inquiry, and it is an important concession to the metacritical challenge to Kant. However, Hegel nonetheless preserves the general contours of Kant's view against the attacks of the metacritics by affirming the "nondiscursive," "pre-linguistic" character of intuition and its own preconditions, and by maintaining (in a certain sense) the autonomy of thought from the contingencies of natural language. Clearly, then, for Hegel, there are quite determinate limits to the role played by signification and language within human cognition, but within those limits, much remains to be said.

Hegel's Systematic Account of Signification and Language

Any reader of the section entitled "Psychology" in Hegel's *Philosophy of Subjective Spirit* must be struck by the degree to which its structure reflects that of Kant's Critical Philosophy. Its two major divisions are "Theoretical Spirit" and "Practical Spirit," and the former is further subdivided into

"Intuition," "Representation," and "Thought," paralleling Kant's distinctions between theoretical and practical reason and the former's subdivision into intuition, judgment, and understanding/reason. Even more, under the heading of "Representation," Hegel emphasizes the faculties of memory and imagination, which also appear in Kant's "transcendental psychology." This overall correspondence becomes especially striking when one compares Hegel's ordering and treatment of the "psychological faculties" with Kant's presentation in the first ('A') version of the Transcendental Deduction.[12] It would be fair to say, then, that Hegel adopted the general architecture of Kantian "transcendental psychology" as the structure of his own discussion of cognition.

Still, Hegel does, in fact, significantly expand and sometimes diverge from Kant's treatment especially with respect to representation, but it is sufficient for present purposes to note that, if Hegel's discussion is not a defense of the 'letter" of Kant's account, it is at least developed within the general "spirit" of the Critical Philosophy and is sharply opposed to the framework underlying the metacritical approach. Although I will not pursue this point in detail in the discussion that follows, I would suggest at the outset that several of Hegel's most conspicuous divergences from Kant's treatment of representation result precisely from the fact that Hegel had come to view the Kantian approach as requiring the intervention of linguistic considerations to assure its very coherence. That is, without the "exteriorization" of intelligence effected by signification and language, Kant's account of representation must remain merely subjective and unable to accomplish its own stated aim of establishing the objectivity of cognition and thought; it would thus continue to be vulnerable to the metacritical challenge. Along the same lines, I would also venture that, once Hegel began introducing signification and language into his account of representation, he saw that certain important emendations of Kant's "cognitive architecture" would be required.

In what follows, I want to show that, in his treatment of psychology generally and representation in particular, Hegel adopts a novel strategy involving a specific sort of "dynamic parallel discourse." Hegel's discussion of linguistic issues, in line with the general heading of "Psychology" in which it occurs, is based upon a sort of "faculty psychology" closely related, as we have already seen, to that of Kant. Its major "moments" are Intuition, Representation, and Thought. Representation is itself further subdivided into recollection (*Erinnerung*), imagination (with three subdivisions), and memory (*Gedächtnis*). Paralleling and intertwined with this discourse of cognitive capacities is a second "significational discourse." The two discourses are related in the following way. Beginning with the faculty of intuition, each successive faculty produces its own "significational counterpart" which (1) serves as its characteristic "objective expression," (2) provides the "content" taken up and internalized by the succeeding faculty, and (3) thus effects the transition from one cognitive faculty to the next. In a sense, then, the "significational discourse" is offset against the "faculty discourse" so that each "significational determination" creates the link and transition between any given faculty and the next.[13] At the risk of employing an expression that sometimes glosses or muddles more than it clarifies, we might say that Hegel offers an integrated "dialectical" account of the relation between cognition and linguistic determinations whereby the development of cognitive capacities is mediated at every point by specific significational elements and, reciprocally, where each form of signification produced by one cognitive capacity provides the transition to the next.

To understand the novelty of Hegel's strategy, we can briefly compare it to two other previous approaches, neither of which could fairly be called "dialectical" or even "integrated." Herder's approach in his *Metakritik* to relating cognitive faculties to linguistic determinations was simply to cite various elements of already existing natural languages as a sort of "linguistic *a priori*" on which the functioning of the various cognitive capacities was based. He did, of course, tend to think of both cognitive capacities and linguistic determinations as having an underlying developmental order, but his account of their interrelations involved more a loose set of empirical-like observations concerning points of intersection rather than a unitary and integrated account of their reciprocal and dynamic influences on one another. By contrast, Fichte proposed what he called a "speculative grammar" to parallel what amounted to his "transcendental psychology." However, rather than showing the ways in which one dynamically interacted with the other, he presented "speculative grammar" as its own "deductive series" which would parallel the "deductive series" of the cognitive faculties. In so doing, he acknowledged, with Hegel, the failure of Kant to accord any role to linguistic matters within the context of human cognition and thought and arguably improved upon the metacritical approach. Still, Fichte's account failed, in this as in other aspects of his philosophy (as famously noted by Hegel in the *Differenzschrift*), to effect a unified and systematic account of the matter.[14]

One further point about Hegel's account of cognition and signification is important to keep in mind. The systematic task of Hegel's discussion of representation is to effect the absolutely crucial transition from the singular, diffuse, and subjective nature of intuition to the universal, integrated, and objective realm of thinking. The trajectory of Hegel's discussion and hence the order of appearance of both the cognitive capacities and their significational expressions is based upon the relative degree to which they have extricated themselves from the determinacy of "externally given content" and entered the realm of the self-determining freedom of thought. As such, Hegel has little to say either about the specific grammatical and syntactical features of natural language or about how individuals come to acquire language (favorite themes of many of his predecessors, including the metacritics). Rather, Hegel's project should be regarded as a genuine "philosophy of language," not a "transcendental grammar" or an "empirical linguistics."

Hegel states that "every stage of spirit is a special individual form and every stage contributes to the concreteness of spirit."[15] We might add that every stage of spirit produces its own characteristic form of expression that provides the basis and transition to the next stage of spirit. This "rule" will govern the following, admittedly schematic, presentation.

As a general and simplified outline of "Theoretical Spirit," Hegel offers the following structure:[16]

Intuition—Image
Representation—Sign, Word, and Language
Thought—Concept (via Memory)

Already it is clear, as mentioned earlier, that the treatment of Representation must bear the entire weight of the all-important transition from Intuition to Thought. Hegel underscores the importance of this section by claiming: "Representation is different from intuition and feeling. But it is also essentially different from concept and thought. It is essential to make this distinction in speculative philosophy."[17] His preliminary presentation also clearly affirms that a proper understanding of the complex role played in this section by signification and language lies at the heart of his argument.

However, after this preliminary outline, when Hegel comes to his more specific discussion, it turns out that Representation, unlike Intuition and Thought, is itself internally complex, that it consists of several different though closely interrelated "faculties." These will provide the actual scaffolding for his detailed consideration of signification and language.

Intuition—Sensuous Image (Bild)

Unlike Kant (at least in his theoretical philosophy), Hegel tends to associate intuition with "feeling" and claims that, "in intuition, I was immersed in immediate being."[18] Like Kant, however, Hegel insists that intuition is "non-discursive," that it does not yet involve the universality (and hence "objectivity') of concepts. It is "pre-conceptual" and thus "pre-linguistic." However, as a capacity of human cognition, it involves a drive to express itself, and this expression is the "image." As Hegel puts it,

> The intelligence, as positing intuition inwardly, posits the content of feeling in itself, in its own space and time, and so the content [of feeling] becomes an image. Image = when the given, which is in the form of immediacy, has sensible content.[19]

The image, that is, is entirely based upon and reiterates the "immediately given (sensuous) content" of intuition. In one sense, the image appears as merely another intuition, but, in another, it is has disengaged itself from the subject's mere "immersion in given content" and "is taken [abstractly] out of the space and time in which it was, and now exists in my space and my time."[20] Hegel goes on to claim that "image means that the intuition is mine" and that "it no longer possesses the complete determinacy or the uniqueness determined by all points (of context) that are possessed by the intuition." The sensuous image, that is, is a copy of the intuition on which it is based but exists not in the externality of the sensuously given but within the subject itself. Freed from the "external" conditions of space and time, it becomes a possession of the subject that the subject can voluntarily reproduce within its own "psychic space and time" and communicate to others through, perhaps, gestures or drawings.

Recollection (Erinnerung) — Psychic Image (or Representation Proper)

Hegel emphasizes the meaning of the term "*Erinnerung*" (to "internalize" or "make inner") in defining "recollection proper" as "the inwardizing of the image in the intelligence, not the disappearance from, but the complete immersion of the image in the intelligence and its connection with an intuition that belongs to me."[21] The internalized or "psychic" image, that is, is Janus-faced: on one side, it remains connected to the original intuition of which it is a copy; on the other, it has become a possession of the subject, which "can for the first time repeat the intuition as it were,"[22] though "in my space and my time."

Recollection thus effects a separation of the "psychical order" of images that can be freely recalled from the immediately experienced sequence of intuitions. Freed from the sensuous particularity of intuition, the "psychic image" "is supported [no longer by its context but] by itself."[23] (Hegel sometimes refers to the "psychic image" as a "representation" in the narrow sense of something that is "made present again within consciousness.") For Hegel, the most important result of this is that "the image that belongs to me has acquired the determination of the universal."[24] It is, of course, not a "universal" in the sense of an idea or concept, but it permits a certain degree of generality so that, for instance, one might draw the image of "a cat" (in a nonspecific, generic sense) rather than "the cat that I see here on my sofa."

Reproductive Imagination (reproduktive Einbildungskraft) — Abstract Representation

Put simply, whereas the function of recollection is, as Hegel famously puts it, to "bur[y] the image . . . in the pit of my consciousness,"[25] that of the reproductive imagination is to retrieve images, now freed of their particular intuitional contexts, so that they are "capable of being expressed."[26] Hegel emphasizes here that, just as Recollection had bestowed a certain sort of universality (or, perhaps better, generality) on the image, the Reproductive Imagination, in calling forth images, makes them "objective to the intelligence, and so the intelligence knows of the object it has reproduced." Hegel sometimes refers to the general and objective image as an "abstract representation," which he regards as the proper designation for what some empiricists such as Locke called "ideas.'[27] This result of the working of the Reproductive Imagination brings us to the threshold of the point where signification proper begins to intervene in Hegel's account.

Productive Imagination (produktive Einbildungskraft or Phantasie) — Signs

Taking over the "abstract representations" produced by the Reproductive Imagination, the Productive Imagination varies and places them in diverse combinations. It is "a free connecting of representations, a presentation that connects the image to the explication of its proper sense — its proper sense is the universal — as processed representation."[28]

To demonstrate how "sense" emerges, Hegel refers to symbol as the simplest example of the working of the Productive Imagination. An "abstract representation," which is still a sort of image, can be paired or associated with another. When this occurs, as when an image of a fox is associated with, say, an image of Odysseus, then the former can be said to function as a symbol for the latter. Hegel tells us:

Symbol is an image, the content of an intuition, but it no longer has a simple, natural sense; rather it has a second sense. The one is the immediate sense of intuition, the second is the [symbolic] sense. In the symbol as such, the intuition as such according to its proper essential content, is the same as what the meaning, the sense is.[29]

Like the role of the image with respect to intuition and recollection, the symbol has a dual aspect: on the one hand, it is an internalized, recollected image; on the other, it has a "second sense" arising from its "productive pairing" with another image or representation.

Expanding and generalizing on such a simple example, Hegel explains the "sign" as the result of "the drive of externalization" implied in the productive capacity of the Imagination. A sign arises when some "external immediate [means]," itself spatial and temporal (Hegel mentions "a sound, a tone, a color")[30] is associated by the Productive Imagination with an [internal] "abstract representation." In so doing, a "second sense" or "meaning" of the sign is produced. A sign, therefore, always possesses a dual aspect: "The one is the meaning, the sense of the sign, that which is represented; the other is that which represents."[31] (Later these two aspects would be called the "signified" and the "signifier.")

Sign-Making Imagination (Zeichenmachende Phantasie) —
Words and Language

Although Hegel sometimes seems to elide this "faculty" with the Productive Imagination, he does, in fact, clearly present it as a third form of Imagination, especially in the 1830 outline of the *Enzyklopädie*.[32] The contrast seems to be that, whereas signs are the result of the operation of the Productive Imagination, the "Sign-Making Imagination" takes these still somewhat discrete signs and places them in various combinations so that they become integral parts—words—of the higher unity of language. As Hegel states, "Immediate things [and here I read him as meaning intuitable signs] acquire a second existence in and through language."[33]

There follows a lengthy and somewhat digressive discussion about the relative advantages of spoken versus written language and, with respect to the latter, about hieroglyphic versus alphabetic forms of writing. We can summarize Hegel's conclusions briefly by noting that he regards "the sign whose externality is time, namely, sound and language" as "much more appropriate to intelligence"[34] and that, of written forms of language, alphabetic systems, which are more directly connected with spoken language, have a decisive advantage by way of simplification and capacity for expressing abstract ideas.

Memory (Gedächtnis)—Names

In order to understand Hegel's complex discussion of the crucial final moment of Representation, it is well to observe that the root of the word he employs (Gedächtnis) is denken, thinking, which will be the next major moment of his presentation. Not to be confused with Recollection (Erinnerung), whose primary task is to "inwardize" the images derived from intuition, Memory operates at the furthest remove (within Representation) from all images. Hegel explains:

> First the object is preserved in the intelligence as image. Like the object, the image has an immediate sensible quality. The name is a second mode [of existence] of the sensible as it has been produced by the intelligence. The name is the determinate existence of the content so that we do not need the image at all; we do not need to bring the image of the content before us.[35]

As noted above, words are linguistic signs which still retain an "imagistic element" alongside their sense or meaning. On the one hand, names have no such connection and are, in that sense, completely arbitrary. On the other hand, "we have the entire content while we have the name before us,"[36] though without having to imagine the content itself. In the name, the entire "content" of intuition and meaning is stripped away, leaving us in the purified realm of "meaningless signs."[37]

Hegel calls that faculty dealing exclusively with names "Mechanical Memory." As he notes, "It appears miraculous that the spirit, this essential freedom at home with itself, relates to itself externally in its [own] inwardness in an entirely mechanical way."[38] And yet, Hegel says that it is "of the greatest importance in relation to thought" to realize that it is precisely this complete detachment from the sensuousness of the image and its particularities that first makes genuine thinking possible. As any reader of Hegel will immediately understand, it is only at the most extreme point of alienation, of the abject emptiness of meaning, that "Thought," a new form of truth and objectivity, can arise.

Some Concluding Reflections

We began by suggesting that Hegel's account of signification and language be considered as a simultaneous response to Kant's dismissal of such issues as relevant to philosophy and the metacritics' insistence that all philosophy resolve itself into *Sprachkritik*. I want now briefly to assess Hegel's response on each count.

The response to Kant: Had Hegel to choose between the two, his sympathies clearly lay with Kant, as one would expect. After all, he adopted Kant's own "transcendental psychology" as his operative framework and, as I have suggested, offered his own revisions of it and his account of signification and language as providing the necessary supplements that would render successful Kant's attempt to establish the objectivity of human cognition and knowledge. Still, it is also true that Kant himself jettisoned the entire approach based on cognitive faculties adopted in the first version of his Transcendental Deduction for a quite different form of presentation that, arguably, could dispense with them. Thus, even if a die-hard Kantian might admit that a discussion of signification and language was required by Kant's first attempt, s/he might still claim that the second succeeds without such an account as Hegel's.[39]

More broadly, however, Hegel's account of the cognitive faculties as well as language and signification is "dialectical," not "transcendental." Though Fichte's original attempt at a transcendental account might also fall to the metacritical critique, a more sophisticated transcendental treatment, such as that of Husserl's, might yet meet with more success.[40]

Surely Hegel was right in thinking that signification and language plays a far more important role in cognition and thought than Kant was willing to admit, as we have learned well in the time separating us from Kant. But one might have hesitations about whether developing a theory of signification and language on the basis of a "faculty psychology" like that of Kant can provide a suitable foundation for such a project. Certainly many present "philosophers of language" would share such suspicions.

The response to Herder and the Metacritics:

Hegel makes two key points against the metacritical attack. The first is his delimitation of the role of signification and language within the context of human cognition. On this score, Hegel seems rather successful, especially in light of the fact that Herder's account was itself beset with paradoxes of its own stemming directly from his "pan-linguistic" stance. The more limited role that Hegel assigns to signification and language allowed him to avoid such paradoxes and shed a good deal of light on issues that are rather muddled in Herder's account, when they arise at all.

The second is that names, properly understood, provide thought with "pure linguistic determinations" freed of all the historical, cultural, and individual particularities that the *Metacritique* alleged to contaminate any philosophical attempt to state universal, necessary, or objective truths. According to Hegel, names, unlike mere words or other signs, are image- and representation-free, hence ahistorical, transcultural, and objective, making them the sole suitable "vehicle" for thought.

Were Hegel right about this, then one of the metacritics' main challenges would be successfully met. But to accept Hegel's view would also entail, for example, that all the determinations of his *Science of Logic* are themselves "names." This would, in turn, imply some claim on Hegel's part about the identity of name and concept, since he is insistent that the determinations of the *Logic* are, first and foremost, concepts. Thus, while Hegel's theory of names might well address the metacritics, considerably more discussion would be required to accept Hegel's view when considering his logical writings. Hegel does not address this question in the *Philosophy of Subjective Spirit* or anywhere else in his writings of which I am aware. That is not to say that such a case could not be made, only that I do not believe Hegel himself (or anyone else) has as yet made it. On this score, I can only conclude that, if Hegel's theory of names was in fact a response to the metacritics (as I have suggested it was), then it raises potentially more difficult problems for other parts of his philosophical view.[41]

To summarize, Hegel's account of signification and language in the *Philosophy of Subjective Spirit* is a novel and thought-provoking effort to resolve an important controversy that had been in the offing since the end of the 18th century. In its general contours, it likely moved the discussion of these issues forward a considerable degree. But it remains somewhat sketchy and overly schematic in its details and, at certain points, may well have created more problems for other areas of Hegel's thought than it resolved. The fact is, one wishes that Hegel had written a detailed and worked out "philosophy of language" to place alongside his philosophies of art, religion, history, and politics. Why he did not and where, if he had, he would have located it within his system are intriguing questions yet to be explored.

Notes

1. LPS, 233.
2. The most comprehensive study of Kant's knowledge of and views regarding linguistic issues, including a detailed discussion of Kant's motives for excluding

them from his critical philosophy, is Jürgen Villers, *Kant und das problem der Sprache. Die historischen and systematischen Gründe für die Sprachlosigkeit der Transzendentalphilosophie* (Konstanz: Verlag am Hochgraben, 1997).

3. *Kants Werke, Akademie-Textausgabe* (Berlin, 1968), vol. 4, 322–23. L. W. Beck's translation of this passage reads: "To search in our common knowledge for the concepts which do not rest upon particular experience and yet occur in all knowledge from experience, of which they as it were constitute the mere form of connection, presupposes neither greater reflection nor deeper insight than to detect in language the rules of the actual use of words generally and thus to collect elements of a grammar (in fact both researches are very nearly related), even though we are not able to give a reason why each language has just this and no other formal constitution, and still less why any precise number of such formal determinations in general, neither more nor less, can be found in it." See Villers for other similar citations.

4. See Jere Paul Surber, *Metacritique: The Linguistic Assault on German Idealism* (Amherst, NY: Humanity Books, 2001), henceforth cited as MC. This volume contains an extended essay on the "metacritical movement" as well as introductions and translations of some of its key texts. Hamann's "Metacritique of the Critique of the Purism of Reason" is translated in full, preceded by a discussion of the quite interesting circumstances under which it was written.

It is also worth noting that Hegel was familiar with this work. His long review of Hamann's writings published in 1828 contains extended quotations from this essay, which Hegel refers to as "very remarkable" and suggests that, though "highly baroque" in style, it is far superior to Herder's work bearing the same title. While Hegel does not directly engage Hamann's views about language (though his insertion of "(!?)" at one point is suggestive), neither does he offer any defense of Kant on this issue. Inconclusive as it is for present concerns, Hegel's *Hamann-Rezension* does provide further evidence that linguistic issues, and the *Metakritik* in particular, were very much on Hegel's mind at the time of his lectures on Subjective Spirit. See G. W. F. Hegel, *Berliner Schriften 1818–1831*, ed. Walter Jaeschke (Hamburg: Felix Meiner, 1997), 291ff.

5. Refer to MC, 85–130, for an introduction and abridged translation of this work. What follows is a brief summary of points made by Herder. See also Surber's introduction for a more detailed account.

6. It seems that part of the spleen underlying Herder's attack arose from the fact that his own son had come under the influence of Fichte's allegedly "atheistic doctrines." See MC, 87.

7. MC, 60.
8. MC, 128.
9. See MC, 99ff.
10. LPS, 207–08.
11. LPS, 212.
12. See diagram 1 at the end of this essay. Burkhard Tuschling's introduction to the German text of LPS (1827–28) provides further evidence for the close connection between Kant's Transcendental Deductions and Hegel's treatment of representation.

13. See diagram 2, where I offer a schematic presentation of the "two discourses" and their interrelations. In devising this diagram and its accompanying discussion, I am well aware of the facts that none of Hegel's textual variants of this section are as clear as one might wish (or, perhaps, as my diagram and discussions suggest), and that there are some variations in themes and treatment among them. In my discussion, I rely mainly on the "transcripts" of the 1827–28 lectures and the final published version of Hegel's "Outline" in *Enzyklopädie der philosophischen Wissenschaften* (1830), ed. F. Nicolin and O. Pöggeler (Hamburg: Meiner, 1969). Although these variations over the course of Hegel's thought about signification and language deserve more attention than they have as yet received, my main concern in this essay is to demonstrate the broader points that, whatever the particular details, Hegel (1) viewed these issues as unfolding in direct correspondence with the various stages of the development of "Subjective Spirit" presented in the sections "Intuition" and "Representation" and (2) regarded them as essential elements of this development. I emphasize the latter point because, in some versions, much of Hegel's discussion of significational and linguistic issues appeared as "*Zusätze*," perhaps creating the impression that they were merely supplemental or peripheral. My presentation is designed to demonstrate that this is most certainly not the case.

14. On Fichte's contributions to this discussion, see Jere Paul Surber, *Language and German Idealism: Fichte's Linguistic Philosophy* (Atlantic Highlands, NJ: Humanities Press, 1996). This volume contains a translation and commentary on Fichte's essay on language of 1795. For Fichte's project of a "speculative grammar," see pp. 127ff. See also Surber's discussion on 21–22.

15. LPS, 215.
16. LPS, 205.
17. LPS, 213.
18. LPS, 214.
19. LPS, 215.
20. LPS, 216.
21. LPS, 217.
22. LPS, 218.
23. LPS, 216.
24. LPS, 217.
25. LPS, 217.
26. LPS, 218.
27. Cf. LPS, 219ff.
28. LPS, 222.
29. LPS, 222.
30. LPS, 224.
31. LPS, 224.
32. Cf. *Enzyklopädie* (1830), 368 (cited above).
33. LPS, 225.
34. LPS, 224.

35. LPS, 230. See the translator's introduction to LPS, 33ff. Jim Vernon, in *Hegel's Philosophy of Languge* (London and New York: Continuum, 2007) also offers a detailed and lucid discussion of the role played by *Gedächtnis* in the form of "mechanical memory" as a basis for the transition from Representation to Thought. Cf. pp. 73ff.

36. LPS, 232.

37. Cf. LPS, 233.

38. LPS, 234.

39. I would venture that one of the major dividing points between many Neo-Kantians and Hegelians would be precisely the issue of whether recourse to a theory of signification and language was necessary in order to establish the necessity and universality of synthetic a priori judgments and, more broadly, human knowledge itself.

40. I have in mind here Husserl's treatment of signification and language in his *Logical Investigations* and *Experience and Judgment*.

41. This is an issue that Vernon, in his excellent recent work cited above, who lays particular stress on the role of names and "mechanical memory" as the necessary and immediate foundation for thinking, fails to address. More generally, unlike him, I am not convinced that it is possible to construct a "Hegelian Philosophy of Language" that would at once be self-consistent, possess a determinate location within Hegel's system, and bear the weight of Hegel's philosophical aspirations.

KANT (Transcendental Deduction "A"):	HEGEL (Philosophy of Subjective Spirit):
Intuition	Intuition (includes "Feeling")
	*******************************
	Representation
	Recollection ("*Erinnerung*")
Reproductive Imagination	Imagination
	Reproductive Imagination
	Productive Imagination
	Sign-Making Imagination
	Memory (*Gedächtnis*)
	*******************************
Understanding (Concept) ["Transcendental Unity of Apperception"]	Thought

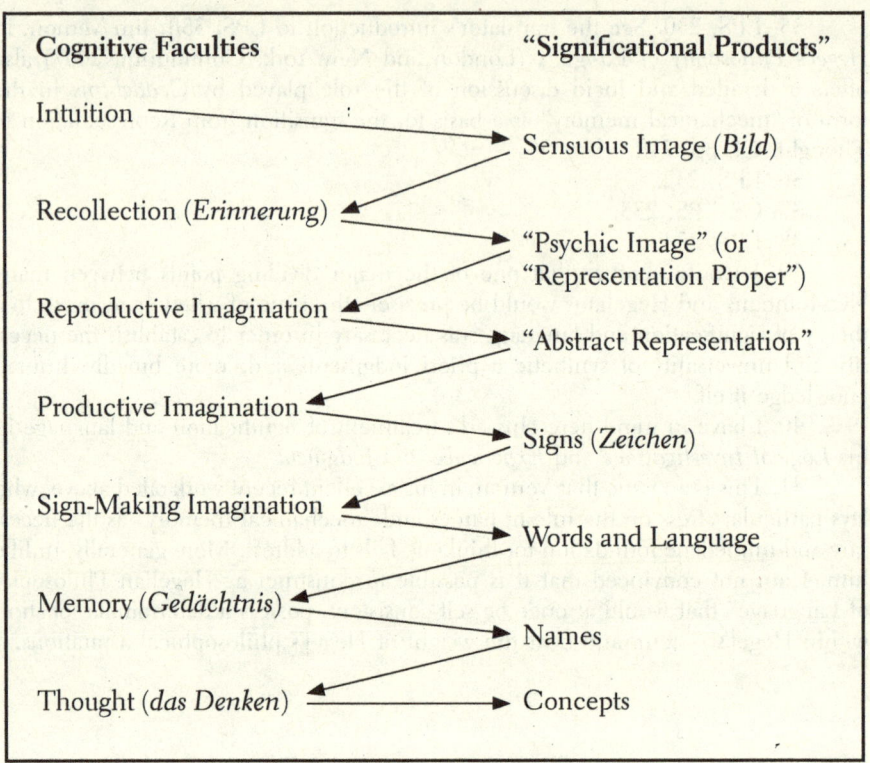

The Psychology of Will and the Deduction of Right

Rethinking Hegel's Theory of Practical Intelligence

RICHARD DIEN WINFIELD

Hegel's *Philosophy of Subjective Spirit* is perhaps the most neglected part of his system, and no portion of that work has lingered in deeper oblivion than its concluding section "Practical Intelligence." That section, however, is doubly significant. First, Hegel's account of "Practical Intelligence" provides an important contribution to comprehending will as it falls within the philosophy of mind. Second, that account brings the *Philosophy of Subjective Spirit* to closure and ushers in the *Philosophy of Objective Spirit*. In so doing, the theory of practical intelligence consummates the philosophy of mind and provides the conceptual prerequisites for normative conduct, the topic of *Objective Spirit*. The theory of practical intelligence thereby constitutes the derivation of the concept of right, the reality of the free will. This means that practical intelligence comprises the will that is not yet truly free, yet furnishes individuals all they need to freely determine themselves.

To understand practical intelligence the different dimensions of willing and the separate accounts Hegel provides for them must be distinguished. Generally, the *Philosophy of Right* addresses the reality of the free will, whereas the *Philosophy of Subjective Spirit* addresses the will as psychologically determined. The introduction to the *Philosophy of Right*, however, restates the development of practical intelligence as it appears in the *Philosophy of Spirit*. This account is not part of the Idea of Right, but rather recapitulates the concluding section of the philosophy of mind that provides what Hegel calls the deduction of the concept of right.[1] Further, the psychological account of will as practical intelligence must not be confused with the logical account of will provided in Hegel's *Logic* and *Science of Logic*.[2] Logically speaking, will is a subject that strives to make itself something which unites subjectivity and objectivity by transforming what confronts it so as to conform to the subject's own determination. As such, will has a determinacy, its aim, which is to be made objective. Because will's aim initially lacks objectivity, the will is subjective and finite, bounded by the objectivity that lies beyond it. Thus will presupposes the self-subsisting independence of the objectivity it sets out to annul. By urging itself on to unify subjectivity and objectivity, will extinguishes its own activity, which only proceeds so long as that unification has not been attained.[3]

Will as mind adds to these logical determinations a natural and psychological concretization. With respect to mind, objectivity comprises a natural world containing the living subject whose own subjectivity has a living, animal-embodied being in the world. That embodiment combines the individual's physiological species being with the psychological dimensions of mind, which have physiological ramifications of their own.

If the involvement of mind and body in volition is evident, whether will as mind is practical intelligence is controversial. This question, which Hegel answers affirmatively, is sometimes confused with whether will necessarily involves thinking, whether will is practical reason. If will does involve thought, then it becomes problematic to attribute will to nonrational animals or children who have yet to develop linguistic intelligence. Because, however, intelligence includes intuition and representation as well as thought, the identification of will with practical intelligence bears upon a more fundamental divide distinguishing intelligence from psyche and consciousness. Then will may be attributed to both dumb animals and prelinguistic children, who lack reason but intuit and imagine.

Granting these possibilities, why should will be practical intelligence and not just an engagement of psyche and consciousness? Underlying this question is the more fundamental question of how will can comprise something irreducible to desire and reason. The famous absence of any word for "will" in classical Greek philosophy reflects the common dogma of Plato and Aristotle that mind can do nothing independent from our desires or our reason.[4] How, then, can action, goal-directed behavior, proceed without subordination to desire or reason? If will is practical intelligence, volition's irreducibility to desire and reason must thereby be explicable.

To determine whether will is practical intelligence requires establishing whether will constitutively involves not just psyche and consciousness, but intelligence. Intelligence unites the features of psyche and consciousness, such that mind relates to its own content as both subjective and objective. This occurs in various ways, involving successive degrees of immediacy and mediation. Intuition immediately relates to a manifold that it intuits to be both its own subjective modification and something immediately given in opposition to its own intuiting subjectivity. Representation internalizes the immediately given contents of intuition and modifies them through imagination without relinquishing the objective reference of what is imagined. Finally, linguistic intelligence enables reason to conceive concepts that are both subjective determinations of the mind's thinking and determinations ascribed objectivity.

Why should intelligence be necessary for volition? Certainly linguistic intelligence is necessary for any acting upon rational principle, since without language and thought, volition could not pursue an end requiring conceptualization. If volition constitutively entailed acting upon the conception of some good or principle of volition, will would be unique to thinking, speaking individuals.

Yet, are there not dimensions of volition devoid of conceptualization, without which acting on principle is not even possible? Willing can hardly pursue rational ends or principles without choosing, that is, committing to some aim. Yet can the choosing will not opt for following urges that relate to purely singular objects and situations, which can be intuited and represented without conceptualization? To choose to fulfill an urge, the individual must comprehend how it can alter the given world it confronts to conform to its aim. Some understanding of the mechanical, chemical, and biological relations of objectivity is required, since otherwise the individual would have no way of understanding what need be done to effect the satisfaction of its urge. Yet, such connections can be anticipated without concepts so long as the individual can recall similar associations, making use of images and general representations. This possibility renders linguistic intelligence unnecessary for choice, but it does not preclude intelligence insofar as intelligence can involve intuition and representation, with or without thinking. If volition cannot proceed without intuitions and representations, and these involve intelligence and not just psyche or consciousness, then volition would be practical intelligence with the possibility of both prelinguistic and linguistic forms.

Hegel does not confine volition to an explicitly thinking activity, but details a series of forms of willing that make possible acting on principle, yet involve prelinguistic intuitions and representations.[5] If this option is to hold up to scrutiny, identifying volition with practical intelligence, but allowing for prelinguistic as well as linguistic forms, prelinguistic volition must be impossible solely with psyche and/or consciousness. Yet given that the psyche and consciousness both involve embodied activity, why should such activity not qualify as volition?

The activity in which the psyche engages is at once mental and physiological, and neither consciousness nor intelligence can proceed without it. This activity involves the mental registering of life processes both internal to the individual's living organism and reflecting its metabolism with its environment. On both accounts, the psyche registers modifications given to its sensibility, monitoring these modifications as alterations of its subjective field of feeling. In so doing, the psyche is not merely passively receptive, but engages in the self-activity of a feeling self that, in feeling its own mental registrations, acts upon itself while interacting with its biosphere. This activity and self-activity does not yet differentiate subject and object. Rather, the psyche modifies its own sensibility by feeling its own feelings, engendering habits through repeated self-registerings of the feeling self. Habituation allows the mind to distance itself from certain of its feelings in function of its own history of self-feeling activity, setting the stage for the psyche to give expression to its feelings in bodily gestures distinct from the physiological embodiment of those feelings themselves. Without feeling, habituation, and expression, the individual would be in no position to detach itself from its given mental manifold, treat any of it as an end, and endeavor to realize that end in the world. Feeling provides the mental manifold for every further function of mind. Habit, enabling the feeling self to inure itself to repeated feelings, allows mind to distance itself from some of its mental contents and retain the imprint of feelings that are not immediately felt. Although this sets the stage for retaining mental contents that could figure as an end to be realized through action, it does not provide opposition to an objectivity in which aims are to be carried out. So long as the individual remains caught in the preconscious self-communion of the psyche, where all determinations are registered simply as contents of mind, there can be no passage from inner subjectivity to outer objectivity, no realization of ends by which volition can operate.[6]

Consciousness provides the needed opposition of subject and object and acts upon its embodied self while engaging with the objectivity from which it distinguishes its awareness.[7] Nevertheless, mere consciousness will not suffice for volition. If the individual is aware only of an opposing objectivity, but not of his or her embodied self, mind cannot entertain ends of its own, nor distinguish whether any alteration in the perceived world is the result of mind's own embodied agency. To have an end, mind must be aware of its own mental contents in face of an objective world in which it comprehends that that content is to be realized through mind's own activity. Further, unless mind can be conscious of and recognize its own embodied self in its active engagement with the world, volition can hardly occur. At most, the conscious mind might experience the correlation of mental contents and objective events as well as the interaction of its body with its biosphere. Consciousness would not, however, be aware of any *practical* connection between its mental contents, such as desires, purposes, and intentions, with the objects it perceives. Consciousness would not thereby be conscious of its mental contents actualizing themselves in objectivity.

Self-consciousness might appear already to involve will insofar as desire sets the individual in a practical relation to objects, entailing action modifying them. Desire, however, figures as a minimal shape of self-consciousness by relating to its objects purely negatively. Desire enables consciousness to be aware of its own self by obliterating the independent subsistence of the object of desire. The object here succumbs to desire, whose consuming appetite relates consciousness to its own self only by removing, albeit in a partial, particular fleeting way, its relation to some independent other. Appetite does not realize an end in the world, making subjectivity objective. Rather it cancels a part of that world, reducing it to the subject.[8]

This empty obliteration is superseded, admittedly, when one conscious individual satisfies another's desire through observable behavior. The acquiescing individual desires the desire satisfaction of the other, but the beneficiary does not yet recognize the desire of its benefactor. The beneficiary does not engage in any volition, since the beneficiary does not itself realize any end of its own. Its benefactor, however, does act to satisfy the beneficiary's desire.[9] Why does this serving activity not qualify as volition and allow volition to occur without intelligence?

Moreover, when parties engage in an evenhanded recognitive desire, where individuals reciprocally serve the appetite of one another, all act to satisfy the desire of another, whose desire aims at their satisfaction as well. Through this recognition, each is indirectly conscious of its own desire, as reflected in the satisfaction provided by its counterpart.[10] Why, then, is the behavior engaged in by each not volition?

The key reason is that the behavior in both cases remains pursuant to quenching appetite, achieved not by realizing an end in a transformed objectivity but by consuming the object of desire. Other forms of recognition may well involve purpose and intention, where ends do attain a positive realization. In those cases, volition will be at play. Here, however, where only self-consciousness is engaged, behavior remains in the thrall of appetite.

What intelligence adds that appetitive behavior lacks are abiding mental determinations that remain both subjective and objective. Whereas appetite may be intentional, confronting an object to be consumed, appetite remains solely subjective. It does not seek to make itself objective, translating its mental content into something nonmental. Desire does not aim to make its object desirous. Rather, desire relates to its objective correlate as an inherent nullity, absorbable into subjectivity. That absorption may well involve the activity of an embodied individual, both feeling and conscious, but that behavior does not aim at making the individual's mental content something objective. For behavior to have an end that it consciously effects in the world, the individual must entertain a mental content that is both its own subjective possession as well as something it recognizes to be objectifiable through the activity of the individual. Only then can it figure as an end, and only then can volition occur to the degree that end-oriented action distinguishes volition from appetitive behavior.

Whether or not the end has any conceptual character, it figures in inverse relation to the mental contents of theoretical intelligence. Theoretical intelligence modifies its own subjective mental content so that it corresponds to given objectivity, obtaining the subjective/objective unity of truth.[11] By contrast, action in pursuit of an end proceeds from a subjective mental content that the individual relates to as something with which it is to generate its own corresponding object by modifying the world to which it belongs.

Despite this inversion, one can expect the differentiations of theoretical intelligence to provide a structural clue to the forms of practical intelligence. Although the end of volition is not knowledge, like knowledge it is a subjective mental content to which objectivity becomes joined. Hence, the different modes by which theoretical intelligence determines its subjective unity of subject and object should bear upon the different ways in which the end of volition can be determined. Since theoretical intelligence has intuitions, representations, and thoughts as the subjective vehicles of truth, volition should have three successive dimensions, whose ends reflect, respectively, intuition, representation, and thought. The first two would comprise nondiscursive forms of volition, while the latter would involve acting in light of concepts.

Conceiving the rational will in all its forms is the task of the *Philosophy of Right*. Before this task can be addressed, the *Philosophy of Mind* must consider the forms of willing that lack full rationality, yet provide the volitional prerequisites of rational agency. If the rational will wills the concept of itself, then there can be two broad types of nonrational wills—one that wills the concept of something other than itself and one that wills no concepts whatsoever, but instead pursues ends that are nonconceptual in content and represented by imagination. The necessity of these other forms of willing will be found in how the rational will emerges from them.

To address these options, it is worth critically examining the threefold delineation that Hegel gives them in his *Philosophy of Mind*. There Hegel outlines three stages that practical intelligence must undergo to reach the threshold of willing itself in its universality. He designates these stages as practical feeling (*praktische Gefühl*), impulses and choice (die *Triebe und die Willkür*), and happiness (*Glückseligkeit*).[12] Each involves a form of willing that does not yet determine itself as rational and free.[13] Instead, they build successive steps in the will's liberation from bondage to external givens to which the will is necessarily afflicted at the outset.[14]

As stages in the conceptual determination of will, these forms have a dual relationship to one another. They stand in a genetic order, in which those conceptually antecedent to the others actually arise prior to those that follow upon them. What gives this genetic ordering any authority is a structural necessity according to which each prior form provides a prerequisite without which what follows cannot operate. Besides forming a genetic ordering, these stages in the will's development may equally concurrently occur. Each preceding stage may be incorporated in those that follow, such that impulse and choice involve practical feeling and the pursuit of happiness contains both practical feeling and impulse and choice. Second, the agent may pursue a later stage while simultaneously engaging in another form of willing.

The initial determination of will should comprise the minimal specification that can be given without any further features of will, but that is ingredient in all the rest. This minimal shape will have a temporal priority insofar as all successive aspects of will must presuppose its occurrence, both in each volition and in the development of each agent's practical intelligence. As such, the initial determination of will cannot be mediated by any volition. Instead of issuing from any act of will, it will have a content given independently of volition. Nonetheless, it will comprise a necessary feature of every volition.

Feeling is mind's most basic aspect, comprising the given modification of mental content to which the psyche relates itself without disengaging and projecting it as something objective. Volition requires that mind have some mental content to be realized in objectivity by the agent, an intended state of affairs that may lie in a resulting product of the individual's embodied activity or simply in a performance by the individual. Before outwardly realizing some such inner content, the individual must register some subjective content *as* an aim, as a mental manifold poised to become subjective *and* objective in face of a world awaiting its realization. Doing so involves consciousness of an opposing objectivity, as well as awareness of the subjective content to be realized. Yet mind must further sense the discrepancy between inner and outer as something eliciting its practical response.

To have a mental content as an aim involves both apprehending that discrepancy and being poised to remove it. An aim is a telos that realizes itself, provided no external inference intercedes. It is not an antecedent cause of volition, but rather the subjective disposition within volition whose presence is a sufficient condition for undertaking the action that will realize it. Otherwise volition would be contingent upon something else, rather than self-initiating. Willing would then be reduced to a mechanistic behavior, in which ends get supplanted by prior causes that have no intrinsic connection to the agent. By contrast, the aim figures as a determining element contained in the process of volition without rendering willing contingent upon something external. Unlike mechanistic movement, which is determined from without with indifference to what kind of thing gets moved, volition only applies to agents who, as such, have living perceiving bodies and pleasures and displeasures. Consequently, volition can remain a process that moves itself, given its specific nature.[15]

In this respect, volition begins with intelligence finding itself to have specific aims, factors that belong to mind, but equally refer to an objectification that intelligence represents to itself and immediately leans toward achieving. Because these aims are, to begin with, immediately given, rather than a product of volition, the will is initially a natural agency, possessing drives, appetites, and inclinations through which it finds itself determined by nature.[16] These given contents are the agent's own, but they equally have the externality of not yet being determined by willing. Because these aims are immediately given, they lack any mediating connections other than the purely formal bond of belonging to one and the same individual. They otherwise stand independent of one another, and the agent can be said to have one as well as another, with, as Hegel puts it, nothing but "also" being their connector.[17]

As immediately and minimally given, the aim of volition has a mental reality that can be aptly characterized as a practical feeling. At the outset of volition, the agent is aware of having an aim in apprehending a modification of its own mental realm that, as immediate, has no relation to other aims or to any practical principles that might qualify its end. Feeling, by itself, informs mind only of its own modifications as immediately given in all their personal singularity. For this reason, feeling can engage the psyche without the intentionality of consciousness or any awareness of the subject-object identity underlying every aspect of intelligence. Nevertheless, once intelligence and consciousness supervene upon the psyche, feeling gets conjoined with conscious perception and intelligent representation. Feeling becomes practical in this wider mental context when mind registers its own immediate singular response to having an aim and perceiving the degree of fulfillment of that aim in the world. Feeling rendered practical is *emotion*. Practical feeling or emotion is practical *intelligence* because it necessarily responds to mind's awareness of the fit of the subjective content of an immediately given aim to the objective state of affairs to which that aim refers. What renders this response a practical *feeling* is the immediacy and personal singularity it possesses. Although the practical feeling is based upon a perception of the world condition that relates to the individual's aim, that feeling directly registers pleasure or displeasure as the case may be, rather than invoking any principle or rendering any judgment.

The pleasure and displeasure of practical feeling are not equivalent to their counterparts when appetite is at stake. Appetite is a relation of self-consciousness insofar as appetite desires the annihilation of the independent otherness of the object of appetite, assimilating it into the subject, who is conscious of itself in virtue of eliminating this other. By contrast, practical feeling takes pleasure in the objective realization of an aim, which involves the individual apprehending how its aim has become something both subjective and objective. Practical feeling comprises the sentiment that occasions such objectification, without yet involving any such action upon the world. Practical feeling can comprise a first form of volition, as well as the threshold for further development, insofar as it has a self-determination, but one restricted to feeling its own sensation of the fit between the given aim of the individual and the world it faces. This fit is not a theoretical matter of insuring that representations match reality, but a practical concern for how far reality matches subjective aim.

As such, practical feeling is formal in that the sentiment it has may possess any singular content.[18] Just as one agent may have different aims from any other, so the common world they face may please some but not others, with aims and corresponding feelings liable to change at any moment. Accordingly, practical feeling, that is, emotion, can accompany every development of practical mind, from the first inchoate urges of thoughtless behavior to the pursuit of aims according with rational principle, but of itself, it comprises simply the subjective sentiment given at the outset of any volition.

Because it forms the subjective starting point of volition, and therefore cannot already be mediated by will, practical feeling will vindicate itself as such through the ensuing action of which it forms the beginning. On the other hand, because practical feeling is given, it is equally determined externally, affected by outside factors that impinge upon it. These include everything in the anthropological formation of the individual that affects its felt wants, as well as every contingent circumstance that bears upon the correspondence of aim and world. The will, as practical feeling, therefore unites its immediate determinate being as an affection originating from without with its character as something that determines its worldly existence through its own nature. Since intelligence has come to treat its own subjectivity as having objective significance, volition's character as self-determining is what *ought* to be. Hence, the foreign determinacy facing the individual *should* correspond with that character. The feeling of this correspondence is the pleasant and the feeling of the lack of correspondence is the unpleasant.[19]

Because the inner determinacy to which the affection is related is still immediate, belonging to my given, natural individuality, it is subjective and can be only felt, lacking any objective determinacy to be sensed or intuited. Since the basis of comparison is a subjective given, to which the externally determined affection should correspond, whether I feel something to be pleasant is in itself no reason for it to be right or good, granted that these are not merely subjective designations.[20]

Practical feeling does not itself *make* subjectivity and objectivity coincide; it rather registers in sentiment the given correspondence between mind's own immediate singular inward content with the existing world it confronts. What confirms the practical, rather than intuitively theoretical character of this self-discovery is that the correspondence become something that ought to be objectively produced by mind. When practical feeling passes over into impulse, mind is ready to make what ought to be its product the result of an actual intervention in the way of the world.[21]

The transition from practical feeling to impulse is immediate since once the agent feels the discrepancy between its aim and the world, it has the urge to remove that incongruence. That urge immediately proceeds from practical feeling because whatever aims the subject finds itself to have and finds unrealized in the world figure as ends only by driving the subject to bring about their fulfillment. Yet, because impulse still precedes the actual achievement of the agent's aim in the world, it is just as subjective as the practical feeling that provides its occasion.

Nevertheless, it is important to distinguish the subjectivity of impulse from that of appetite. As Hegel points out, impulse differs from appetite in two correlative respects.[22] First, appetite is simply a function of self-consciousness, caught within consciousness' constitutive opposition between subjective and objective. This is exhibited in how appetite makes consciousness aware of the self in the purely negative act of obliterating some independent object of desire by consuming it, thereby assimilating it into the subject. Second, because appetite produces nothing subsisting, but instead eliminates some object, appetite is a merely individual, fleeting engagement that provides a momentary singular satisfaction that disappears once it is achieved. Impulse, by contrast, is a function of intelligence, which, as such, always concerns something both subjective and objective. Consequently, whatever satisfactions impulse provides have the inherent durability of an objectively embodied end. To the extent that the satisfaction of impulse involves pleasant feelings, these comprise an extended series of satisfactions corresponding to the persisting embodiment of the end to which impulse drives the agent. Nonetheless, as Hegel notes,[23] because the content of impulse derives from the subjective singularity of practical feeling, the universality each impulse has in relation to its enduring satisfactions remains particular. Although the agent, in acting upon impulse, secures a relatively enduring fulfillment lasting beyond the momentary satisfaction of appetite, this still remains something different from the fulfillment of the agent's other impulses, not to mention those of others. Consequently, not only is there no necessary conformity between the impulses of different subjects, but the impulses of each agent have no intrinsic harmony with one another.

Moreover, each impulse is susceptible of multifarious realizations. On the one hand, the fulfillment of an impulse may vary according to changes in the situation intuited by the agent. On the other hand, one and the same situation can allow for various possible fulfillments of the same impulse. Accordingly, although each impulse is particular in character, it is universal in relation to the plurality of its possible fulfillments, which are contingent upon both what circumstances confront the agent and how the agent perceives and reacts to them.[24]

Hence, if any aim is to be realized, the agent must commit to some impulse rather than another, as well as to some specific option for fulfilling the selected impulse. The contingent plurality of impulses confronts the agent with choosing among them and their realizations in order to carry through any volition. If the individual were unable to make this dual selection, impulse would remain no more than an instinctual drive. Nonetheless, instinct need not have the last word. Intelligence provides the individual with sufficient resources to engage in the double determination of choice whereby the agent opts for some impulse as well as for some determinate way of acting upon it. Intuition and representation enable any individual to be aware of its urges, consider them in distinction from one another and in relation to the world, and imagine a plurality of options for fulfilling one or another. The habituation of the psyche already provides a mastery of the body, whereas the subject-object opposition of consciousness and intelligence's awareness of contents that are both subjective and objective enables mind to tackle the translation of subjective aim into objective realization. On these bases, the recourse to choice is inescapable. Nothing can be willed unless the agent decides which impulse to follow and how to fulfill it.

Practical feeling thus engenders urges from which volition must choose. If that choice were contingent upon antecedent conditions, the teleological character of impulse would be defeated. Although the impulse might tend to drive the individual to commit actions for the sake of some aim, if that tendency could never realize itself unless subject to some external necessitation, behavior finally would be decided by that contingency. What saves volition from such reduction to a mechanical process is the groundlessness of choice. Choice is self-initiated, opting from among impulses without being impelled to do so. Reproductive and productive imagination provide practical intelligence with representations of its different impulses and their possible implementations, and mind's power of attention allows for focusing upon one option to the exclusion of others, with or without the contribution of discursive reflection. On this basis, practical intelligence need only take the further step of making the chosen impulse its own and embodying it in directed action.

Choice, however, does not generate the impulses from among which it chooses. These impulses are contents given to it, leaving choice formal, exercising the same capacity no matter what it chooses. This is the case because what can be chosen cannot be derived from the form of choosing, which is open to an indeterminate range of independently given options. Although choice is dependent upon a given array of impulses in order to have anything from which to choose, its choice is otherwise independent of external necessitation. For this reason, choice can remain purposive in character, precipitating action that is done not because of any antecedent condition, but because of what end has been chosen.

Although purpose is instrinsic to choice, it would be a mistake to confuse the logic of choice with teleology. Purposive action follows from choice, but choice itself does not opt for an end as a realization of some antecedent end. Choice instead independently decides what end to seek in the first place. This exercise of freedom, however, is formal insofar as choice does not engender its ends, but selects them from among given alternatives. Because choice does not engender the options it chooses among, it is a faculty whose potential to choose is always actualized in whatever particular course of action gets chosen. As such, choice is a natural volition, having a character given antecedently to every exercise of will. This natural faculty is able to stand over and above all the options from which it is free to choose, including both its different aims and the different ways of implementing each. Instead of being immediately captive to any particular urge and any particular satisfaction of that urge, choice can select at will from their multitude and their multitudinous realizations. Nonetheless, because choice does not possess any intrinsic ends, but must find the content of its ends in the independently given array of urges, the freedom of choice is purely formal.

This incongruence between the particular content of given ends and the indeterminacy of the choosing self makes the determination of choice a poor semblance of self-determination. Self-determination involves reflexivity whereby determiner and determined are one. By contrast, in choice, none of the contents chosen among can correspond to the will, just as in none of them the will can be truly itself, as opposed to something external.[25] Substituting one option for another can never remove this discrepancy, for each choice is just as externally given as any other. Holding to the indeterminacy of indecision is no remedy, for the will that hesitates to choose remains an empty subjective capacity that fails to determine itself.[26]

Significantly, the capacity of choice requires no discursive intelligence. Feeling, intuition, and imagination are sufficient for mind to present itself with the options of impulses and implementations from which to select. For this reason, both dumb animals and prelinguistic children can choose, provided they have enough intelligence and bodily control to imagine their options and decide which to follow. Indeed, without the prelinguistic natural choosing will, individuals would be unable to decide which commonly observed objects to designate to one another, or which intuitable factor to employ as a sign for that purpose. Once, however, the choices are made initiating linguistic communication, agents can choose with thought.

Drives and inclinations, as well as the circumstances affecting their fulfillment, are all given without any mediating principle guaranteeing their successful and harmonious satisfaction, be it by one individual or many. Insofar as the pursuit of one drive may hinder the pursuit of others, the choosing will finds itself embroiled in a morass of conflicting impulsions.[27] Can the will somehow escape the conflicted pursuit of particular impulses, despite the abiding formality of its choosing agency? The turn to happiness provides the one remaining stratagem for practical intelligence.

To will to be happy may not involve willing on principle, but it does require representing an end that transcends the singularity of a particular impulse. Choice, as such, simply directs action to some particular fulfillment of an impulse to the exclusion of others. Yet since choice is equally free of bondage to the impulse it elects, whatever choice is made is but an instance of a general capacity that can always pursue something else. To act, the agent must choose some particular aim, yet each choice is ready to give way to some different option, ad infinitum. The natural will might seem condemned to this endless repetition, in which each choice is followed by an equally dispensable successor. Yet the agent imagines its own predicament, simply by being aware of all its own ends and choices. The practical intelligence of the choosing will can, therefore, aim to fulfill its impulses in their totality, to the extent that this is possible. To do so, practical intelligence must make its aim happiness.

This might seem to require full-fledged thought, insofar as happiness has universality, like a class under which its members are subsumed. Happiness, however, subsumes all the independently given impulses and their projected fulfillments under its encompassing end. The harmonious realization in which happiness seeks to unite them is posterior to these impulses, whose empirically given content provides the unity of happiness with its filling. To pursue happiness, the agent must therefore *imagine* how to accomplish this compatible general goal, reflecting upon both the given plurality of drives and the contingent circumstances for achieving their global satisfaction.

Nonetheless, imagining happiness is not analogous to any single pleasant feeling signifying the satisfaction of a single drive. Happiness is a universal end, aiming beyond any momentary satisfaction to a totality of enjoyment. As such, the ideal of happiness is something universal, standing higher than all particular impulse satisfactions. Yet, because happiness comprises a universal satisfaction to which the choosing individual aspires, it lacks any necessary concrete filling of its own, but depends upon the contingent variegation of given impulses and circumstances to provide the material whose total satisfaction it aims to accomplish.[28] Thereby conditioned upon the subjectivity and feeling of a particular individual, the end of happiness is itself particular and contingent.[29] What is happiness for one individual need not be the happiness that individual seeks at a later time, let alone match the happiness sought by anyone else.

Because impulses have a given particularity, as well as a contingent transience, their fulfillments stand in potential opposition to one another. The pursuit of happiness cannot involve affirmative commitment to every impulse fulfillment. Instead, opting for happiness requires mediating the conflict of impulse realizations. This entails fulfilling those impulses that can be implemented in harmony with one another but, where this is impossible, sacrificing some impulse satisfactions in favor of others. Deciding how to do this involves grappling with the qualitative and quantitative differences of impulses and their satisfactions. Because these are variable and contingent, no objective universal prescriptions can be given. Instead, each agent must ultimately rely upon subjective feeling and preference to decide wherein happiness is to be sought.[30] Whatever the subject resolves, the pursuit of happiness remains a problematic undertaking, where no choices can secure an objective fulfillment of impulse in general.[31] However happiness is sought, some impulses remain unfulfilled and frustrated by the fulfillment of others, while new impulses arise calling for further action.[32]

Because happiness promises a general fulfillment of impulse, it cannot be aimed at unless one is able to entertain a universal end, which must be thought to be pursued. Consequently only agents with linguistic intelligence can represent happiness as an end and seek to be happy. Nonetheless, acting for the sake of happiness is not equivalent to an exercise of free will, or what might be called practical reason. Practical intelligence, whether choosing to fulfill particular impulses or to attain happiness, lacks three correlative features constitutive of actual self-determination: a unity of form and content, objectivity, and freedom as an end.

The pursuit of happiness, like the pursuit of particular impulses, lacks a unity of form and content because the willing of each of these ends is different in form from the ends themselves. In each case, the achievement of satisfaction is a result of action, making general happiness as well as particular pleasures consequences of a willing that extinguishes itself in fulfilling these ends.[33]

Further, the ends of impulse and happiness are subjective, being relative to the given inclinations of the individual and still lacking objectification in actual fulfillments. These inclinations, taken individually or integrated into the goal of happiness, have no necessary relation to those of any other agent, nor any necessary satisfaction. The happiness of each individual may just as well impede the happiness of others as have its fulfillment blocked by the pursuits of other agents or other externalities.

This predicament reflects how the pursuit of happiness and acting on particular impulses fails to have freedom as an end. So long as action aims at impulse satisfactions that are distinct from the activity that brings them about, willing lacks the reflexivity that enables a free will to will its own freedom, that is, to be self-determined.

Although practical intelligence retains these three deficiencies throughout its development from practical feeling to choice and the pursuit of happiness, mind has hereby attained all it needs to bring closure to "Subjective Spirit" by ushering in the reality of freedom comprising "Objective Spirit's" domain of normative conduct.

Hegel suggests that for freedom to be actual, practical intelligence must relinquish its particular determinacy as well as the abstract individuality of choice.[34] Although happiness to some extent removes the particularity of impulse by comprising a general satisfaction of all impulses, that general satisfaction still rests upon the given content of impulses, to which happiness still relates. Similarly, although happiness comprises a totality of desire satisfactions, all remain contingent givens external to the faculty of choice employed to select how to be happy. In this sense, choice just as much gives itself these aims in pursuing happiness while leaving these particular aims without any necessary connection to its pursuit of happiness. What overcomes the particular givenness of the ends of happiness and the abstract individuality of the agency of practical intelligence is the will's aiming at its own universal determination, its concept. By willing itself as its end, the will determines itself by itself and in terms of itself. As end of itself, the self or unity of the will concretely contains its whole content, which is itself as self-determined. In this way, the form and content, the concept and object of the will become identical.[35]

In so determining itself, the will is the *actual* free will in two interconnected respects. First, the self-determining will is not a capacity, like the faculty of choice, which is merely potentially determining. Insofar as the will that wills itself as free does so only in the activity of realizing its own concept, it is inherently actual. Second, because the free will is what it determines itself to be, it does not exist apart from its characteristic activity. The free will is therefore an actuality, not a faculty, capacity, or potentiality.

When the will wills itself as free, it corresponds to its object by determining that object and being determined in function of that object. Just as theoretical intelligence determines itself to conform to its object, so the free will determines itself to accord with its object—itself as self-determining. Similarly, just as practical intelligence determines its object to conform to intelligence, so the free will determines its object—itself as free—to accord with the agency that aims at this its end. Both types of accordance simultaneously apply since what gets determined and what does the determining coincide in self-determination.[36]

This coincidence of determiner and determined in free willing eliminates the abiding subjectivity that afflicted practical intelligence so long as it did not aim at self-determination by willing its own concept. By pursuing particular impulses or their integration in happiness, practical intelligence aimed at something different from itself, insuring that no necessary connection can hold between its volition and its ends. With the form of willing differing from its content, the object of willing is extraneous to what is inherent in volition, to its concept. The ends of willing, therefore, remain particular and contingent, rather than genuinely universal and rational. The will is left other-determined rather than self-determined and lacks any necessary objectivity.

Self-determination, universality of end, unity of form and content, and objectivity thus all go together. When practical intelligence succeeds in making these features its own, mind achieves an objectivity of its own, a reality of freedom.

These connections underlie Hegel's claim that the will is the true free will only as thinking intelligence.[37] In every case of self-determined conduct, the will wills itself in its universal determination. In willing this its concept, the will makes its end what is intrinsic to itself, rather than how it is contingently determined. Only then does the will will nothing but itself and achieve an objectivity that is its own. For this reason, the thinking will is not only self-determined but just as much true and objective. The free will is true insofar as what it wills is identical with itself, in accord with its concept.[38] The free will is equally objective insofar as it has realized itself without retaining a subjectivity alien to its content in the way in which the choosing will remains an abstract capacity whose selected ends derive from something external.[39] The objective will contains truth because the will has won an objectivity in accord with its concept when it achieves self-determination.[40]

Hegel's *Philosophy of Right* is the comprehensive development of how the thinking will, willing itself as true and objective, involves willing oneself as a bearer of rights, exercising a prerogative of choice that is universal. Rights can only be engaged in through recognition of and facilitation of the same prerogative on the part of other agents. Every exercise of rights is a lawful willing, exhibiting a type of agency common to all bearers of rights within the correlation of right and duty where every entitled volition proceeds in respect of the equal opportunity of others to engage in the same type of willing. Within the practice of rights, each participant wills its own artificial agency as a right holder, making the type of choices (e.g., dispositions of property, moral conduct, family activity, social involvements, and political engagement) whose ends are specific to the lawful practices to which they belong. Although all participants will in relation to other agents, this relation to other is not a restriction upon their willing of themselves, but rather the enabling condition that allows them all to realize the self-determination in which they are correlatively engaged. In relating to other bearers of rights in respect of their entitlements, each participant exercises its own entitlement and determines itself as the autonomous agent it can permissibly be in that context. Self-related in its relation to other, the free will is truly infinite and fully actual.[41] The other volitions to which it must relate in exercising its rights only refer the self-determined will back to itself, because what others do in exercising their rights is respect the rights of their peers. Hence, each self-determined will confronts an objectivity ratifying, rather than bounding, its own freedom. This objectivity contains its own self-determination in lawful relation to that of all other participants in the exercise of rights. Because these relations exist in acts of will, the free will is only in the activity of its self-determination. The moment it withdraws from that activity, it reverts to the finite, subjective capacity of practical intelligence, which all agents possess independently of their participation in conventions of right. Practical intelligence's faculty of choice can, however, always reenter the lawful practice of self-determination when interactions of right are reengaged by a plurality of agents. That move can not be undertaken unilaterally. It is instead an intersubjective undertaking whose coordinated exercise of choice comprises the practical transition from practical intelligence to objective spirit. In both theory and practice, it brings the philosophy of mind, that is, the philosophy of subjective spirit, to closure.

Notes

1. G. W. F. Hegel, *Werke 7: Grundlinien der Philosophie des Rechts oder Naturrecht und Staatswissenschaft im Grundrisse* (Frankfurt am Main: Suhrkamp Verlag, 1970), § 2.

2. G. W. F. Hegel, *Wissenschaft der Logik: Die Lehre vom Begriff (1816)*, ed. Friedrich Hogemann and Walter Jaeschke, *Gesammelte Werke*, vol. 12 (Hamburg: Felix Meiner, 1981), 277–283, and Enz. (1830), §§ 233–34.

3. These aspects of the logical determinacy of the good indicate that will per se cannot qualify as self-determined in several respects. First, will has its subjective content prior to the activity by which will makes objectivity conform to itself. To be self-determined, will would have also to determine its own content through its activity. Then, in determining objectivity, will would be determining itself. That requires, of course, that the objectivity in question does not remain standing over against the will as something independently given. Significantly, Hegel's entire analysis of practical intelligence addresses the will insofar as it has yet to achieve self-determination. Objective spirit, by contrast, addresses the reality of the free will, which is an objectivity determined by itself.

4. As John McCumber observes, "the classical Greek moral vocabulary famously has no word for "will." To Plato and Aristotle, that we could actually do something that goes against both our desires and our reason is simply unthinkable, because those are the only things in us that can lead to action at all." See John McCumber, *Time in the Ditch: American Philosophy in the McCarthy Era* (Evanston, IL: Northwestern University Press, 2001), 105.

5. In § 8 of the *Philosophy of Right*, Hegel maintains that the formal opposition of subjectivity and objectivity as external immediate existences comprises the formal will as self-consciousness. Although this might suggest that will involves merely self-consciousness, Hegel points out that the relationship of consciousness comprises only the appearance of the will, which no longer comes into consideration to the degree that spirit (intelligence) is what here lies at issue. See Hegel, *Grundlinien der Philosophie des Rechts*, § 8.

6. Enz. (1830), §§ 399–411.
7. Enz. (1830), see §§ 413–15.
8. Enz. (1830), §§ 426–28.
9. Enz. (1830), §§ 430–33.
10. Enz. (1830), §§ 434–36.
11. Enz. (1830), §§ 445 and Hegel, Werke 10, Z to §445.
12. See the addition to §469 in Hegel, *Werke.* 10.
13. In § 8 of the *Philosophy of Right*, Hegel claims that the differences between the forms of will are comprised by what particularization the will gives itself in moving beyond the abstract universality of its point of departure. This applies generally to both the stages of volition leading to the free will and to the different types of self-determination constituting the different spheres of right. See Hegel, *Grundlinien der Philosophie des Rechts*, § 8.
14. Why the will need be bound to givens at the outset is reflected in the logical emergence of the concept, where self-determined determinacy emerges when the difference between determiner and determined eliminates itself in the course of the development of the categories of essence. Because self-determined determinacy arises once what is determined and what determines becomes indistinguishable, self-determination necessarily arises not from itself, but from an antecedent development. As a result, self-determined determinacy must further develop so that it can be what it has determined itself to be, and thereby be consistent

with itself. This progressively occurs when the concept gets determined by its own constitutive factors in judgment (e.g., where the universal becomes determined by the particular and the individual), and further when this determination becomes mediated by its own factors (e.g., when judgment gives way to syllogism, where factors of the concept are mediated by another factor—the individual is universal through its particularity). See Richard Dien Winfield, *From Concept to Objectivity: Thinking through Hegel's Subjective Logic* (Aldershot: Ashgate, 2006), for a detailed investigation of these stages in conceptual development.

15. Charles Taylor gives an important analysis of these differences between mechanistically determined behavior and volition (action) in chapter 2 of his *Explanation of Behaviour* (London: Routledge and Kegan Paul, 1964), 26–53.

16. As Hegel puts it, the will is first only free in itself, only the immediate or natural will. See Hegel, *Grundlinien der Philosophie des Rechts*, § 11.

17. Hegel, *Grundlinien der Philosophie des Rechts*, § 11.

18. Enz. (1830), § 471.

19. Hegel, *Werke 10*, Z to § 472.

20. Hegel, *Werke 10*, Z to § 472.

21. Hegel, *Werke 10*, Z to § 469.

22. See the addition to § 473 of Hegel, *Werke 10*.

23. Addition to § 473, Hegel, *Werke 10*.

24. So Hegel describes each impulse as something universal and indeterminate with various objects and manners of satisfaction. See Hegel, *Grundlinien des Rechts*, § 12.

25. Hegel, *Grundlinien des Rechts*, Z to § 15.

26. Hegel, *Grundlinien des Rechts*, § 16.

27. Hegel, *Grundlinien des Rechts*, § 17.

28. Hegel, *Grundlinien des Rechts*, § 20.

29. Hegel, *Grundlinien des Rechts*, Z to § 20.

30. Enz. (1830), § 479.

31. Kant labels imperatives of happiness assertoric, rather than problematic, because he regards happiness to be one end actual in all rational agents. Kant recognizes, however, that only counsels of prudence can be provided to guide the pursuit of happiness, given the subjective contingency of what fulfillments one will judge to be part of one's happiness. See Immanuel Kant, *Groundwork of the Metaphysics of Morals*, trans. H. J. Paton (New York: Harper and Row, 1964), Ak. 415–16, 82–84. Admittedly, any rational agent with understanding can represent happiness as an end. Nevertheless, not only is the realization of happiness always unattainable with any finality, but individuals need not aim at happiness simply in virtue of acting on impulse. The pursuit of happiness requires a specific development of choice, which all thinking individuals may be able to undertake, but which they may ignore by simply choosing impulses in their isolated singularity.

32. Enz. (1830), § 480.

33. When Aristotle identifies happiness as an activity for its own sake consisting in virtuous conduct, he is conceiving something fundamentally different

from happiness as it figures within practical intelligence. Aristotle is conceiving something ethical, involving a self-sustaining association with objective ends, pursued in common by members of a community that already realize the ends in question. Such ends are objective both by being universal to all individuals who fulfill their roles in the community by jointly pursuing them and by being such that they can only be sought by individuals who belong to a community that embodies those ends.

34. Enz. (1830), § 480.

35. By uniting concept and objectivity, the will exhibits the logic of the Idea, which is why objective spirit can be characterized by Hegel as the Idea of freedom. By contrast, practical intelligence exhibits only the concept of freedom, still subjective and formal.

36. Accordingly, the actual free will, whose emergence brings closure to the *Philosophy of Subjective Spirit*, is characterized in Enz. (1830), § 481 as the unity of theoretical and practical spirit.

37. Hegel, *Grundlinien des Rechts, Anmerkung* to § 21.

38. Hegel, *Grundlinien des Rechts*, Z to § 21, § 26.

39. Hegel, *Grundlinien des Rechts*, § 26.

40. Hegel, *Grundlinien des Rechts*, Z to § 26.

41. Hegel, *Grundlinien des Rechts*, § 22.

The Relation of Mind to Nature

Two Paradigms

Philip T. Grier

The two paradigms that I propose to explore here are, somewhat loosely, the Hegelian, and a certain strand of the 20th-century analytic tradition. By "paradigm" I mean either a theoretical framework to govern empirical investigations of a problem, or, alternatively, a distinctive conceptual analysis or formulation of some problem. More generally, one might refer simply to alternative philosophical "traditions." Characterizing actual philosophical traditions requires attention to the historical, the rhetorical, as well as the philosophical aspects of an intellectual practice, sometimes in equal measure. All of these will figure in the essay that follows. Despite the significant elements of history involved, the ultimate motivation for this inquiry was a curiosity about the contemporary configurations of these two traditions, the extent to which they could be viewed as commensurate or incommensurate, and consequently, the profitability (or unprofitability) of a prospective dialogue between them.

Introduction

The first of the two paradigms for the investigation of mind's relation to nature might be thought of as the Comprehensive one, as it designates the broadest conception of the problem, the outlines of which can be originally discerned in the texts of Plato and Aristotle.[1] In the modern period that same general conception is clearly framed as a central problem in the German idealist tradition, culminating in Hegel's highly complex attempted resolution of it, which was one of the principal aims of his system.

The comprehensive paradigm of the relation of mind to nature involves two distinct but interconnected branches of argument: the first attempts to explain how mind can be understood to have arisen in the context of the natural world, while the second attempts to show how *that world* can be comprehended as such *by* the mind depicted in the first branch of the argument. More simply put, what is required is both an account of the constitution of mind from the standpoint of nature, as well as an account of the constitution of nature from the standpoint of mind. One of the most succinct formulations of this problem was supplied by T. H. Green 125 years ago, in the opening sentence of his *Prolegomena to Ethics*: "Can the knowledge of nature be itself a part or product of nature?"[2] Fifty-four years ago, Errol Harris adumbrated the position in terms of an epigram: "The mind is in the world and the world is in the mind."[3] In referring to this first paradigm as the "Comprehensive" conception of the problem, I mean simply to indicate that it requires that *both* branches of the problem be pursued to satisfactory solutions and that the two solutions must turn out to be mutually consistent aspects of a single overarching conception of the nature of the real.

By the second, or Narrow, paradigm I intend to refer to theories of the so-called "mind-body problem," in contemporary parlance, which construe the issue much more narrowly as simply the question of how a mental event can be related to a brain event, where the latter is construed as physical. At first glance one might suppose that this "Narrow" problem is just the first branch of the "Comprehensive" problem taken by itself without reference to the second branch. If so, one might presume that the energies being invested in debate and research on this Narrow paradigm might in the long run make some sort of contribution to a solution of at least half of the Comprehensive problem. I submit that this would not be philosophically or historically accurate, because the two paradigms stem from radically distinct philosophical traditions, do not share truly convergent aims, and conceive basic terms of the problem such as "mind" in ultimately incompatible ways. Finally, one project, the Comprehensive one, is grounded in systematic philosophy; the other is grounded as much in empirical psychology as philosophy.

Historically speaking, once the second branch of the Comprehensive problem had been effectively dropped from the agenda by philosophers such as Moore and Russell around the beginning of the twentieth century, the remaining first branch, now reconceived in a quite different and simplified form as the "mind-body problem" could then be referred back comfortably and naturally into the 17th-century Cartesian context, and its outlines then easily traced through the early modern British empiricists, and thence into the 20th-century development of empiricism. This is the version of the history of philosophy that is exceedingly familiar as the standard background story for much of 20th-century analytic philosophy. This maneuver had the double effect of shrinking the apparent terms of the mind-body problem into the dimensions of an exceedingly familiar, if troublesome, old Cartesian shoe and simultaneously making it possible to ignore or circumvent the post-Cartesian history of the German idealist tradition, within which the more ancient Comprehensive problem in both of its branches had been reinstituted.

The thesis I plan to advance here is that amid the continuing frustrations encountered by attempts to "solve" standard forms of the narrower "mind-body" problem in 20th-century anglophone philosophy, there is little reason to suppose that the Narrow problem could ever yield a satisfactory resolution of any of the deeper philosophical issues raised by the Comprehensive conception of the problem.

The Relation of Mind to Nature in Hegel

Perhaps the most basic point that should be made concerning Hegel's approach to the Comprehensive problem is to acknowledge the circular structure of his philosophical system. In Hegel's account of the relation of spirit to nature, nature is not only a *presupposition* of mind or spirit, but is in a specific sense also already *implicated by* spirit. As Hegel said, "Spirit, just because it is the goal of Nature, is *prior* to it. Nature has proceeded from spirit: not empirically, however, but in such a manner that spirit is already from the very first implicitly present in Nature which is spirit's own presupposition."[4]

In this way Hegel's account can be seen to accommodate both branches of the Comprehensive problem. The first branch of argument is accomplished (at least minimally) if one commences reading his system at the *Philosophy of Nature* and follows it through at least as far as the emergence of subjective spirit in the first part of the *Philosophy of Mind*. This reading provides an account of the emergence of mind from nature in terms of which spirit turns out to be the truth of nature. The second branch of the argument is accomplished, in effect, by a reading that commences at Absolute Spirit, proceeds through the *Logic*, and culminates in the *Philosophy of Nature*. In this second reading mind (Absolute Spirit) is conceived as the nexus within which nature as a fully developed and explicit categorial structure is realized and revealed as a complex, hierarchically ordered, whole of mutually adjusted parts, ordered in terms of internal relations, explicitly realized only at the level of mind or spirit. The circular nature of this system ultimately guarantees the strongest possible coherence between the outcomes of the first branch of the argument and of the second: namely a subject-object identity of mind and nature.

The stages of Hegel's account of what I have termed the first branch of the Comprehensive paradigm, or the constitution of mind from the standpoint of nature, need not be summarized in detail here, as they were expounded with admirable clarity by Richard Dien Winfield in a recently-published article.[5] I will simply point to some of them here, as Hegel recounts them at the end of the *Philosophy of Nature*, anticipating the more detailed exposition that follows in the *Philosophy of Mind*.

Hegel's account of the emergence of mind begins at the stage of *animal organism*, at the level of *psyche*. The animal as organism is characterized by the possession of *members* existing in relation to an implicitly unitary psyche, an "*inwardly reflected* self of *singularity*," which "stands in relationship with an inorganic Nature, with an outer world."[6] Such an "inwardly reflected self," providing the basis in *feeling* for an "inner" and an "outer" of nature,[7] develops into the relation of *self-feeling*, and thus implicitly a relation to the external world as distinct.

However, this most primitive manifestation of mind must not be conceived as one term of a dualism of mind and nature. Rather, as Winfield points out, Hegel's identification of psyche "as the outcome of nature leaves mind inherently connected to a physical world in which there is life."[8] Quoting Winfield further,

> Hegel here presents minds not just as a result of the animal organism but as incorporating that organism as a constitutive element of mental life. On this basis, mind is necessarily a living entity, not merely in the world but metabolically interacting with it. Whatever theoretical challenges this point of departure may involve, it precludes the dualist problems of connecting a disembodied mind with nature . . . By being in part an animal in the world, mind never faces the dilemma of dealing with an

ontologically incommensurate domain . . . Instead, action is the self-activity of a being that always involves animal physiology.[9]

Hegel further thematizes *life* as the existence of the *speculative Concept* in the form of the animal organism, as a *concrete* realization of the speculative Concept, by contrast with which all of inorganic nature stands revealed as *abstract*.[10] "Structure," Hegel tells us, "as alive, is essentially process,"[11] but it is as such "abstract process, the structural process within structure itself, in which the organism converts its own members into a non-organic nature, into *means*, lives on itself and produces its own self" such that each member is reciprocally end and means.[12] This process has for result "the simple, immediate *feeling of self*"[13] contrasted with *externality* as a negation, and issuing in a feeling of *lack*.

The feeling of lack produces an *urge*, which is the activity of getting rid of the defect, the manifestation of an *end* or *purpose*, and is as such *instinct*. Through instinctive activity, the animal organism overcomes the negation of externality, assimilating the materials necessary for its survival. But because the animal organism does not have ends which are for itself, instinct is therefore "a purposive activity acting unconsciously."[14]

As Winfield has argued in very careful and persuasive detail, the functioning of *psyche* does not presuppose or require *consciousness*. Whereas the standard procedure with the Narrow paradigm is to identify mind with consciousness, Hegel, according to Winfield, instead conceives mental reality as "involving three successively determined processes: the psyche, consciousness, and intelligence, all of which involve life but are not reducible to it." These three processes form "successive stages in the self-constitution of the totality of mind."[15]

Hegel's account of the relation of mind to nature proceeds in terms of a dynamic principle of logic operative throughout the universe, implicit at the level of nature, explicit at the level of spirit, ordering the whole as a scale of forms in which each phase presents itself as a summing up of the whole to that point, and is in turn taken up in the successive phase, in a process that continues until the whole has reached fully explicit self-manifestation as the completed and self-sufficient system of the Real, in which each part is constituted by its relations to all the rest. Nature and mind thus turn out to be two significantly overlapping phases of a single continuous, self-developing process. This conception can also be compared with Plato's and Aristotle's assumption that "there is a *logos* in the nature of things which is identical with the principle of reason in our minds."[16]

The constituting of nature from the standpoint of mind, the second branch of the Comprehensive problem, can be most succinctly grasped from the perspective of the final section of "*Absoluter Geist*"[17] at the end of the *Encyclopedia*, where Hegel describes philosophy as "the self-thinking Idea, the knowing truth."[18] Whereas nature was initially to be understood as only implicitly organized by the idea, the recapitulation of the idea of nature from the standpoint of absolute spirit reveals it as the middle term of a syllogism "that has the *logical* as its grounds, its starting-point, and *nature* as the middle that joins *the mind* together with the logical."[19] The unity and coherence of the world as experienced is thus accounted for by the activity of the Concept. *That* it should come to be known is of course ultimately a result of the activity of the rational intellect manifest in the form of absolute spirit.[20] *What* comes to be known is that the self-determining of thought in the form of the Concept, culminating in the Absolute Idea, is also the self-determining of being,[21] the ultimate subject-object identity.

To reiterate two subsidiary but crucial points: First, the continuous overlap of categories or phases in the scale of forms entails among other things that the categories of nature and mind are not mutually exclusive, but must be conceived as overlapping in significant measure.[22] Hegel's conception is thus, among other things, a thorough-going naturalism, albeit of a distinct type. (The more usual conception typically found in various versions of the Narrow conception of the mind-body problem (at least initially) is that the physical and the mental are entirely distinct, which renders the possibility of a gradual or phased emergence of one from the other either inconceivable or at best thoroughly mysterious).

Second, the earliest traces of mind become discernible at the phase of *animal organism*, and as Hegel develops his account of the emergence of mind, it becomes clear that it could only operate in the context of *organic life*. *Life* then must figure as a fundamental category in the conceptual scheme, as it does for Hegel, and it cannot be treated as an incidental property, as is the case in so many contemporary Narrow theories of the mind-body relation.

The Fate of Internal Relations

Given the crucial role played by the speculative Concept within both branches of Hegel's argument concerning the relation of mind to nature, it is obvious that no such account would be possible save in terms of the internal relations whereby the various elements or phases comprising both nature and mind could be understood to develop into a genuine, coherent whole, the concrete universal. In a sense, Hegel's entire conception rests upon the foundation of internal relations in the form of the dialectically self-developing Concept.

In the anglophone philosophical universe such conceptions of mind and nature were seemingly swept away around the turn of the century by a new philosophical perspective that appeared to abolish internal relations entirely, as constituents either of mind, or experience, or the natural world. This new perspective was of course put forward by Moore and Russell in their assault upon "Idealism," the position that Peter Hylton has dubbed "Platonic Atomism."[23] Certain aspects of Russell's Platonic Atomism were of course only a passing phase in a kaleidoscope of positions through which he subsequently moved, but I will argue that other aspects of it have remained influential to the present, especially with regard to the Narrow conception of the mind-body relation.

One of the central motives for Russell's appropriation of Moore's Platonic Atomism was of course that it provided Russell with a means of demonstrating the applicability of his newly developed mathematical logic to the world. The central claim of that new theory was that the world was *constituted of* externally related atomic propositions, meaning in effect that the new formal logic was in principle competent to formulate any truth concerning that world.

Russell (following Moore) declared that all relations were *external*, thus apparently ruling out the very possibility of internal relations. As the world is composed of *propositions*, each of which is conceived as an objective and independent entity, its truth or falsity is independent of its relations to any other proposition and equally independent of any acts of judging. In this new doctrine there was "no overt concern at all with the nature of thought or the mind, or of experience, in any sense."[24] All such problems were declared to be of merely psychological, not philosophical, interest. The concern of philosophy was with "what was true about a given subject-matter; whether it [could] be known or not [was] a separate question, relevant to psychology rather than to philosophy."[25] Minds were viewed in effect as "devices" capable of "registering" logical facts through direct acquaintance; any further details of the process whereby this takes place were left for the psychologists to explore. One might argue that after a few decades' delay, this division of labor was accepted literally in the emergence of cognitive science.

The atomism presupposed by Russell's new doctrine, combined with the denial that there could be any degrees of truth or falsehood whatsoever (i.e., each proposition was either wholly true or wholly false), appeared to rule out any possible version of a dialectically developing holism structured by internal relations. Holism, on the other hand, would seem to be a necessary characteristic of any of the various idealisms that Russell and Moore meant to eliminate. Russell repeatedly seemed to imply that his new philosophical perspective had in some sense "refuted" the very possibility of idealism, because his new logic and its apparently successful solutions to certain problems in the philosophy of mathematics were incompatible with idealism. However, as Hylton pointed out, Russell's defense of his new system of logic rested in significant measure on his new philosophy of Platonic Atomism, and the latter simply *presupposed* the incoherence of idealism. Russell offered no direct refutation of the thesis of internal relations.[26] Hence, Hylton concludes, "Russell's appeal to logic and mathematics against Idealism is circular."[27]

As Hylton further points out, when Russell later attempted to introduce the concept of a propositional function into his own system, his justification for it proved inadequate, because it required the "idea of one entity presupposing or being dependent upon others," which is precisely what the idealists had meant by "internal relations." However in the metaphysics of Platonic Atomism, "each thing is what it is, independent of every other thing; there is no room here for the idea of one entity being dependent upon another."[28] According to Hylton, Russell never acknowledged the need to revise his earlier metaphysics in this connection: "For Russell to acknowledge the full implications of his use of the idea of presupposition would be for him to undo the most fundamental elements in the rejection of Idealism."[29]

Notwithstanding the question-begging nature of Russell and Moore's sally against the thesis of internal relations (which has come to be more widely recognized only relatively recently), as the 20th century rolled on, their attack upon idealism appeared more and more successful in the rhetorical sense. With the apparent success of Russell and Moore's critique of internal relations, and with the triumph of analytic philosophy[30] having become nearly total by the end of World War II, the comprehensive problem of the relation of mind to nature was essentially set aside as belonging to an outdated conception of the philosophical project and replaced by the much narrower "mind-body problem."

To be sure there were always individual philosophers who remained unimpressed by Russell's "revolution" and continued to pursue philosophy in the broader sense, but these had become rather few in number by the midcentury. One of them of course was Errol Harris, whose seminal work, *Nature, Mind and Modern Science*, published in 1954, set the agenda for a very rich succession of contributions which, among many other things, could be described as reinstituting what I have termed the "Comprehensive paradigm" of the relation of mind to nature.

Another event in the fifties that has only rather recently come to be more fully appreciated was Wilfrid Sellars' lengthy essay "Empiricism and the Philosophy of Mind." That essay, with its persistent emphasis on the importance of Kant's dictum that "intuitions without concepts are blind," develops a full-blown attack on the claim that there are *non-conceptual* states of awareness which could count as the acquisition of knowledge/beliefs (e.g., through perception), *in the absence of any inferential relation to other beliefs*. Instead, "to treat something as even a candidate for knowledge is at once to talk about its potential role in *inference*, as premise and conclusion."[31] To speak of *inference* is, needless to say, to speak of a kind of internal relation.

Sellars' essay can now be seen to have had some very significant predecessors, as well as successors. In both Hegel and T. H. Green, the emphasis on Kant's "intuitions without concepts are blind" takes the more full-blooded form of an attack upon the ultimacy of the very distinction between intuition and concept. Two important successors, John McDowell and Robert Brandom, have of course significantly advanced the same general point of view, the former by denying that there is any such thing as an "extra-conceptual Given" involved in belief formation,[32] and the latter developing a systematic account of belief formation as invariably "inferentialist" as opposed to "representationalist."[33]

This once "old" but now apparently "new again" philosophical attitude that the world can in itself be conceptually constraining of thought, has an interesting implication for Russell's denial of internal relations. If both mind and world are conceptually structured—above all when the structuring Concept is the same for both—relations are inevitably both *internal and external*, and Russell's philosophical "revolution" loses essentially all of its excitement. As Redding points out in a discussion of McDowell's work, "If judgment can be rationally constrained in empirical experience it must be the case that what does the constraining is both worldly *and* conceptual, and it was Hegel who provided a way of thinking how this can be so."[34] In other words, the excitement surrounding Russell's claim depended on the assumption that the (external) world was in some way radically other than mind,[35] and upon reflection, approximately a century later, this assumption has come to seem dubious once again to a growing circle of philosophers.

The "Narrow" Mind-Body Problem

At this point I will attempt to summarize the salient features of what I have been calling the Narrow paradigm, that is, the so-called "mind-body problem" as it developed through the second half of the 20th century. Clearly one of its proximal sources was the Platonic Atomism of Bertrand Russell in the first full flowering of his anti-idealism. Its other primary inspiration was of course the program of scientific naturalism that was gradually absorbed by anglophone philosophy from the Vienna Circle and its successors. (To be sure, both of these histories have accumulated so many twists and turns that it would be impossible to summarize them here.)

As contemporary representatives of this Narrow paradigm I shall rely, somewhat randomly, and for a variety of reasons, upon the works of Thomas Nagel, Colin McGinn, Owen Flanagan, and John Searle. First, all of them presuppose that the physical and the mental are, at least in the first instance, nonreducibly distinct characteristics, and thus squarely confront the challenge of accounting for their relation as a genuine problem (as opposed to merely presupposing the reducibility of one to the other). Thus, they explicitly confront the ensuing puzzles concerning the relation of one to the other: how one could be said to give rise to the other, supervene upon the other, be "identical to" the other on reflection, or be said to constitute a "knowledge of" the other. Finally, in the face of such puzzles, some of them are willing to countenance the possibility that certain puzzles may not be soluble on the terms proposed. (I will not bother with eliminationist or resolutely reductionist views, nor with any of the straightforwardly computational theories of mind, as I tend to agree with Nagel that these will prove to have been "a gigantic waste of time").[36]

Finding an acceptable formulation of the Narrow paradigm poses one immediate problem. Because it is not obvious that any reasonable version of the paradigm is without insuperable difficulties, any formulation one picks may appear suspect as a straw man. In this connection, it is not encouraging that Colin McGinn, who might be fairly regarded as firmly committed to this paradigm, has concluded that any understanding of how consciousness is related to brain states is "cognitively closed" to us, and to any other possible beings with minds generally similar to ours,[37] that is, that "we do not and cannot grasp the nature of the property that intelligibly links" physical changes in the brain with changes of consciousness.[38]

Despite these various problems, if we remain sufficiently general, the outlines of the Narrow version of the problem can be recognized as quite familiar, and can be loosely described in a series of reasonably noncontroversial steps.

First Step: A Distinction between the Mental and the Physical

First, the Narrow version of the problem begins with an acknowledgment of some philosophically important distinction between the physical (material) and the mental. The mental ('consciousness'), where further specification is sought, is standardly picked out by reference to 'qualia' and these, in the purest form of the problem, are regarded as available only to first-person experience, or subjectivity (though of course there have been various attempts to treat these as equivalent in some circumstances to third-person events).

The other term of the problem has been subject to a much wider range of proposed definitions, ranging from the very schematic, such as Descartes' "corporeal substance," to 18th- and 19th-century conceptions of "matter in motion," to early 20th-century conceptions of the "physical" involving energy fields, and so on. In the mid-20th century, Herbert Feigl offered two definitions of "physical" which were still being quoted by Thomas Nagel as late as 1979. One of these was roughly equivalent to "publicly observable," and the other to "scientific."[39] The common impulse behind most of these attempted definitions is of course to identify the physical with whatever is presupposed by contemporary science as the real basis of causal influences operating in nature.

Recently attention has been focused more typically upon the brain as a biological organ, or the "living brain," (e.g., by Searle, McGinn, Nagel and Flanagan). Galen Strawson has pointed out a salient problem here, however, reminding us,

> When aspiring materialists consider the living brain, in discussion of the 'mind—body problem,' they often slide into supposing that the word 'brain' somehow refers only to the brain-as-revealed-by-current-physics. But this is a mistake, for it refers just as it says, to the living brain, i.e., the living brain as a whole, the brain in its total physical existence and activity.[40]

Strawson is surely correct that most proponents of the view in question have implicitly been referring to the brain-as-revealed-by-current-empirical-science, and this is a crucial bit of abstraction.

Still more recently, as in the work of A. R. Damasio,[41] attention has occasionally shifted to the more sophisticated (Spinozistic) view that the content of mental experience must be explained by relation to states of the body as an organic whole [Spinoza: "The object of the idea constituting the human mind is the body"[42]], and not simply to the brain, (as though the brain were somehow the terminus of a chain of physical causes originating in the world, and only what is causally registered in the terminus could be supposed to register in the mind).[43]

It should be noted that this entire standard conception of the mental/physical distinction, operative in nearly all recent treatments of the mind-body problem, has been radically called into question by Galen Strawson. He has argued, in a series of substantial articles, that the standard philosophical uses of the terms "physicalism," "materialism," and "naturalism" in recent decades have all been badly misconceived and have turned long-established philosophical usage on its head. In recent philosophy of mind by "physicalism" or "naturalism" has been intended "the view that everything mental—and indeed everything that concretely exists—is physical." However, Strawson insists that *real* physicalism, *real* naturalism are simply attempts to acknowledge what really exists; but the one "entirely natural phenomenon whose existence is more certain than the existence of anything else" is *experience*.[44] Thus, according to Strawson any nonconfused usage of the term "physicalism" would constitute an acknowledgment that whether or not there exists anything nonmental, the reality of the mental cannot be called into question. Therefore he concludes that "much of the present debate about the 'mind-body' problem is beside the point."[45]

Second Step: The Relation of the Mental to the Physical

The first instinct of many theorists of the mind-body relation (in the category under consideration) is to suppose that there must be some causal connection between brain states and mental states, but this supposition runs into the immediate difficulty that the causality in question could not be simply physicalistic or naturalistic. Nevertheless, the temptation to tell some causal story remains strong. For example, Colin McGinn winds up hypothesizing that there is a "hidden structure" of consciousness, unavailable to introspection by consciousness, which is causally connected to brain states by some property P, where that property P "is responsible for the capacity of matter to form the basis of consciousness, or for the capacity of consciousness to take its rise from matter."[46]

On Searle's view, consciousness "is just an ordinary property of the brain in the way that digestion is a property of the stomach."[47] However, just as "solidity" refers to a higher level phenomenon of the behavior of the many molecules comprising a table, or "liquidity" refers to a higher level phenomenon of many molecules of water, "consciousness" refers to a higher level phenomenon of the activity of brains. He believes that we should seek causal explanations of the higher level phenomenon in terms of the lower,[48] a view that he insists is neither dualistic nor reductionist.

Flanagan reserves the term "consciousness" as a name for "a heterogeneous set of events and processes that share the property of being experienced."[49] As such it is the name of a set of processes, and not a thing or a mental faculty. He also supposes that consciousness has a complex structure that will require the coordination of phenomenological, psychological, and neural analyses for further explanation. He terms his theory "neurophilosophical" in that it tries to mesh "a naturalistic metaphysic of mind"[50] with a gradually progressing science of the brain. Ultimately, he supposes the mind will turn out to be the brain. For now he supposes that mind and brain are "one and the same thing seen from two different perspectives,"[51] and that sensory qualia will prove to supervene upon patterns of neural activity.

Nagel is inclined toward a dual aspect view, in terms of which something would turn out to be capable of having both physical and mental properties, without claiming to have any very precise understanding of how that might be the case. He further supposes that the mental properties would turn out to be at least *supervenient* upon the physical properties. Given these assumptions, he also accepts the implication that some form of *panpsychism* would turn out to be true,[52] a position recently defended in much greater detail by Galen Strawson.[53]

Third Problem: The Content of Mental Experience

Perhaps the most telling indicator of the limitations of the Narrow conception of the mind-body problem can be found in its implicit account of what might be termed the "constitution" of mind. More precisely, what one actually finds falls well short of any possible account of the constitution of mind proper and is at most a view about the *types of content* that characterize mental experience. On any of these standard accounts, mind is supposed to be composed of "sense data," "raw feels," "red patches," "preconceptual sensory givens," and the like. Not only is this is a dominant feature in discussions of mind in much of the analytic literature, but it is also the usual one encountered in the cognitive science literature: an assemblage of discrete, atomistic "bits" of (mental) experience which will supposedly, when fully understood, turn out to be equivalent to a mind in some commonsense understanding of it. As John McCrone points out, "The reason why the philosopher's favorite example, the color red, seems to stand as the ultimate challenge to a theory of consciousness is that it is as near to a structureless and discrete brain state [*sic*] as we can imagine."[54] Any more complex "bit" of mental activity, "such as picturing a rhinoceros or hitting a tennis ball" would make it more difficult to direct our attention away from the essentially relational aspects intrinsic to the event. In other words, the red patch appears to represent an atomistic bit of the "stuff" out of which minds are conceived to be composed. The implicit atomism of this approach is of course the counterpart to the atomism of Russell's external world, in other words, mind "naturalized," and would appear to be what is called for by any standard scientific naturalism.

At least three challenges immediately arise for such a conception of "mind." First, the plausibility of this "naturalized" version of mind ultimately rests upon the assumption that there are in fact "bits" of raw sense experience, "raw feels," to be had, relations among which can be conceived to be merely external (atomistic), where any story concerning their eventual registration in the mind must initially proceed in purely causal terms, given that such bits of sensory data are supposed to be preconceptual. However, if McDowell's (and Hegel's and Green's and Sellars') denials that there *are* any such "preconceptual givens" is to be taken seriously, then this conception of "mind" falls at the first hurdle.

If we nevertheless do suppose that mind can be pictured as containing preconceptual bits of the Given, a second very curious implication arises. Within such an intrinsically atomistic image of the mind it becomes difficult or impossible to make sense of the problem of the *unity and coherence* of the world as experienced. The problem I have in mind here is essentially the same as the one Kant took himself to be addressing with the doctrine of the transcendental unity of apperception. One would not expect a follower of Russell or a scientific naturalist to adopt Kant's purported *solution* to this problem, much less Hegel's, but one is entitled to ask what becomes of the *problem itself?* Within the purview of the Narrow paradigm, has the problem not simply disappeared? The evidence suggests that the problem has been abandoned as without interest.

Thus, it is unclear in what sense any mere concatenation of atomistic bits of the Given in experience could constitute the basis for mind. Such a conception simply could not amount to a mind in any genuinely intelligible sense, as a nexus for the *comprehension* of the world, since any minimally qualified comprehension of anything deserving to be called a "world" would necessarily be *holistic* in a strong sense.

In place of a concept of mind as the nexus of a holistic comprehension of the world, much less of a mind which in any sense could be conceived as *active* in *synthesizing* or *constituting* that world (whether in Kantian or Hegelian or Husserlian senses), there is a conception of mind as purely passive, in no way creative.[55] But if so, what becomes of the mind's necessary activity in the *synthesis* of coherent, enduring objects from the fragmentary, perspectival elements of perceptual experience, much less of the elaboration of these into a unitary world? A solution to this problem was central for the projects of Kant, Hegel, Husserl, and any number of other philosophers working in these related traditions.

One looks in vain for a counterpart within the Narrow paradigm; the passive, atomistic conception usually encountered there simply could not amount to a mind in any genuinely intelligible sense. Along these lines John Findlay made the apt comment:

> All such solutions spring from a peculiar inability to see that consciousness just is, or at least is, the bringing into a focus of indivisible contemporaneity of what, from another point of view may be successive and dispersed, and that a world in which, perhaps per impossibile, there were only mutually external happenings in space and time, would be a world of which we could not be conscious, in which there could be no such thing as conscious experience at all.[56]

Conclusion: The Two Paradigms and Their Fates

If the substance of what I have attempted to argue above can be defended, then it would follow that the Comprehensive and the Narrow paradigms must be regarded as fundamentally disparate, notwithstanding the appearances of a coincidence of interest in the problem of the relation of mind and body. The conceptions of "mind" and "body" (or "nature") within each of the two projects are so distinct, and the projects themselves so disjointed, that no genuine convergence appears likely. Translations of the conclusions reached within one research paradigm into statements genuinely intelligible in the other will remain problematic.

If one looks over the landscape of contemporary research that might be described as relevant to the mind-body problem, first it appears that most of it is conceived in terms of what I have called the Narrow paradigm, with all of its associated limitations. This remains true if we restrict our view just to philosophers. Empirical research proceeds apace under the umbrella of "cognitive science," which covers two major groups of researchers, one continuing to work on the problem of machine intelligence (a massive two-volume history of which by Margaret Boden has just been published.)[57] The other group consists of the burgeoning industry of brain imaging, the motives and activities of which are by now too varied and numerous to be easily catalogued. In the absence of a compelling philosophical paradigm to guide such research, it is unclear what can be expected from it. Many appear to be motivated simply by commitment to a program of scientific naturalism.

To summarize, there are several crucial respects in which the two paradigms remain fundamentally incommensurate:

1. In the Hegelian paradigm, any adequate account of consciousness presupposes the emergence of the preconscious phenomena of *psyche* as a distinct phase in the development of *animal organism*, as a manifestation of *life*. Minds are conceived as incorporating animal organism as a constitutive element of mental life. As such, mind itself is a *living entity* "not merely in the world but metabolically interacting with it."[58] "By being in part an animal in the world, mind never faces the dilemma of dealing with an ontologically incommensurate domain. . . . Instead, action is the self-activity of a being that always involves animal physiology."[59] Hegel's conception, strongly influenced by Aristotle's *De Anima*, precludes the possibility of any metaphysical dualism from the outset. It presupposes that *life* is a fundamentally important, constitutive category of being, in the absence of which his account of mind would not be conceivable.

    In the analytic tradition, by contrast, one finds (with some limited recent exceptions) a consistent rejection of "neo-vitalist" attitudes as irrelevant to the solution of the "mind-body problem." The motive for this position, evidently, lies in the desire to defend a reductionist conception of the scientific enterprise, to which, supposedly, the mind-body problem will ultimately yield. Given the many critiques of such reductionism that have been launched in recent decades from so many quarters, one wonders why the rejection of "neo-vitalism" should still be thought to be crucial. Continued retention of this "ban" on "neo-vitalism" however renders the two paradigms essentially incommensurate in this respect.

2. In consequence of the first point, within the Comprehensive paradigm the categories of nature and mind must be understood to overlap in an essential way. This overlap is manifest from the level of animal organism, including the *psyche*, all the way through *consciousness* and the succeeding phase of *intelligence*. (It is also possible to argue that the overlap of mind and nature continues throughout the entirety of *Geist* in Hegel's conception, but this latter claim is not essential to the immediate point at issue). This conception of the method of philosophical analysis as presupposing the overlap of classes in a scale of forms is of course borrowed from Collingwood, and his defense of it in *An Essay on Philosophical Method* deserves to be much more widely appreciated than it appears to be.[60]

Such a conception of the overlap of classes is generally not to be found among contemporary analytic writers on the mind-body problem. The closest approach that can be identified might be the endorsement of *panpsychism* by writers such as Thomas Nagel and, more recently, Galen Strawson. In their writings the assertion of panpsychism appears to be driven by a desire to overcome the otherwise insuperable difficulties of metaphysical dualism, though in practice it appears to have less to offer in the way of a solution than a pursuit of Collingwood's notion of an overlap of classes.

A more interesting development is visible in McDowell's recognition that a drastic revision in the prevailing conception of nature is necessary in order to make sense of the possibility of "spontaneity" in the realm of moral decision. He advocates a return to an Aristotelian conception of nature as the background to a theory of "practical wisdom" in terms of which we can understand that

> [e]xercises of spontaneity belong to our way of living. And our mode of living is our way of actualizing ourselves as animals. So we can rephrase the thought by saying: exercises of spontaneity belong to our way of actualizing ourselves as animals. This removes any need to try to see ourselves as

peculiarly bifurcated, with a foothold in the animal kingdom and a mysterious separate involvement in an extra-natural world of rational connections.[61]

This is one of a number of recent evidences that could be cited of a growing recognition that Aristotle's ethics and metaphysics may contain some important possible solutions to some of the familiar impasses of contemporary thought.

3. Collingwood's presentation of a distinctive pattern of reasoning appropriate to, or rather definitive of, philosophical inquiry can of course be regarded as a restatement in more contemporary terms of the essential forms of Hegel's speculative logic. Without such a logic, articulated in Collingwoodian or Hegelian terms, it is difficult to see how a solution to the Comprehensive problem of the relation of mind to nature would be conceivable. As argued above,[62] Hegel's account of the relation of mind to nature proceeds in terms of a dynamic principle of logic operative throughout our conception of the universe, implicit at the level of nature, explicit at the level of spirit, ordering the whole as a scale of forms in which each phase presents itself as a summing up of the whole to that point, and is in turn taken up in the successive phase, in a process that continues until the whole has reached fully explicit self-manifestation as the completed, self-sufficient system of the Real. Given the ultimate identity of thought and being in Hegel's system, the structuring of thought is equally the structuring of being, hence the dialectically self-developing Concept is conceived as the actual dynamic principle of the whole.

Given that the analytic tradition took its origins from Russell's rejection of any such pattern of reasoning, and has instead been rooted in formal mathematical logic throughout, this must remain one of the chief points of incommensurability between the two paradigms,[63] and it is difficult to imagine that changing. It is however interesting to note that in his recently published *Analytic Philosophy and the Return of Hegelian Thought*, Paul Redding devotes an entire chapter to recent lines of inquiry into the concept of contradiction by a number of logicians, stemming from the work of Graham Priest, that begin to open up the territory of Aristotelian logic once again, and possibly to set the stage for a more constructive reexamination of Hegel's uses of the idea of contradiction.[64]

4. Finally, as I have attempted to document throughout this chapter, there remain at least two distinct paradigms within which the relation of mind to nature can be explored in contemporary philosophy, and only the one that I have termed "Comprehensive" could be said to incorporate the full range of philosophical problems actually inherent in an adequate account of the relation of mind to nature.

In conclusion, I will draw attention once again to the fact that a few individual philosophers have never lost sight of the Comprehensive paradigm and have always worked explicitly within it. One of these is Errol Harris. Not only did he commence his public philosophical career with a strong restatement of this philosophical problem, but it has remained an explicit concern of a long series of important books he has published on a variety of topics in the ensuing fifty years and more. Quite recently he published yet another work, this one focused entirely on the problem of consciousness. It is one of the more important treatments of this topic from the perspective of the broad problem of the relation of mind to nature of which I am aware in the current philosophical literature. In this latest work, *Reflections on the Problem of Consciousness*,[65] he provides an exposition of his account in a continuous dialogue with many of the most prominent contemporary philosophers and scientists dealing with the problem. I will conclude by quoting a substantial passage from that work:

> The fundamental proposition of the position reached is that the universe is an indivisible whole of systematically inter-related parts ordered in accordance with a principle of organization which (as in all other wholes at varying levels of completeness) specifies itself as a scale of forms increasing in adequacy to the principle of wholeness governing the system. It follows that the principle is dynamic, because any partial manifestation, depending as it does for its nature and behavior on the other parts with which it is interdependent (as they are likewise among themselves), will demand complementation and display a nisus towards the whole. Each phase of the whole is itself a provisional whole at its appropriate level, but, being provisional, it is not strictly complete. The human organism is such a whole, highly complex

and at an advanced stage of the biological level. But at no stage is a complex adequate to the principle of wholeness if the relations between its parts and processes are merely implicit. This is the case throughout the scale up to the biological, where the relations are effective and make themselves evident, but not to themselves, only to an observing mind. Full completion requires *explicit* realization of all relations. The immanent nisus to completion, therefore, drives the complex to the explication of its internal relations so that they become recognizable as such. But this is possible only if they come to consciousness, which they cannot do except by registering their interdependence in sentience and by the living organism's turning in upon itself and attending to those elements in its bodily feeling most crucial to its self-maintenance, survival and reproduction. Consciousness is thus the dialectical phase subsequent to the complex biological wholeness of the evolved organism (or the teleological requirement of its nisus to completion).[66]

Notes

1. See for example, Errol Harris, *Nature, Mind, and Modern Science*, the Muirhead Library of Philosophy (London: George Allen and Unwin, 1954; N.Y.: Humanities Press, 1954), 63–113. Reprinted in 1968; reissued by Routledge, 2004. Available in French as *Nature, Ésprit et science moderne* (Lausanne: L'Age d'Homme, 1979).

2. An excellent new edition has recently been published as T. H. Green, *Prolegomena to Ethics*, ed. David O. Brink (Oxford: Oxford University Press, 2003); see p. 13.

3. *Nature, Mind and Modern Science*, 44.

4. PN, §376 Z.

5. Richard Dien Winfield, "Identity, Difference, and the Unity of Mind: Reflections on Hegel's Determination of Psyche, Consciousness, and Intelligence," in *Identity and Difference: Studies in Hegel's Logic, Philosophy of Spirit, and Politics*, ed. Philip T. Grier (Albany: State University of New York Press, 2007), 103–27, (the Presidential Address at the 2004 meeting of the Hegel Society of America). For a fuller account of these matters see Richard Dien Winfield, Hegel and Mind: Rethinking Philosophical Psychology (Basingstoke, England; New York: Palgrave Macmillan, 2010), and also his The Living Mind: From Psyche to Consciousness (Lanham, Md.; Plymouth, UK: Rowman & Littlefield Publishers, 2011).

6. PN, § 350, and Z.

7. PN, §§ 351, 352.

8. Winfield, "Identity, Difference," 107.
9. Ibid.
10. PN, § 353 Z.
11. PN, § 356.
12. Ibid.
13. Ibid.
14. PN, § 361.
15. Winfield, "Identity, Difference," 107–08.
16. Errol Harris, *Nature, Mind, and Modern Science*, 417. He was himself quoting Dorothy Emmet, *Whitehead's Philosophy of Organism* (London, 1932), 46.
17. Hegel, PM, "C. Philosophy" (§§ 572–77). Hereafter, in this chapter, PM.
18. PM § 574.
19. PM § 575.
20. Such absolute knowing cannot be supposed to be the work of individual subjective spirit alone, of course, but presupposes the development of objective spirit, the socially mediated development of reason, as an essential phase in the development of absolute spirit, and the philosophical comprehension of the truth, which is its ultimate outcome.
21. For a particularly clear explication of this basic claim, see Stephen Houlgate, *An Introduction to Hegel: Freedom, Truth and History*, 45.
22. Collingwood draws out this conclusion from his insistence that all genuinely philosophical discourse involves the overlap of classes: "Hence no object of philosophical thought can be rightly conceived as a mere aggregate, whether of logically distinguished elements or of spatial or temporal parts; the parts or elements, however proper it may be to distinguish them, cannot be conceived as separable; and therefore it is impossible that such an object should be either put together out of parts or elements separately preexisting, or divided into parts or elements which can survive the division; for either of these would imply that the connexions between the parts are accidental, whereas they must in reality be essential." R. G. Collingwood, *An Essay on Philosophical Method* (Oxford: Clarendon Press, 1933), 52.
23. Peter Hylton, *Russell, Idealism and the Emergence of Analytic Philosophy* (Oxford: Oxford University Press, 1990), 108.
24. Hylton, *Russell*, 108. As Errol Harris remarked in discussing Russell's later philosophy, "In fact, nowhere in Russell's philosophy does one find any very clear conception of the nature of mind; one rather gets the impression that his constant endeavour is to eliminate it from the world altogether." Harris, *Nature, Mind, and Modern Science*, 287.
25. Hylton, *Russell*, 109.
26. Indeed it is difficult to conceive what might serve as a genuine argument for such a conclusion. According to Hylton, "by far the strongest argument that Moore has against internal relations" was provided in *Principia Ethica* (34–35). There he argues that, contrary to Aristotle's well-known pronouncement that a hand severed from a living body is not a hand, if we conceive the severed part to

retain all the causal properties that it had while it remained a living member of the organic body, then the severed member would be exactly what it was when it was attached. (In other words, apparently, if we are willing to think of the severed hand at a sufficiently high level of abstraction and counterfactually, then it *would* be a hand). Hylton concludes that Moore has succeeded in showing that "causal dependence is all that we need in order to give an account of what the Idealists would have called an organic unity" (see Hylton, *Russell*, 122). However it seems more likely that Moore's argument would be found persuasive only by someone already willing to accept his distinctive presuppositions; otherwise it would appear to be question begging.

27. Hylton, *Russell*, 116. Hylton continues, "Unless one already accepts Platonic Atomism—or at least rejects Idealism—the new logic will not appear to have the status which it must have if it is really to show that mathematics is fully coherent and consistent." (At the same time, Hylton does not regard the circularity of Russell's position as undermining its intellectual appeal in the prevailing circumstances.)

28. Hylton, *Russell*, 326–27.

29. Hylton, *Russell*, 327.

30. Hylton argues that, strictly speaking, analytic philosophy did not originate in the doctrines of Platonic Atomism per se, but rather in Russell's subsequent attempts to unravel various problems posed by Platonic Atomism. Cf. Hylton, *Russell*, 280ff.

31. Robert Brandom, "Study Guide," in Wilfrid Sellars, *Empiricism and the Philosophy of Mind* (Cambridge: Harvard University Press, 1997), 123.

32. "We should understand what Kant calls 'intuition'—experiential intake—not as a bare getting of an extra-conceptual Given, but as a kind of occurrence or state that already has conceptual content. In experience one takes in, for instance sees, *that things are thus and so*. That is the sort of thing one can also, for instance, judge." John McDowell, *Mind and World* (Cambridge: Harvard University Press, 1994, 1996), 9. It is worth noting, in historical perspective, a significant overlap between McDowell's arguments and those of T. H. Green in his 1883 *Prolegomena to Ethics* (chap. 1, 34–44 and passim) in pursuit of some of the same general conclusions.

33. Robert B. Brandom, *Making It Explicit* (Cambridge: Harvard University Press, 1994); see, e.g., 93.

34. See Paul Redding, *Analytic Philosophy and the Return of Hegelian Thought* (Cambridge: Cambridge University Press, 2007), 51.

35. One is reminded of Errol Harris's observation that "the empiricist is pathologically anxious to avoid contamination of the real with mind." *Nature, Mind, and Modern Science*, 417.

36. Thomas Nagel, *The View from Nowhere*, 16. If nothing else, all of these approaches at bottom simply set aside or circumvent the central issue of the relation of mind to nature.

37. Colin McGinn, *The Problem of Consciousness*, 3ff.

38. Ibid., 20.

39. "By 'physical1 terms' I mean *all* (empirical) terms whose specification of meaning essentially involves logical (necessary or, more usually, probabilistic) connections with the intersubjective observation language, as well as the terms of this language itself." "By 'physical2' I mean the kind of theoretical concepts (and statements) which are sufficient for the explanation, i.e., the deductive or probabilistic derivation, of the observation statements regarding the inorganic (lifeless) domain of nature." Herbert Feigl, "The 'Mental' and the 'Physical,' " in *Minnesota Studies in the Philosophy of Science*, vol. 2, *Concepts, Theories, and the Mind-Body Problem* (Minneapolis: University of Minnesota Press, 1958), 424. See also Thomas Nagel, *Mortal Questions* (Cambridge: Cambridge University Press, 1979), 183.

40. Galen Strawson, "Real Materialism," in *Real Materialism and Other Essays* (Oxford: Oxford University Press, 2008), 22.

41. See for example, *The Feeling of What Happens: Body and Emotion in the Making of Consciousness* (New York: Harcourt Brace, 1999).

42. Spinoza, *Ethics*, trans. Samuel Shirley (Indianapolis: Hackett, 1992), part 2, prop. 13.

43. On this view, one supposes that the mind is being tacitly regarded as equivalent (crudely speaking) to a counter, or an indicator, which is capable of being incremented or decremented in accordance with electrical impulses originating in the electronic circuitry to which it is wired, *but where nothing in that circuitry can monitor and respond to the status of the counter* (and therefore the "mind" is not capable of exerting influences upon the "brain").

44. Galen Strawson, *Real Materialism and Other Essays* (Oxford: Clarendon Press, 2008), 7. He continues on the following page: "My use of the words 'physicalism' and 'materialism' is non-standard relative to their use in the last fifty years or so, because many philosophers in this period have used them—and still use them—in such a way that it follows from the truth of physicalism or materialism that there's no such thing as experience. This is, however, a very recent use. None of the many and great materialists of past times held this view. Their view, as materialists, was (in Locke's words) that matter might think, i.e., that experience itself, conscious experience conceived of in a wholly realistic, non-reductionist way, might be a wholly physical phenomenon. It was only in the twentieth century . . . that 'materialism' and 'physicalism' came to have this extraordinary meaning (though never for all), in a way that allowed the debate about physicalism to become completely unreal."

45. Ibid., 20.

46. Colin McGinn, *The Problem of Consciousness* (Oxford: Blackwell, 1991, 1993), 58.

47. John Searle, *Consciousness and Language* (Cambridge: Cambridge University Press, 2002), 2.

48. Ibid., 33.

49. Owen Flanagan, *Consciousness Reconsidered* (Cambridge: MIT Press, 1992), 220.

50. Ibid. For a more detailed critique of Flanagan's views, see Errol Harris, *Reflections on the Problem of Consciousness*, vol. 3 in Studies in Brain and Mind (Dordrecht: Spring, 2006), 43ff.

51. Flanagan, *Consciousness Reconsidered*, 220–21.

52. Nagel, *The View from Nowhere*, 47–49.

53. See Strawson, "Realistic Monism: Why Physicalism Entails Panpsychism," in *Real Materialism and Other Essays*, 53–74.

54. John McCrone, *Going Inside: a Tour round a Single Moment of Consciousness* (London: Faber and Faber, 1999), 305.

55. Hylton, *Russell*, 111.

56. "Translator's Introduction" to Edmund Husserl, *Logical Investigations*, trans. J. N. Findlay, vol. 1, 7.

57. Margaret Boden, *Mind as Machine: A History of Cognitive Science*, 2 vols. (Oxford and New York: Oxford University Press, 2006).

58. Winfield, "Identity, Difference and the Unity of Mind," in Grier, ed., *Identity and Difference*, 107.

59. Ibid.

60. Errol Harris has tirelessly reminded us of this, as a continuing refrain in many of his works.

61. John McDowell, *Mind and World*, 78. See also 78–84, 108–110, 181–82, and *passim*.

62. See the section "The Relation of Mind to Nature in Hegel," above.

63. For a thorough examination of the implications of a commitment to these differing conceptions of reasoning, see Errol Harris, *Formal, Transcendental and Dialectical Thinking: Logic and Reality* (Albany: State University of New York Press, 1987).

64. Redding, *Analytic Philosophy*, chap. 7, "Hegel and Contradiction."

65. Errol Harris, *Reflections on the Problem of Consciousness*, vol. 3 in *Studies in Brain and Mind* (Dordrecht: Springer, 2006).

66. Errol Harris, *Reflections*, 158.

Contributors

Marina F. Bykova is professor of philosophy in the Department of Philosophy and Religious Studies and the editor in chief of the journal *Russian Studies in Philosophy*. Her research interests lie in the history of the 19th-century continental philosophy, with a special focus on German idealism and theories of subjectivity developed by Kant, Fichte, and Hegel. She has authored three books and numerous articles on Hegel and German idealism. Her works have been published in Russian, German, and English.

Philip T. Grier is the Thomas Bowman Professor of Philosophy and Religion Emeritus at Dickinson College. Among recent publications he edited *Identity and Difference: Studies in Hegel's Logic, Philosophy of Spirit, and Politics* (2007), and translated and edited the two-volume commentary on Hegel by the Russian philosopher Ivan Il'in (*The Philosophy of Hegel as a Doctrine of the Concreteness of God and Humanity*, 2010 and 2011). He is a past president of the Hegel Society of America.

Jason J. Howard is associate professor of philosophy at Viterbo University. He has published articles on Hegel, Kant, and Schelling and was recently awarded a research fellowship from the D. B. Reinhart Institute for Ethics and Leadership for his work on conscience.

Simon Lumsden is senior lecturer in philosophy at the University of New South Wales, Sydney, Australia. His research is primarily concerned with German idealism, poststructuralism and the relation between these traditions. He has published papers in these areas in journals such as *The Review of Metaphysics, Inquiry, Philosophical Forum,* and many others.

Glenn Alexander Magee is associate professor and chairman of the Philosophy Department at the C. W. Post Campus of Long Island University. His publications include *Hegel and the Hermetic Tradition* (Cornell University

Press, 2001; revised second edition 2008), *The Hegel Dictionary* (Continuum, 2011), and *The Cambridge Handbook of Western Mysticism and Esotericism* (editor; forthcoming from Cambridge University Press in 2013).

Nicholas Mowad received his PhD *cum laude* from Loyola University Chicago in 2010, after which he accepted a visiting professor position at Georgia College and State University. He has written several articles on Hegel, including a chapter in *Hegel on Religion and Politics* (State University of New York Press), and an article in *Environmental Philosophy*.

Angelica Nuzzo is professor of philosophy at the Graduate Center and Brooklyn College, CUNY. Among her recent books are *Memory, History, Justice in Hegel* (MacMillan 2012) and *Ideal Embodiment: Kant's Theory of Sensibility* (Indiana 2008).

Jeffrey Reid is professor of philosophy at the University of Ottawa. He publishes on Hegel and early German romanticism in both English and French. He has contributed numerous articles to scholarly reviews and collections and is the author of the first French translation and commentary of Hegel's review of K. W. F. Solger's *Posthumous Writings and Correspondence* (1997), *L'anti-romantique: Hegel contre le romantisme ironique* (2007), *Real Words: Language and System in Hegel* (2007), and an introduction to philosophy entitled *Great Philosophers: A Brief Story of the Self and Its Worlds* (2009).

David S. Stern is professor of philosophy at Hamline University. A former vice president of the Hegel Society of America, he has published articles on Kant, Hegel, and Kierkegaard, as well as a number of articles on social and political philosophy.

Jere O'Neill Surber is professor of Philosophy and Cultural Theory at the University of Denver. He has published numerous books and articles on 19th- and 20th-century German and French philosophy and cultural theory, especially focusing upon linguistic thought within these traditions. He has been a visiting professor at such institutions as Katholieke Universiteit-Leuven, Johannes Gutenberg Universität-Mainz, and Tromsa University (Norway). He is also a former vice president of the Hegel Society of America.

Italo Testa is assistant professor at the Department of Philosophy of the University of Parma. He has edited a number of books on Hegel, critical theory, and social philosophy, and is author of "Hegel critico e scettico" (Il Poligrafo 2002), "Teorie dell'argomentazione" (Bruno Mondadori 2006), and "La natura del riconoscimento" (Mimesis 2010).

Mario Wenning is assistant professor at the University of Macau as well as Humboldt Research Fellow at the University of Frankfurt. In addition to his publications on critical theory, German idealism, and Daoism, he has also translated authors such as Jaspers, Schmitt, and Sloterdijk

Robert R. Williams is Professor Emeritus of German and philosophy, University of Illinois at Chicago, past president of the Hegel Society of America, Fulbright Research Professor, author of *Tragedy, Recognition and the Death of God: Studies in Hegel and Nietzsche* (Oxford 2012), *Hegel's Ethics of Recognition* (California 1998), and *Recognition: Fichte and Hegel on the Other* (SUNY 1992) and translator of *Hegel's Lectures on the Philosophy of Spirit 1827* (Oxford 2007).

Richard Dien Winfield is Distinguished Research Professor at the University of Georgia. He is the author of *Reason and Justice* (1988), *The Just Economy* (1988), *Overcoming Foundations: Studies in Systematic Philosophy* (1989), *Freedom and Modernity* (1991), *Law in Civil Society* (1995), *Systematic Aesthetics* (1995), *Stylistics: Rethinking the Artforms after Hegel* (1996), *The Just Family* (1998), *Autonomy and Normativity: Investigations of Truth, Right and Beauty* (2001), *The Just State: Rethinking Self-Government* (2005), *From Concept to Objectivity: Thinking Through Hegel's Subjective Logic* (2006), *Modernity, Religion, and the War on Terror* (2007), *Hegel and Mind: Rethinking Philosophical Psychology* (2010), *The Living Mind: From Psyche to Consciousness* (2011), and *Hegel's Science of Logic: A Critical Rethinking in Thirty Lectures* (2012).

Index

action/activity, xi, 10, 11, 13, 26–28, 30–32, 34n30, 48, 73–74, 76, 122, 130–131, 133, 135, 137n37, 142, 148, 151–152, 156, 158–159, 170, 172, 202–206, 208, 212–216, 218, 219n3, 220n15, 220n33, 227, 228, 236–238
agency, 146, 149, 150–152, 205, 207–208, 214, 216–218
animal magnetism, 51n21, 55–67, 83, 110
anthropology, 2–14, 15n4, 15n19, 16n35, 17n68, 20–21, 25–28, 38, 40, 42, 44–45, 50n15, 52n38, 56, 62, 87, 88, 90, 93, 100n3, 102n25, 102n29, 103n40, 104n50, 104n52, 108–112, 115, 118n1, 152n5, 153n8, 153n9, 186, 210
Aristotle, 1, 2, 10–11, 26, 34n30, 84n6, 84n13, 92, 100n4, 104n50, 109, 157, 158, 167, 175n10, 178n49, 202, 219n4, 220n33, 224, 227, 238, 240, 243n26
autonomy, 121, 123–125, 128–131, 135n6, 142, 149, 151, 157, 160, 164, 166–167, 172, 176n33, 218

Bertold-Bond, Daniel, x
Boumann, Ludwig, ix, x, 42, 102n28
Bourdieu, Pierre, 123, 129–130, 132
Brandom, Robert, 123, 231

consciousness, x, 6–7, 22, 27–30, 38–39, 41, 48, 50n15, 56, 61, 63–65, 74, 76, 80, 88, 92–93, 104n52, 111, 113, 117, 121, 125–127, 133, 135n2, 135n10, 141–142, 158, 182, 186, 192, 202–205, 208–209, 211–212, 219n5, 227, 232–239, 241–242
corporeality (Leiblichkeit), 3, 6–8, 11–14, 19, 22, 48, 75–76, 88

de Sousa, Ronald, 77, 82
deVries, Willem, x, 33, 33n3, 35n42, 73, 81, 84n9, 86n39, 136n19
dreams, xi, 40–43, 45, 48, 50n15, 57, 62–63, 92, 94, 95–96, 102n28, 103n35, 104n50, 113, 117
dualism, 12–13, 21–24, 26–27, 31, 33, 33n9, 34n17, 34n30, 35n36, 121–122, 124, 156, 226, 235, 238, 239

embodiment, 7, 11, 15n10, 16n42, 24, 26, 28, 30–32, 34n16, 34n30, 73, 76, 107, 129, 143, 186–187, 202, 204–206, 208, 211, 226
emotion, x, 71–83, 84n23, 109, 112, 209–210

feeling, x, 13, 22, 26–30, 32, 37–50, 50n13, 50n15, 53n51, 54n55, 56–57, 60–61, 65, 71–83, 88,

251

feeling *(continued)*
    91–100, 103n41, 103n44, 104n48, 108–109, 112, 118n8, 124–128, 130, 131–134, 186–187, 190–191, 199, 204, 206–216, 226–227, 236, 242, 245n41
Ferrarin, Alfredo, 34n30, 73–74, 175n10
Fichte, Johann Gottlieb, 8, 67, 126, 147–148, 151, 153n22, 164–165, 171–172, 177n37, 178n56, 178n61, 184, 189, 195, 197n6, 198n14
Findlay, John, ix, 237
Flatt, J. F., 43–45, 52n31, 52n32, 52n34
Foucault, Michel, 111, 116–117, 118n8, 123
freedom, 1, 8, 12, 16n28, 34n30, 38, 60, 109, 111, 118n6, 121, 123, 124, 127, 131, 135n2, 135n6, 142–149, 151, 155–179, 180, 194, 213, 215–218, 221n35

Habermas, Jürgen, 123, 140, 169
habit, habituation, x, 27, 28, 29, 31–33, 34n30, 38, 40, 48, 50n15, 72, 74–76, 84n23, 97–99, 103n41, 104n52, 105n59, 109, 121–135, 136n26, 136n27, 136n34, 137n37, 204, 212
Harris, Errol, 224, 231, 241
Herder, Johann Gottfried, 62, 181–187, 189, 195–196
Hylton, Peter, 229–230

imagination, 39, 41, 43, 47, 184, 188, 192–193, 199–200, 207, 212–213
immateriality, 5, 9, 11, 14, 17n69, 19–22, 24, 26, 32, 34n19
intuition, 40, 46, 49, 77–78, 122, 182, 184–194, 198n13, 199–200, 202–204, 206, 212–213, 231, 244n32

Kant, Immanuel, 1–3, 7–12, 14, 15n4, .16n41, 21–22, 39–40, 43–44, 52n29, 52n34, 53n41, 67, 71, 104n50, 107, 112, 116, 121–124, 129, 131, 134, 135n6, 147–148, 152n2, 153n22, 164, 176n33, 181–191, 195, 196n2, 197n4, 197n12, 199, 220n31, 231, 236, 237

madness/insanity, x, xi, 40–41, 45, 48, 51n23, 53n41, 61, 80, 87, 95–100, 104n50, 104n52, 105n54, 105n62, 107–108, 110–117, 118n6, 118n8, 119n14, 125
master and slave, xi, 110, 142, 145, 149, 160–163, 177n47
materialism, 12–13, 33, 234, 245n40, 245n44
McDowell, John, 122, 231, 236, 239, 244n32
memory/remembrance, x, 39–40, 111, 116–1,17, 188, 190, 194, 199n35, 199n41
mental, 13, 23–24, 30–31, 33, 73–74, 81, 107, 110, 125, 185, 204–206, 208–209, 224, 226–228, 232–236, 238
metacritics, 182–190, 195–197
monism, 12, 23, 33n9, 137n45

naturalism, 13, 23, 25–26, 28, 31, 33, 34n18, 228, 232, 234, 236, 238
nature, 1–9, 11–14, 15n3, 15n13, 16n38, 19–33, 35n30, 38, 40, 45, 56–57, 62–64, 66, 87–100, 100n3, 101n19, 102n24, 102n25, 102n28, 102n29, 103n39, 103n40, 104n52, 105n53, 107–117, 121–135, 135n2, 135n10, 137n45, 158, 159,

175n14, 208, 223–242, 244n36, 245n39

Paralogisms, 3, 9, 22
paranormal, xi, 44–45, 56–61, 64–65
Petry, Michael, ix, x, 17n69, 38, 42, 51n15, 52n38, 53n49, 61–62, 68n20, 118n1, 118n6, 176n23
physiology, 57, 59, 61, 65, 71–76, 80–83, 115, 186, 202, 204, 227
Pinkard, Terry, 123, 135n6
Pippin, Robert B., 155–156, 170–172, 174n2, 174n3, 176n33
practical feeling, 76–78, 82, 207, 209–212, 216
practical intelligence, 201–204, 207, 209, 212, 214–218, 219n3
psychology, x, 2–4, 6–11, 13, 14, 15n4, 20, 27, 38, 40, 42–45, 50, 52n35, 52n40, 71, 79, 84n2, 84n23, 86n42, 108–110, 116, 181, 186–189, 195, 224, 229, 242n5
psychology, empirical, 9, 11, 42–45, 50, 52n35, 52n40, 224
psychology, rational, 2, 9–11, 14, 15n4

recognition, xi, 3, 110, 139–143, 145–152, 154n32, 155–174, 205–206
representation, 39–42, 47–48, 77–78, 92, 181–182, 185–194, 196, 197n13, 199–200, 202–204, 206, 209, 212
Russell, Bertrand, 225, 229–232, 236, 240, 243n26, 244n27

Schleiermacher, Friedrich, 45–47, 49, 53n54
Schubert, Gotthilf H., 55, 60, 62–65, 67, 68n30, 69n31
second nature, 25–26, 28–29, 32, 35n30, 35n34, 121–122, 124, 128–132, 134–135, 135n5, 160, 170

self-consciousness, 28, 30, 32, 48, 104n52, 139–152, 154n32, 160, 163–166, 168–170, 205–206, 209, 211
self-determination, 8, 76, 110, 122, 123–124, 127, 129, 135, 145, 159, 164, 175, 190, 210, 213, 215, 216–218, 219n3, 219n13, 219n14, 228
Sellars, Wilfrid, 231, 236
signification, 182, 187–190, 192, 195–196, 198n13, 199n39
sleep/sleeping/sleepwalking, 23, 25, 39–45, 48, 56, 61, 64, 87, 92, 94–97, 99, 103n35, 103n45, 104n50, 104n52, 105n53, 110, 112–113, 133
soul /body (soul and body) 2–3, 5–6, 10–12, 14, 15n4, 19–20, 22–23, 28–30
soul, 2–14, 15n4, 17n69, 19–33, 34n19, 35n36, 37–50, 51n15, 51n23, 53n51, 56–57, 59–61, 63–66, 72–80, 82, 85n34, 87–88, 90–100, 100n4, 102n23, 102n24, 102n25, 102n28, 103n39, 103n40, 103n41, 103n44, 104n52, 105n53, 105n54, 108–109, 111–117, 119n8, 124–127, 130–131, 135n2, 135n10
  actual soul, 26–27, 29, 38, 56, 88, 90, 95, 97, 99, 104n52, 108
  dreaming soul, 37–50, 108, 112
  feeling (or sentient) soul, 26–27, 29, 37–38, 40–50, 50n13, 50n15, 53n51, 56–57, 60, 65, 74, 88, 93–97, 99, 103n41, 103n44, 108, 118n8
spontaneity, 28–29, 34n30, 39, 41, 57, 122–123, 130, 134, 239
Strawson, Galen, 233–234, 239, 245n44

volition, 80–81, 133, 202–213, 217–218, 219n13

will, 60, 76, 79–80, 83, 124, 127–128, 131–134, 164, 201–202, 207–208, 210, 213–214, 216–217, 219n3, 219n4, 219n5, 219n13, 219n14

Williams, Robert, x, xi, 2, 3, 15n3, 15n7, 17n68, 37, 42, 47, 48, 51n15, 53n52, 71, 108, 110, 118n6, 142, 152n5

Winfield, Richard D., 74, 226, 227

Wolff, Michael, 2, 3, 6, 13, 16n47, 19, 23, 30